Murphy, Karen

A house full of
kids

A House Full of Kids

A HOUSE
FULL OF KIDS

Running a Successful Day Care

Business in Your Own Home

Karen Murphy

Beacon Press   Boston

Grateful acknowledgment is made to the following: Mary Wegmann of the Family Life Education and Psychology Department, Peninsula College, Port Angeles, Washington, and Helen Kolff of Seattle, Washington, for permission to include "A Few Hints — Communicating with Your Child About Sex," "Normal Sexual Development in Children: Major Landmarks," "Books on Sexuality for Children, Ages 3-9," and "A Bibliography for Parents on the Sex Education of Their Children"; John Wrobleski for permission to include his "Children's Book List"; The Sexual Assault Center, Harborview Medical Center, Seattle, Washington, for permission to include "What To Do If Your Child Has Been Sexually Molested" (originally prepared with support from the Law Enforcement Assistance Administration, U.S. Department of Justice) and "Sexual Abuse Within the Family."

Beacon Press books are published under the auspices
of the Unitarian Universalist Association of Congregations
in North America, 25 Beacon Street, Boston, Massachusetts 02108

Published simultaneously in Canada by
Fitzhenry & Whiteside Limited, Toronto

(hardcover) 9 8 7 6 5 4 3 2 1
(paperback) 9 8 7 6 5 4 3 2 1

Library of Congress Cataloging in Publication Data

Murphy, Karen, 1945-
    A house full of kids.

    Bibliography: p.
    Includes index.
    1. Day care centers — United States.   2. Day care
centers — United States — Management.   I. Title.
HV854.M87 1983   362.7′12′068   82-73961
ISBN 0-8070-2302-7
ISBN 0-8070-2303-5 (pbk.)

Drawings by Lori Rapport

To my wonderful and supportive family, Terry, Brianna, and Sean, and my extended family, the day care home network

Acknowledgments

The day care parenting experience has stimulated my personal growth, and the material in this book emerged from the experience of working with day care families and children. The community of day care families gave me moral and practical support; their concern for my needs and their confidence motivated me to write this book. The loving support of my husband, Terry, who assumed many of the household duties, and the understanding and independence of my children, Sean and Brianna, allowed me the necessary time and environment for writing. This provided me with the rare opportunity of sharing five years of my life with a much larger community of women and families. I would also like to express my gratitude to my parents, Harold Adams and Marguerite Anderson, to my grandmother Elvira Manion, and to Ruth and Henry Goodman, whose home served as my earliest training ground in the care of young children. I hope that readers will gain a greater understanding of the day care home from *A House Full of Kids,* and that this knowledge will increase the sense of satisfaction and worth among day care providers as well as offer a valuable guide to those contemplating this rewarding occupation.

Those who recognize the value of a writer's first book are especially important. My agent, Sandra Dijkstra, recognized the need for this book, and I thank Sandra for her energetic presentation to the publishing world, without which the book may not have been published, and for her continuing warm support. I also thank Joanne Wyckoff, my editor at Beacon Press, for her invaluable assistance, continuing enthusiasm, and belief in *A House Full of Kids* and for her encouragement throughout the publication process. Susan Oleksiw provided excellent editorial assistance. I extend appreciation to Beacon Press for its faith in this book, and to all the members of the staff who have worked in concert toward publication.

Contents

If this were all you knew about a job, would you be interested?
Hundreds of these positions are available now all over the country.
Many more are created every day. The job: home day care
operator. The only qualifications are those above. The rest is
mythology.

Being a home day care operator doesn't call for a saintly person
who loves children, or one who has unusual patience. It doesn't
take mother earth. It *does* take a lot of motivation, and a willingness to learn effective and positive methods of teaching and
handling children.

Everything you need to know to create this position for *you*
is in this book.

Introduction

If you are a parent, this book is for you — regardless of whether you think you want to run a day care home. Every parent at some point confronts the question of day care. In the 1950s the question was simply "Who will watch the children while I recover from the flu?" Today the question and its answer are not as simple.

Today parents are looking for day care for any number of reasons: they need to work full time for financial reasons, their child needs peer contact, or they need time to be alone or to meet other obligations. Most parents will look for day care services and either not be able to evaluate what they find or not be satisfied with what is available in their communities. Most will go looking for a myth — a supermother who seems to be divinely gifted for the care of children. When mothers and fathers fail to find such a day care mother, they still measure the options against the myth and are disappointed. Few parents know at the outset what makes for good day care. If you see yourself among these parents, you have probably started wondering what the best option is. The answer is you.*

Day care is a lucrative and rewarding business, but few women consider running a day care home to be a viable financial alternative to working outside the home. Yet today, more women than ever before are college-educated, have young children, and need to support their families. These are the women who should consider running a day care home as a way to meet their financial needs and to find satisfaction in providing a service to the community.

---

*Though many men are also capable of providing good day care in a home, sexual discrimination works two ways; our society does not trust men with children and it is therefore very difficult for a man — unaided by a woman — to run a day care home today. For this reason alone I will speak of the provider as a woman throughout this book.

Some women run day care businesses because they cannot — or think they cannot — do anything else to support their families. These women feel trapped by circumstances. This is not a good environment for them or for the children in their care. Others want to earn a little extra money for the family, to have children for their own children to play with, or to alleviate boredom. These women do not see day care as a business; they feel that charging a fair price for day care services is immoral and unwomanly. But they quickly find that the benefits — a little extra money, play-mates, or whatever — are not worth the energy and work that any business requires. Fortunately, these women quickly give up the business and find other ways to meet their needs. And there is perhaps a very small group of women who provide day care because they love all children and enjoy the fun and self-esteem. Though this is the provider we all look for, she is for the most part a myth.

The women I consider the best candidates for day care provider are still few, but their numbers are growing. These are the women who (1) have young children; (2) are career-oriented; (3) are highly motivated by money; and (4) want to be home with their own children during the early years. These are the qualities that will bring a strong commitment to the day care business and therefore to the care of individual children. The committed day care mother can provide the consistency and secure environment that every parent wants for his or her child. In this kind of home children will find fair treatment, acceptance, and a stable peer group — a far more realistic and valuable goal than the mythical super-mother who loves all children equally.

I stress that day care is a business, and until this is understood by women throughout the country day care will not attract the kind of women who can offer the best child care, the kind of women we would trust with our children. Day care is not baby-sitting; it is not a substitute for a "real" job. It is demanding work for which the provider should receive a proper financial return. The provider sacrifices the privacy of her home and perhaps an outside career to guarantee mature guidance and care for children; parents who understand this (and most do) should be willing to pay a reasonable fee.

A successful day care provider can expect to earn from $12,000 to $18,000 during the first year of business. This is a salary range comparable to that of most beginning professionals, including draftspeople, designers, dieticians, social workers, college teachers, and computer programmers, and one that is well deserved by the provider. Furthermore, as a result of operating a day care home, the provider can actually end up with more of her earned income after taxes than salaried employees do, because she does not have to pay for such things as child care, suitable clothing, transportation, parking, or lunches.

The financial rewards in day care are important because they underscore the seriousness of the provider's involvement and the professional relationship between the provider and the parents. The provider wants her business to run smoothly and successfully; the parents want a healthy environment for their children. These are the ingredients of a successful relationship between provider and parent, and provider and child.

In addition to the financial rewards, the day care business has other, more subtle benefits. After the harried and stressful first months of providing day care, my philosophy began to crystalize. The methods I developed to deal with a large group of children began to show in the children's behavior. I was pleased with the results, and so were the parents. I was learning about what is important to children — how they learn and what they really needed from me, as opposed to what they and I thought they needed in the beginning. Parents began to consult me on specific problems they had with their children; behavior problems in certain children disappeared; and I found a competency in my own judgment that I had not experienced before. Day care quickly became a source of great satisfaction, and I received unconditional support and appreciation from parents.

The most obvious benefit, and the one most important to me, was learning that I can support my family when times are hard. Learning this has given me a greater sense of personal security and strength that has altered other areas of my life. I now make decisions and choices from a feeling of strength and understanding.

The service of the day care provider to the community in general is gradually becoming known beyond the circle of families with children in day care. Adults who choose to perpetuate myths will ask, "Why don't you get a real job?" However, parents, teachers, and other professionals who work with families and children will hold you in high esteem and admire you for the job you do. You will be the first to recognize a troubled family or a troubled child, and you might be the best person to help that child deal with the difficulties in his or her life — separation and divorce are the most common today, but there may be others.

This book is designed to teach you how to offer the service of a day care provider — how to start and run a day care business in your home — and, at the very least, how to assess any day care home. I will take you every step of the way: choosing the number and ages of the children you want to care for; deciding whether to seek a license; determining fees, expenses, and taxes; finding day care children and selecting those suited to your style of day care home; handling children during the first few days; caring for infants; teaching eating habits; dealing with toilet training and sexual awareness; teaching independence and values; identifying the necessary materials and equipment and arranging your home, and defining rules and reasonable limits. Because day care can be such a significant factor in the lives of the day care families, I have included two chapters on special aspects of day care to enrich and secure the day care home in the families' lives. Above all, you will learn how to control your level of income, how to work with parents and children, and how to use the resources available in your city or town.

The different methods of working with children described here are the result of my experience with day care and are the methods that I found to be most effective in accomplishing an immediate goal, such as solving a discipline problem, while also working toward the more important goal of the child's growth and independence. In the beginning I searched many resources and parenting guides for advice on how to deal with specific problems; some of these sources have become ready tools, and I strongly recommend them: *Between Parent and Child,* by Haim Ginnot; *How to Parent,* by Fitzhugh Dodson; and *P.E.T.: Parent Effectiveness Training*, by Thomas Gordon. If you are familiar with these books, you may recognize their influence in the following pages.

There are many different ways to run a day care home — as many ways as there are people. Each home reflects the values and goals of the provider. In the chapters that follow I have used my day care home as the touchstone and the norm. My day care home is best described as a large family environment, a home with sometimes more then ten children. Although most providers will not want to care for so many children, the problems encountered in any day care business are generally the same regardless of size. The size of the group of children is a choice for you alone to make, and one that will reflect your goals and your values. My particular biases will be clear as you read through the chapters: I prefer to see children developing freely through play and peer interaction; I prefer to see children sharing and helping; I prefer to see children discovering their feelings rather than pretending they have no so-called bad feelings; I prefer to see children becoming independent rather than remaining safe at all costs; and I prefer to see children letting their minds come alive through imaginative play rather than restricting their activity to adult-organized table games, crafts, and reading lessons, for which many children have little enthusiasm. These preferences should give you a clue to my methods of disciplining. Only one needs prior explanation: I believe in the method of taking time out to calm excited emotions. Children in my home take time out when they fuss or throw a tantrum; they are taken to a room where they can fuss or cry until they are finished. This method, like many others, takes everyone in the day care home into consideration, and as you read through these pages you will see how effective a tool it is. As you consider and plan your own business, you will develop your own methods — your own key words for talking to the children, your own favorite games to play with them, and your own style of dealing with parents and children.

Running a day care business will have an effect on you and the rest of your family during the hours outside of day care. When you begin a day care home you will have to choose carefully how to use the time and energy that remains after children have been picked up. Is housekeeping very important to the peace and security of your family life? If it is, then you will want to insure maintenance of this standard in some way. Are there other members of the household who might assume a larger share of the daily and weekly chores? You will be working full time at a very demanding job and you will be tired at the end of the day.

You will be able to do some of the housework during day care hours, but perhaps you will want to hire someone to come in to do certain jobs. I found that trading some housecleaning work for limited day care was a very successful arrangement for everyone involved. Is gourmet cooking expected daily by 6:00 P.M.? Forget it, or hire a cook. No one will be able to spend much time in the kitchen preparing dinner before closing time. Children are so interested in kitchen activity that it is unlikely that you can accomplish much unless you begin your dinner preparation right after breakfast. I found that I needed more evenings out when spending five days a week with children in the house. You will have more energy and interest in your day care business if you pay attention to your need for adult stimulation and relaxation. This expense is not frivolous if it raises your spirits and keeps you going; it is an investment.

If your own children are infants, beginning a day care home will be an easy adjustment and will usually be a delightful addition to the infants' life. Your children will be more tired and less demanding. They will nap longer and more soundly and they will profit from association with the day care children. You must be especially careful to treat your children the same way as the others, since all the children will be quick to feel favoritism. The result of favoritism is a lack of trust in the adult from the excluded children, while favored children may feel guilty or superior. All will recognize the inconsistency and resent it.

Older children adjusting to day care in their home may have some feelings about their loss of privacy and personal property, which you can minimize by allowing your children to select belongings and toys to reserve as personal. Keep these items on a shelf in the closet, and allow day care children to use them only with permission from your children. If these items are brought out during day care time, it is with the knowledge that they will be shared. My children decided that their individual bunk beds would be private space; one of them seemed to need this space and retained it, while the other did not need this private space and freely offered it for use by the day care children in their games. To ensure the happiness of all, you will want to assess your own children's needs and make adjustments in the day care environment to meet them.

If you have children over three, they will profit from a discussion about the difference between day care time and family time. Some activity or behavior is acceptable during family time but is not appropriate during day care time. This difference is easily understood and accepted by children when they know that they still have family time and privacy when day care hours are over.

If after reading this book you are still hesitant about providing a home yourself, I strongly recommend finding a day care home in your area and offering your free services, first to observe, then to take over for short periods, and finally to operate for two or three consecutive days. Of course, your home and your children will be different. Children in another home will not interact with you in the same way as those for whom you provide continuous care, and your own children will act differently in their own home with you as the day care mother. But this experiment will help you test what you have learned from this book and your own ideas about the day care business.

Author's Note

The drawings of children's play furniture, tire swings, outside jungle gym, porch gate and the tipless step should not be used as blueprints. Consult a carpenter, architect, or other experienced professional for plans to build such structures to meet safety requirements.

1

Choosing Your Style

Let us assume you have decided to enter the day care business. How do you start? To run any successful business, you need to know as much as possible about that business before you start, and you need to know where your business will fit into the network of businesses like it. Your style of day care home will reflect your choices from a wide range of possibilities, but first you must learn as much as you can about what is possible. You begin by surveying your competition—who are they and where are they? Next you consider the individual factors that distinguish one day care service from another—the number of children, their ages, child-rearing philosophy of the provider, and so on. Finally you consider the different options that appeal to you and you choose your own style, one that will reflect your abilities, your interests, and your philosophy.

The Competition

You need to learn who is offering day care services in your community in order to know who is seeking day care, what services seem most successful, what rates are acceptable, what philosophies are followed, and what kind of support network is available for day care providers.

First contact the state and local offices that keep track of day care services. In most cases, this will be your state's department of social or health services. This office will usually have a list of every person who has expressed an interest in offering licensed day care and will also have information about any other day care referral services in your area. Also contact church and civic organizations that might sponsor day care services. Make a list of the day care homes and centers in your area, listing those closest to your home first and those farthest away last.

Second, call the day care homes and centers and ask the adult in charge if you may visit the home or center for an hour and discuss what they offer as a service. Make specific appointments for visits; a provider may invite you to drop in at any time, but you should try to avoid inopportune times such as the lunch hour or closing time. You want your visit to occur when children are engaged in activities; this will give you an opportunity to assess the provider's philosophy and involvement with the children.

Third, prepare for your visits by making up a list of questions to ask each provider. I used a general survey form on which I could record providers' answers plus my own views (see the survey form below). The survey covers basic information, such as number of children, equipment, and rates, as well as my assessment of the attitudes of the children and other matters. Add any other questions that concern you or may be especially relevant to your area. One question not included here is why a child is in day care. You will probably find that a child is in day care because both parents work, but this is not always the case. You may also want to know if most of the parents work in one area. Does the day care service cater to a specific employment group? I found that living near a university meant I would always have a certain number of children whose parents studied or worked at the university.

Fourth, visit as many homes as possible, interviewing the providers according to your survey questions. During these visits you will be not only gathering information but also making important business contacts. The information you gather will help you run your own business, and the business contacts may supply you, through referrals, with your first day care children.

Fifth, organize and review the information you collected during your survey. You should now know the different options available in your area. Which homes are in high demand? Why are some homes in need of children? Are these very young businesses or are the fees too high? Is there a problem with the location or with the quality of care? Are there too many homes located in a small area or in a neighborhood with few young families? Did you like what you saw? Do you have ideas about how you would do things differently? If you answered yes to the last question, you are

Day Care Home/Center Survey

Name
Address
Phone

(When using the 1–10 rating scale, 1 and 2 = poor, 3 and 4 = fair, 5–7 = good, 8 and 9 = very good, 10 = excellent.)

beginning to define your own style. Regardless of how you feel about the various homes and centers you visited, keep the survey information; this is a basic resource for later years when you feel you should refer a prospective client to another day care service.

Factors and Preferences

If you have conducted your survey of the competition carefully, even with only a limited number of homes, you now know that the variations in day care service are limited only by the imagination of the individuals involved. Each service is different, and each reflects the values and preferences of the individual provider. Nevertheless, you can isolate the factors that have the most obvious influence on determining a style of service. As you consider each factor and your personal preference, you will begin to narrow the options to the few that are best suited to you. The main factors distinguishing various day care services are the definition as a home or center, the philosophy according to a method or the provider's personality, the number of adults, the types of children, the ages of the children, the number of children, full-time or part-time day care, the inclusion of additional employment for the provider, the type of space, and rates.

Homes and Centers

In your survey, the most obvious difference you probably encountered was between a day care home and a day care center. There are several important differences between these two kinds of services which are apparent to adults and even more apparent to the kids, judging from how they act. Sometimes children come to a day care home after having attended a day care center. They usually refer to the previous situation as "school." After being with me for a few weeks, I hear them talk about coming to "Karen's house." The differences in attitudes are related to the differences in the two environments.

Centers usually divide their population into spaces based on age. All the children in one group will be the same age, and children will spend most, if not all, of the day in this large group (twenty kids or so). Usually more than one adult is present, and those adults will take on the role of teachers, not the role of parents. The setting is obviously not a home; there are no spaces reserved for adult living and no bedrooms where family members sleep. A cook may spend all her time in the kitchen preparing meals but not interact with the children at all. Children in a day care center receive most of their instruction as part of a large group. Furthermore, they respond to this kind of environment by looking to the external forces of teachers to guide them.

In a day care center or school the children expect adult authority to intervene at every point, and they do not seem to exercise the same self-control and self-discipline they exhibit in a day care home. They expect the control and discipline to come more from the environment. They are often presented with table activities or organized, adult-led games. The adults in the center are there specifically to attend to the children; this is the expectation of the children as well as of the teachers. A day care center may concentrate on teaching external skills such as reading, social behavior in groups, and controlled use of time.

A good day care home will be a sharp contrast to any day care center. In my day care home, the children see me not as their parent but rather as *a* parent who will treat them in much the same way as their own parents. Children know they are in a home, and therefore they know that a certain range of behavior is acceptable. They know what kind of discipline will be used by a parent, and they come to regard the other children as siblings to some extent. Children living with younger day care siblings learn as a matter of course that even the youngest baby is an individual with his or her own personality and value. With attention and effort, the adult can ensure that there is little or no stereotyping based on age or sex. Without any formal instruction, children learn to consider each member of the group as an equal with intrinsic value and entitled to consideration and respect. Older children become more sensitive to and appreciative of younger children, and younger children look to them for assistance, guidance, and protection. The younger children quickly lose any fear or sense of intimidation that they may have acquired from previous negative experiences with an older child in another setting. Their self-esteem increases when they experience respect and consideration from older children. Separating age groups of children breeds distrust, misunderstanding, and unnecessary barriers, as does separation in adult society of groups of people based on differences. In a good day care home it would be hard for a child to feel isolated or overlooked, because the developmental differences in the children are so great that each child must be addressed individually.

Children at home do not expect to be supervised and guided in their activity every moment of the day. Knowing that "home" means more freedom and less structure than in other settings, children use their built-in set of rules and apply self-discipline. They expect to solve more of their own problems, to create their own diversions, and to apply behavior standards learned at home. They spend a lot of time on the floor, taking clothing on and off, moving furniture around. Most of this kind of child-created activity is thought not to be appropriate for the day care center or school setting but is appropriate in a home.

I have a strong personal preference for the day care home, because it accepts children as children and gives them their own choice of activity while allowing them to develop strong relationships with other children. This acceptance and bonding is characteristic of the day care home. If this appeals to you, you will want to organize your business around the *home* environment. If the qualities of a day care *center* appeal to you — more structure and external teaching — you will want to plan your business around that idea.

Method and Personality

Visiting a number of day care providers will have given you a good idea of the variety of approaches in use in day care services. Some will follow a definite method; others will run their day care home according to their natural responses to children. Each will probably have given some consideration to the question of what approach to take. Some of the approaches you will like, and others you will dislike. Be open to the possibilities and choices you see.

My approach is based on my preference for developing certain qualities in a child's life and can be adapted to most forms of child care. This approach, which I call attentive noninterference, involves much more peer interaction than more standard modern approaches, and embraces many of the early American educational principles found in the one-room schoolhouse and the large family. Older children teach younger ones not only skills but also attitudes and expectations. Older children gain in this exchange by acquiring an expanded capacity for responsibility and appreciation for younger children. An adult is there when really needed but is involved in other activities with other responsibilities. This discourages unnecessary dependence on adults to solve problems, and gives children a chance to see adults performing adult tasks.

The individual personality of the day care provider is important only to the extent that she can do the following:

1. project acceptance of children
2. implement methods fairly and consistently
3. maintain reasonable expectations for children
4. accept the environment children create for their activity
5. maintain emotional stability
6. discourage unnecessary dependence
7. communicate effectively with parents about their children

Beyond these skills, the personality of the provider is of minor importance in ensuring a good day care environment. It is the kids and their interaction that will determine their happiness and emotional health. When you see providers whose style you admire, do not think that you could not do as well or would not respond in this or that particular way. The children's interaction will promote individual growth and healthy group dynamics. Wishing you were more artistic, relaxed, cheerful, playful, loving, patient, or organized is not useful. You are who you are, and you do the best you can. Make the choices defining your day care business in such a way that you will be able to respond as well as you can. Concentrate on implementing the methods and practicing the seven skills listed above. None of the wonderful personality traits you do or do not have will ever be an adequate substitute for the positive experience children gain from healthy peer interaction.

The Number of Adults

In most day care homes there is only one adult; in day care centers there may be several. If you intend to operate a day care home for many children, perhaps more than eight or nine, you may want to consider hiring an assistant.

You will probably want to begin alone, building your business slowly and carefully with only as many children as you can handle alone. If you plan to expand your business to a point where you will need an assistant, you should consider what responsibilities you will give him or her. Will you want another adult or a younger person? Will the assistant work full-time or part-time? If you decide to keep the business small, you can reserve the option of an assistant for the summer months or school vacations.

Regardless of age or specific responsibilities, an assistant must have good judgment, a good driving record, an understanding of children, and a child-rearing philosophy compatible with yours. If there is a college or university in your area, you should investigate the possibility of hiring a work-study student. Most students have restricted schedules during the academic year but are available for more hours during the summer. You can find out about student help by calling the college or university financial aid office or student employment service. The school will supply you with a contract, and you will be able to hire one or more students, depending on the college's policy. The contract enables you to interview students and receive reimbursement for part of the student's pay. Other possible assistants include retired relatives of day care children, a mother with young children, a neighbor, or a mature high-school student.

During the summer months an assistant will enable you to offer a more varied program of activities for the older children — field trips to parks, beaches, zoos, and other places — while the younger children remain in the day care home.

Types of Children

Perhaps the last question people ask themselves when considering a day care business is what kind of children they can handle, but this should be one of the first questions. You cannot realistically be all things to all people, but you can be a good provider to several different types of children.

Consider your own personal limitations carefully and realistically to clarify in your mind the kinds of children you can work with. Do you have the exceptional patience and generosity that enables you to take children with major problems, such as emotional disturbance or physical handicaps? Mild retardation and severe health problems in children demand much more from the day care provider. Do you have the skills needed to develop and maintain a good working relationship with the parents of children with severe problems? Some parents will need family counseling to help them deal with their feelings, attitudes, and day-to-day problems. Taking a child you are not equipped to handle, or do not have the extra patience to teach, is not fair to the child. Child, parents, and you would soon learn that the child should be moved, which sometimes causes feelings of failure for all of you and often long-lasting guilt and feelings of rejection for the child. The child may feel that he or she is not lovable or is bad. In the end you have a damaged child, angry parents, and a regretful day care provider. Protect your reputation and children by accepting for day care only those children who will be happy in the environment you offer, making sure also that the parents see the value in that environment and choose it not because of laziness or expediency, but because they support your methods and rationale.

If you do choose to take children with special needs, will you limit yourself to children in this category, or will you try to integrate one or two children with special needs into a larger group of children of average capacities and needs? This kind of service can be especially beneficial to all children involved, allowing them to develop broader understanding of the different talents and needs of a wider variety of individuals. The child with special needs gains from having the opportunity to learn from other children and to enjoy positive peer relationships.

Whatever choice you make, it should be based on your willingness and ability to meet the needs of the children you do accept into your home. Be honest with yourself and with the parents who seek your day care for these children.

Ages of Children

You have probably already started to think about what ages of children you would prefer. Do you love small babies, or are you bored by them? Do you prefer independent three-year-olds, or more responsible five-year-olds? In part, the ages of children you select should reflect what you feel most comfortable with. Age also affects, to some extent, the hours you choose, which I discuss separately below. If you only want children over age five, you will probably be working part-time during the school year and full-time during school vacations.

You may want a mix of different ages. In my day care home I take children from two months to ten years of age. Children from six to ten years are in school from 9:00 A.M. to 3:30 P.M.; and are in my home for a short time in the morning and from 3:30 to 5:30 in the afternoon. There can be many benefits from mixing children of different ages: younger children receive support from older children and learn from them; older children learn to show consideration and patience for young ones and also learn to love and enjoy them.

If you decide on one particular age group at the outset and later feel you want greater variety in age, you can accept children of different ages as your business grows. Whatever decisions you make now can easily be modified as you go along. You will find, however, that most children over age three in day care homes have been in those homes since they were less than two years old. For this reason it is likely that you will take children under two even if you prefer to have all older children.

Number of Children

The number of children you can care for will be determined by your abilities and by the ages and personalities of the children. You will probably not know how many children you can handle until after you have started your business with two or three children and added other children one by one, making sure that each child adjusts to the group and the group adjusts to the new child. Some children will be self-sufficient and undemanding, and you will be able to handle several children like this. Others will require greater attention. One child who is "difficult" by your definition (whatever that may be) may make the entire business seem impossible; that child may have to move to another day care service. The number of children you decide to care for at any given time will have to be balanced against the personalities of the children. If you have two or three difficult children and want to keep them, you may have to give up accepting other children until the difficult ones move on to school or grow into another stage.

Before you settle on an absolute figure, keep in mind basic rules of safety and your ability to handle a group. If all the children are mobile, are they protected from accidents in your home? Can you watch all of the children who require supervision? Do the older children follow instructions the first time? The second time? If you are caring for young children who require close supervision, you will want to take fewer children than if you are caring for a mix of children that includes older ones who accept more responsibility for their own behavior.

Full Time or Part Time

The number of hours you work should be strictly up to you, but it will probably take one or two years before your business is finally arranged the way you want it. If you choose only school-age children because you only want to work in the afternoons, you will probably not have much trouble controlling your time, except during school vacations. Any preschool child will probably require care for more hours than you are willing to give on a part-time schedule. In the beginning you will have to be flexible about hours, until you develop a group of parents interested enough in your service to accept your restrictions on time. When I began day care, the first child came as early as 6:15 A.M. and the last child stayed as late as 7:15 P.M. It was fully two years before I was able to limit my hours to 8:00 A.M. to 5:30 P.M. and maintain a full group of children at my desired rates.

No matter how strictly you define your hours, and no matter how many parents accept your time limits, there will always be one or two who are late in picking up their children, at least once. If a parent is late more than once, I speak with him or her about the importance of my family time. I might say, ''There is very little time left in the day for me to relate to my children individually. If there are playmates in the house, my children will have nothing to do with me. So please be sure to pick up your child by 5:30." I have never used a late fee to force people to pick up their children on time. This is their responsibility, and their adherence to the fixed time shows respect for me. Late fees may be effective in some instances, but I think they also give parents the feeling that it is acceptable to be late — just costs an extra buck or two. By the end of the day I do not want any overtime money; I want to spend time with my *own* family. I also prefer to have a more personal, friendly relationship with day care families.

Additional Work

Some day care providers want to combine their day care service with additional work. If you prefer a structured day care center for preschool children, additional work will not be feasible. All your time and energy will be taken up by the requirements of maintaining that structure. For other day care providers, additional work will be a necessity. An important ingredient of my approach — attentive noninterference — is having some other activity that appears to demand my attention. Typing is perfect. I can hear all that goes on. I process this information automatically, screening out all the ordinary play and picking up on the problems and how the children are handling them. It appears to the children that they are pretty much on their own, but they can see me and hear the typewriter and they know that I am available should they have a real need. Jumping up and down from the typewriter might seem to be a frustrating way to operate, but instead I feel quite frustrated when there is no typing to provide me with the cover I need to keep out of the way. If an adult is completely available to the children, it is very hard for the children to depend on their own resources and imagination to work out their activities and difficulties.

Whatever additional work you choose, it should be an activity that you can abandon quickly when the children need you. The activity itself must present no danger to children. Working with crafts materials might seem harmless, but the materials could include paints or metals or glue dangerous to small children. Whatever you leave on a desk or table must present no hazard to a meandering two-year-old or a curious six-year-old.

Space

You do not need a lot of space to run a day care service. If you live in a house or apartment with access to a yard, you have enough space for a day care home. A day care center usually involves a more formal definition of space, sometimes a separate building or space in a church or civic building. Although I have worked in a day care center located in a large church basement, I will confine my discussion here to a day care home.

During the years I was involved in day care at home, I simply gave over my home to the day care children. The diagram of my house on page 192 illustrates one possible way of using the space in a small home to accommodate a large number of children. You need a room where children can use their play materials freely, an area for a lunch table and chairs, and a quiet area where the children can take naps. I believe children should be encouraged to play outdoors as much as possible, and a back yard can be fenced in for younger children or left open for older children. The details of arranging space to suit children of different ages is discussed separately in Chapter 11.

Rates

Day care is a business, and this must be kept in mind. The rates you charge must reflect the value of the service you offer and enable you to feel that you are being adequately compensated for the work you perform.

You will want your rates to be competitive with those of other day care homes; you can reexamine the answers to your survey questions to get an idea of prevailing rates. Generally, higher rates are charged for babies than for toilet-trained preschool-age children. Your rates will also depend on the income you want to generate and the number and ages of children you are willing to take. If you decide, for example, that you want to earn $1200 per month with preschool-age children, you can charge $325 per month per child for two children under two years old and $275 per month per child for two three-year olds and accept four children. Rates are more fully discussed in Chapter 3, "Dollars and Sense." The point to remember when setting rates is that you are performing a valuable service for families in your community, and inadequate compensation will undermine your self-esteem and the parents' perception of your service. If a parent does not feel that his or her child is worth a reasonable investment of $200 to $400 a month, you can refer him or her to one of the many day care services you found during your survey. If you maintain a professional level of care, parents will respect what you do and think your rates fair.

Sample Styles

You have now considered the major factors determining different styles of day care services and should have a good idea of your preferences and abilities. Each choice you make will define your particular style to some degree, until you ultimately develop a distinctive style that reflects your values and interests. How comfortable you are with your chosen style will determine how happy the children are in your day care home. The number of possible styles is limited only by your imagination and the variety of people in this world. To help you on your way to developing a style that is best for you and your future day care children, let us look at some possibilities. I will consider briefly three distinct types of day care homes that can be integrated into the fourth type, and therefore will devote more attention to the last.

Nursery Style

This is a style for women who have a baby of their own or like having small babies to take care of. The day care baby may arrive at 8:00 A.M. and remain until noon, if the provider works part-time, or until 6:00 P.M., if the provider works full-time. The hours of care, of course, can be set by the provider, depending on how long she wants to spend with three or four infants. Infants adjust easily to day care, and the provider will probably find herself tired from caring for infants but free of the problems of adjustment that arise with older children. The provider's practical concerns will focus more on the physical care of the child and the supervised play than on free interaction of children.

Preschool Play Group

A day care provider may decide to accept only children between the ages of three and five and thus eliminate the extra attention that younger children require. At this age children are interested in planning and carrying out their own activities and can be watched from a distance. If the provider feels strongly about providing a structured learning environment, she may supervise group activities and define those activities more strictly. Children at this age, however, are learning to develop their own interests and abilities and may feel confined by a structured day care environment.

After-School Care

After-school care is probably the easiest approach for a day care provider. It can include early morning care before the schools open; school-age children may arrive at 8:00 A.M., brought by parents on their way to work, and leave for school at 8:45 A.M. It is unlikely you will be able to avoid early morning care in some states, since elementary schools generally do not allow children on the grounds until 9:00 A.M., when adults are available to supervise them.

The children will return for two or three hours in the afternoon, after school closes and until their parents pick them up. Although school-age children are used to the structured environment of a classroom, it is unfortunate if the provider continues this style in her home. These children should have the opportunity to play freely and creatively and do what they want to do, within reasonable bounds, after several hours in a classroom.

Large Family Environment

The style I chose and used successfully is a variation on the large family. As the name implies, this kind of home is run as you might expect one parent to run a family with about ten to twelve children aged from two months to about nine years. There are several sets of twins in this hypothetical family, and the group age configuration might look like this: two months, 7 months, 14 months, two years, two and a half years, three three-year-olds, two four-year-olds, and four after-school kids aged five to nine. As the oldest children in this day care home move on to more school-oriented programs or their parents are able to piece together after-school activities to replace day care, new children are added — usually from the bottom of the age group — so that the youngest children will have age peers by the time they are about two and a half.

In addition to the age span of the children, I have defined several general principles of my style that convey to parents my personal values and the kind of attention children will receive in my home.

Television. Television denies children the opportunity to develop their own imagination and abilities. I advise parents at the first meeting that television viewing will be limited to one hour per week. I allow this much television because there are times when I need to tie the children down to preserve my sanity.

Food. I have found that the food I serve is an important attraction to families: no junk food, no sugar, no preservatives, and no red meat. Though my family enjoys red meat occasionally, there is no need to serve red meat during day care. Children can be persuaded to eat raw vegetables, fruits, and other nutritious foods and will do so willingly once the habit is established. (Eating habits are discussed in detail in Chapter 7).

Housekeeping. The relaxed housekeeping standards and general child-related clutter are signs of the child-centered atmosphere of my home. The space has been taken over by the interests and activity of children. All adult, breakable ornaments and valuables have been stored for the duration of the day care years. We live in a day care home — the kids are the most important thing here. This is the message my home conveys.

The purpose of my style is to inculcate in children certain basic values that will serve them in their future years, and these values are expressed in the personal way I care for the children, through attentive noninterference, and the freedom I allow them.

Responsibility within a community. Children are encouraged to give and receive help and support from peers in a multi-age setting with a minimum of adult interference but constant adult awareness.

Application of the Golden Rule. Children are taught to treat others as they want to be treated; this means no one is excluded from a game, and no one gets preferential treatment during day care, including my own children.

Development of nonsexist and nonracist attitudes. Children are taught by example and experience to accept and value individual differences; stereotypic social views are discouraged.

Acceptance of fair, consistent discipline. Children learn to understand, accept, and follow fair rules and discipline as part of the basis for a smooth-running group and healthier peer relationships.

Understanding the basic ecology of life. Through attitudes and rules regarding toys, materials, animals, plants, and food, children learn ecological relationships and environmental values. When children ask, "Why can't I squash the bug?" I have an opportunity to teach the relationship between natural resources and human and animal life, the balance of nature and the finite character of resources. Through such an understanding children learn to not waste or damage materials. It may be easier to answer a question by saying, "Because I said so," but this does not really answer the question, and besides, teaching values is much more fun than giving pat answers.

Not all families will want to place their children in this kind of environment, but many will. Most important, these values, like yours, will reflect your ability to care for other people's children as carefully as you care for your own. No parent will expect you to love that child as much as you love your own, but the parent does rightfully expect you to value the child and be fair and considerate.

To give you an idea of what care is like in a large family environment, follow me around my house to see what I see and feel what I feel during a typical day care day.

The first parent and child arrive at 7:50 A.M. (ten minutes early, but an exception I have agreed to). I am probably in bed. My husband, Terry, leaves the house at about 7:55 A.M., and I roll out of bed as he walks out the front door. By 8:00 A.M. I am in the kitchen (usually dressed in a muumuu) making breakfast for Brianna and Sean, my children. Brianna begins to play with Paul, the early bird. I instruct her to go into her room and dress before she starts playing. I say, "Paul, please stay out of the other room until Brianna and Sean are through dressing, because they will just play and not get dressed." At 8:05 A.M. Joanna, aged one and a half, arrives with her mother or father. She may protest loudly as Mom makes a hesitating attempt to take her sweater and hat off. She prefers to hang on to them for a while and take care of them herself. Joanna's mom tells Joanna to wave from the window as she goes out the door. If Joanna is having trouble dealing with her mom's departure, Sean usually comes running, and encircling her with his gentle arms, he reassures Joanna, "Your mama will be back tonight to get you. It's okay. Let's wave from the window." Joanna may continue to fuss until her mother drives off, then she immediately turns from the window and chooses a puzzle. Sean and Brianna come to breakfast while I prepare lunchboxes. Six children arrive between 8:10 and 8:40. At 8:40 I call, "School time, Orca kids." (Orca is an elementary school nearby.) "Zip your coats. Don't forget your lunches. Have a good day." Two five-year-olds rush out the door. I then call the next group, "Latona kids [another elementary school], time for school. Zip your coats. Don't forget your lunches. Kristi, do you have the note for your teacher? Have a good day." Three more schoolchildren leave, including my son, who gives me a hug and kisses anyone under chin height on the head on his way to the door. Phase one completed.

Phase two begins. Preschoolers continue to arrive until about 10:00 A.M. I am usually in the kitchen doing dishes and listening to classical music on the radio. I have found that my favorite music, reggae and blues, is too stimulating for the children, as it is for me too. I greet the kids from the kitchen as they arrive one by one. Parents and kids call a greeting as they come in the front door. Each child greets each new arrival. Usually at least one child stops his or her activity and goes to the new member, offering to help with a coat or hang up a sweater. This is not done out of a concern that the child needs help, but rather is a show of affection and welcome. Some kids run to the kitchen to give me a hug, but most ignore me after the initial greeting and get right into the swing of whatever the other kids are doing. By 9:30 A.M. there are blocks all over the rug and two or three kids playing with them. In another room the kids' dress-up clothes are strewn about, with favorite costumes adorning the bodies of two or more two- to four-year-olds. Someone may ask me to reposition the platforms of the climbing gym, or there may not be any need at all for me to help or interfere in the activity. If I hear an escalating argument, I interrupt and deal with it (see Chapter 9).

For the most part, this group of six to eight kids, aged one and a half to four years, will play very happily with only moderate noise until about 11:00 A.M. They come to announce to me throughout the morning that they "need to go pee or dump." None of this current group needs help with the toilet routine, but they seem to want me to know that they are taking care of business. Occasionally they make other reports on activities; some kids report to make sure that any activity is acceptable. It may take an especially controlled child many months to relax and begin to exercise internal judgment. I may have to tell a new child, "I don't expect you to tell me everything that everyone else is doing. If you are worried about someone getting hurt, then you can help. If you need to, come and tell me about it. But you don't have to worry about most play. It's okay to play with your friends and use the toys without telling me or asking me." I think I must have said this about twenty times a day to one child during her first month.

The arrangement of play materials assists children in making appropriate choices. Puzzles for the youngest children are on the lowest shelves, while more difficult puzzles are kept a little higher. All the children understand the rules about various items: Finish any puzzle that you take out. Put it away before taking out another. Put one toy away before taking out something else. Sometimes, though, especially with toys such as blocks, other children become involved and it does not make sense to put materials away as each child finishes. These toys make up the mess that is picked up at clean-up time.

The children occasionally ask permission to wash their hands because they know that I am consistent in my restriction of water play in the bathroom. They do not want me to mistake their hand-washing for play. They also ask if it is okay to play outside after a rain. I check the yard gates as the first child goes out, since the children have become very independent and self-motivated in their activity.

When I finish in the kitchen, I go to the typewriter and begin typing. Keeping my ears open and processing all I hear, I give invisible, constant attention to the group dynamics under way. The phone often rings with potential customers, and visitors frequently come and go, picking up or dropping off typing work. Children enjoy greeting, questioning, and sending off "typees," as we call them, with great enthusiasm. It is usually not necessary for me to become involved in this interaction. Typees are curious and amused with the children and are rarely, if ever, annoyed.

Parents sometimes question my ability to get any typing done with "all these kids," but they don't seem to mind this other business activity in conjunction with day care. I suppose if a child were unhappy here or came home repeatedly with scratches or bruises from fights, parents' attitudes would be different. As long as things seem to be going smoothly — happy play in progress, meals taken care of, kids rested as they should be, warm relationships between me and the children — parents are quite satisfied and do not question the method.

At 11:15 I stop typing and call, "Clean-up time." If Eric and John, the four-year-olds, are here, it is usually not necessary for me to do much. I go to the kitchen and begin lunch. If the children are between one and three years of age, they require my verbal coaching. It is a rare group that will happily comply with the clean-up call, even after several weeks of closely supervised pick-up activity. With a group of children of various ages, you will probably have to assign pick-up tasks from the kitchen as you make lunch. I put the older children in charge of tasks requiring longer attention: "Eric [age 4], you are in charge of the blocks; Paul [age 3], you are in charge of getting the blocks over to Eric so that he can stack them. Naomi [age 2], please pick up all the toy-box toys in this room; Joanna [age 2], please pick up all the Legos and put them in the Lego box. Naomi, please pick up the dinosaur next to the blue chair. Play time is over for now. Jennifer [age 4], please put the tops on all the felt pens and check to see if those tops are on tight. Naomi, play time is over, it is time to clean up. Please pick up the ball in the corner and put it in the toy box." It is amazing what you and the kids can accomplish while you are making lunch.

Occasionally I have to leave the kitchen to present myself physically to a child who is testing my dedication to his or her participation. When a child refuses to contribute effort, I simply pick him up and deposit him, like a sack of potatoes, without anger or affection, in the other room. I tell him, "Stay in here until you are ready to come out and help. We will save some things for you to do." It seems that inviting the child to go into the other room until he or she is ready to help gives the child too much control over this situation, and he or she is more anxious to come out if put there by the adult. If the child does not emerge within two or three minutes to help, I go to the room and invite him out, saying, "Are you ready to come out and help with clean-up?" I have never received a negative answer. If you should get one, I would advise leaving the child until he *does* want to come out; be sure to reserve some picking up for him to do before he sits down to lunch.

As soon as the toys are all picked up, I sweep the whole area, then turn on some requested music for "dance time." The children jump and wiggle around with glee while I finish preparing lunch. At 11:45 Tony arrives from kindergarten and Eric goes wild with excitement. Those two together take more space and make more noise than five children. For this reason it is important to me that lunch be ready and the children seated at the table before Tony walks in the door.

I serve an appropriate portion of food to each child: little bits for Jamaica and triple portions of everything for Tony. I remind them, "Finish your firsts before you ask for seconds." As kids finish — Tony first, Paul second, Joanna next — they leave the table and play in the other room or outside until everyone is finished. If I allow children to play within eyesight or earshot, the slower children will not finish lunch. I generally have to coach the slow eaters by saying, "Have another bite, Eric; have another bite, Jamaica." By 12:45 everyone has finished lunch and is again playing.

At 12:50 I call a toddler and send him to the bathroom before diapering and tucking him into his cot. At 1:00 I call, "Nap time, shoes in the bucket, everyone go pee." One child needs to be called again. I will probably have to stand over this child while she ever so slowly removes her shoes. Without my attention she will drift off to play with anything within reach. I talk the children through the bathroom and into their designated sleeping places. Most need only the first cue, "Nap time." I ask each child if he or she has used the bathroom before I turn off the light and close the door. Naomi needs to hear me say, "No playing around now. It's nap time. No talking or getting up until you have slept. When you get up, come out very quietly so you don't wake anyone who needs more sleep." Magically, they all go to sleep by 1:15.

I have one or two five-year-old children who no longer need naps. These kids choose a quiet activity or play outside during nap time. I allow only one child in the bathroom at a time during naps to make sure that play noise doesn't wake sleepers. Naomi is the first awake, at 2:45 P.M. every day. By 3:30 all the children are awake, some sitting quietly on the couch looking half-asleep. I am typing. Slowly the children begin to interact and to initiate play.

At 3:30 three schoolchildren arrive, hang up their coats, and flop down on the couch. I ask, "Have a good day?" If someone is grouchy, I try to uncover what happened on the way home or at school and get that out of the way so that a negative school experience does not interfere with the day care play to come. At 3:45 another group of schoolkids arrives, walking and by bus, from two nearby elementary schools. Schoolkids grab a little one for hugging and kissing as they arrive, then begin inviting each other into games they make up. They spend a lot of time negotiating and deciding who gets to be what first. Often someone is not satisfied with her or his lot and comes to complain. We discuss what happened and the options. If it seems that the child has truly been victimized by the group (which is rare), I go with her to back up a request for reconsideration. The group as a whole has in the past decided that no one should be excluded from a game, that make-believe games can be expanded to include all who want to play. If at any time there is a protest about including any child in a game, we simply stop and meet again to discuss the previous decision; we inevitably come to the same conclusion. Because no one wants to be left out at a future date, they come to a consensus that all must be allowed to play.

I am at the typewriter again, listening. The kids know where to find me. They know that I will drop my typing instantly if I am needed. They also know that I will not drop it if I am not really needed. The kids move in and out of small play groups, from one activity to another, during the afternoon, with small skirmishes now and then.

At some point in the afternoon I usually pass around a plate of fruit. If a child comes to ask for a snack, I may put that child in charge. I instruct him, "Peel the bananas, then break them in half. Wash the apples; call me to core them. Pass them around. There are two pieces of fruit for each person." If a game of House is in progress, I may slice carrots into thin circles and offer them as a prop for the "mom" or "dad" to serve to other players. Sometimes I serve frozen peas, sliced raw broccoli, or other vegetables. Kids will often pounce on unpopular raw vegetables if they are integrated into a game.

Parents pick up two of the youngest children early, about 4:30 P.M. The parent comes in and greets me at the typewriter, which sits on my desk near the window next to the front door. Now it's time to get ready to go. Maybe Jamaica has her shoes and socks on. During the first month she did not; she was always looking for her socks. After that month she had her socks on; she had learned the importance of putting all clothing removed during play into the bucket — a four-gallon plastic pail where kids keep shoes and socks together. About the time I gave up day care, she had her shoes *and* socks on when her mother came — a major achievement. If a parent shows up earlier than usual, chances are he or she will sigh and say, "Where are her shoes and socks?" They are supposed to be in the bucket, but it may take weeks to teach a new child to put them there. The children start a game in the other room, take off shoes and socks, and throw them on the floor. Other kids come in and kick them around, and they are soon lost under the couch. This level of disorder is the result of my style, and if it is recognized as such, it will be accepted by parents. When a parent is impatient or annoyed with misplaced clothing and toys, I address him or her directly. I say clearly, "My priorities are not flexible. In order to teach peer interdependence and increase individual responsibility and skills, I feel that a little disorder is not only tolerable but even necessary."

At about 5:15 P.M. it is clean-up time again. This time there are many older children and clean-up seems to happen almost on its own. I then sweep again or vacuum. After everything is put away the children continue to play or have another dance session. At 5:30 tired parents descend on the house claiming their children. Often a parent just wants to sit down and talk. I enjoy this and always find time to listen and visit with parents as they come in the evening. I have had little adult contact and stimulation all day and I am ready.

I have given you a detailed look at the large family style of day care because it is the style I know best and clearly the one I think best for children. You have now seen enough of the different possibilities to know what you would like to do.

Your Style

On the basis of your survey of day care homes and observations of different ways of caring for children, you are ready to choose your style. Clarify in your own mind why you have chosen one style rather than another. This will enable you to speak honestly and realistically with parents who want to use your service, and will help you avoid getting into a style or pattern that does not suit you. You may have to be flexible on some choices early in your day care business, until you find children and parents suited to your style, but if you keep your specific goal in mind, you will gradually find that you have a day care service that fits the ideal description you work out now.

General Standards

By now you have a good idea of the general standards of all day care businesses, and you should be willing to follow these standards regardless of the specific style you have chosen. Every parent has a right to expect a certain basic level of care that often is not articulated but underlies the contract, or verbal agreement, between the provider and the parent. Some of these standards are no different from the common sense you use in your own home for your own child, but they are an important element in the basic quality of a day care business.

Provide Child Care on All Days the Parents Need Care

This means that you will be expected to provide a calendar of holidays you will take. If you want to take days in addition to the most traditional, nationally recognized holidays, you will be expected to make alternate arrangements for those families needing child care. I occasionally arranged for two or three children to spend a day with a fourth child at that child's home when only a few parents worked on a holiday. Parents are often glad to have their children visit other children, and the children enjoy this arrangement immensely. My families paid by the month, and the helpful families did not expect financial compensation but were glad to be able to help arrange vacation time for me. When I was unable to arrange this kind of visit, I hired one or two competent adults, depending on the number of children, to take over while I was gone.

Provide an Appropriate Substitute When You Are Ill

If you hire an assistant, being sick may not be a problem — in most cases, you have a built-in substitute. On the other hand, if you work alone, you might find it difficult to find a substitute. The best answer might be parents for whom you provide child care. Many professionals have enough flexibility in their work schedule to help you out when you really need it, provided you do not need help too often. Other possibilities are grandparents or your own mother, another woman in the neighborhood who is home with her children, and a friend of a day care parent.

You must next consider what to do with yourself when you are sick. In my case, we converted our garage into a guest house, which housed the day care assistant most of the time. While the assistant was substituting for me, I used her apartment to rest in. It might be possible for you to use a friend's couch, go to a motel, or in some cases use your own bed and make other napping arrangements for the day care child who usually sleeps there. If you are very sick, you will move all the children who use your bedroom at nap time to other places in the house. It is a good idea to plan before you get sick where you will go and who will take over. You may find that you do not get sick anymore, except on weekends. I was sick enough to stay in bed only two weekdays in five years. Something keeps you going when you have to keep going.

Provide Care for Children Who Are Marginally Ill

When children begin to show symptoms of illness such as colds or twenty-four-hour flu, the other kids have already been exposed and it is too late to remove the child to protect others. If you have a comfortable place for a mildly sick child, the parent will certainly appreciate your enabling her or him to go to work. Even more serious illnesses requiring medication are usually not contagious after a short period of treatment, and child care can then be resumed. It is important to have a clear understanding with all parents about your policy on the care of sick children. Although state regulations will generally prohibit you from taking care of sick children and require that you immediately isolate the child and call parents at work to have him or her picked up, there are times when you cannot reach the parent, when the parent cannot come, or when the child feels bad but is not extremely ill and will actually be happier in day care than at home in bed. In the case of vomiting, conjunctivitis, a high temperature (over 103°), or complete "crumminess," it is certainly wise to send a child home. With something like chicken pox, the sooner a child has it, the better; by the time symptoms appear everyone has been exposed and will come down with it (if they have not already had chicken pox) in seven to twenty-one days. Of course, more serious illnesses cause prolonged or severe discomfort, and you will not be able to accommodate these in the day care home. The best rule of thumb is to ask the doctor and the child (in that order) about coming to day care.

The provider will sometimes be responsible for administering medicine or treatment. It is very important to continue the treatment or medication as long as the doctor directs. Ear infections and pinkeye are notorious for reappearing after premature discontinuation of medication. The same is true of head lice. Although head lice are not as common in day care homes as they are in centers and schools, you will want to deal immediately with this problem. Be sure that the parent of the infected child uses prescription medication rather than over-the-counter lice shampoo, and that the infected child does not return to day care without a treatment of prescription shampoo. Then check the back of each child's head at the hairline for nits (lice eggs, which appear as very small white or brown specks attached to the hair about one to one and a half inches from the scalp). Nits often take up to two months to appear after the first discovery, so it is important to keep on top of this problem for several months. Lice are usually transferred through combs, brushes, hats, coat hoods, and bedding. It is wise, therefore, to avoid communal use of these items.

Provide a Safe Environment

In general, the provider should use locks and safety latches on doors at the tops of stairs and on medicine cabinets, knife drawers, and cupboards for cleaning and other chemical items. Check your yard for poisonous plants, sharp sticks, and other items that might easily be used dangerously in play. Keep unused electric outlets covered and secure porch and yard areas for wandering toddlers. Install smoke detectors, and refrain from smoking during day care hours. Use seat belts for all children on field trips. Be sure that all of these safety considerations are in full use at all times.

Let Parents Know When Children Are Having Problems

This is an area that requires unusual tact and good judgment. You do not want to cause unnecessary problems in a family, but you want to alert parents to continuing or serious difficulties with a child. You may be able to locate appropriate resources for a family before you make your concerns known.

Prevent Children from Hurting Themselves and One Another as Much as Possible

In addition to providing a safe environment, you will exercise veto power over activities that you consider hazardous — perhaps some climbing, throwing, or sliding, when these activities are not appropriate to the environment. You will enforce rules and a behavior code that respect each child's right to play without fear of harm from other children or adults.

Maintain Your Own Emotional Control at All Times

There will be times when you are overtired and frustrated, but if you recognize that the cause is within you, not in the children, you will keep your perspective and maintain a good environment.

Meet Basic Physical Needs of the Children, Such as Diaper Changing, Feeding, and Clothing Appropriate to Weather

Commit Yourself to Providing Day Care for Some Time

Six months is probably a bare minimum for a family seeking day care, but you cannot realistically commit yourself to more than three years. Do not expect or ask for a commitment from families. If you do, you are bound to be disappointed when your most trusted parents suddenly announce they have to move.

These general standards combined with an awareness of your abilities and preferences will enable you to set up and run a professional day care business. As your business grows you can vary your style and the details of your service according to your day-to-day experience. You will be part of a network of day care providers offering an important service to your community.

2

To Be or Not to Be Licensed

Most states have adopted laws requiring a person who cares for children not related to her or him to apply for and receive a license before assuming the responsibility of providing day care. Some states have recently altered their regulations to apply only to persons caring for four or more children unrelated to the provider. Rules and regulations are in flux at present. These standards can vary considerably depending on state budgets.

What is a license? It is a document issued by the relevant state or local agent stating that the holder of the license has complied with the state or local requirements for operating a day care center or day care home, which may then be defined according to the relevant law as a home limited to a certain number of children under a certain age. In most states the provider is required to exhibit the certificate in a prominent place for the benefit of prospective clients or anyone else entitled to know about the provider's certification.

As more and more people offer day care services, state and local agencies are pushing to regulate these services and maintain some measure of control, either through licensing or registration. Anyone who even calls an agency for information is often pressed to supply his or her name and come to the office to receive information, or is urged to have mail sent to a home address. This in itself is an indication of government interest in controlling all aspects of child care and may or may not be constructive for the person seeking information.

The decision to apply for a license is an individual one and must be made after a careful review of the relevant information. You must consider the assumptions you have about the benefits of a license and the requirements for qualifying for one.

Myths About Licensing

Licensing is a major concern of state and local agencies and of parents and providers because of a variety of misconceptions and myths regarding child care and licensing.

The first myth is that a licensed home is a safe and high-quality home and an unlicensed home is not. This is probably one of the gravest and most dangerous myths of day care. A licensed home is one that has been checked and will be checked again, periodically, for basic safety and fire hazards and for paperwork and record-keeping. There is no guarantee that the safeguards required by the health department, fire department, or social services department are observed or utilized during any of the other days during the year. A home operator without a license may be more conscientious and responsible about implementing safety measures and maintaining them throughout the year. I prefer to be primarily accountable to myself, the children, and the parents. I do not need a superparent. Day care home associations have long been battling state and local agencies all over the country about eliminating costly and intrusive licensing and replacing it with voluntary registration, which would provide more complete listings of day care to the public and guidance for day care homes in need. This program would cut the state cost of surveillance and would give responsibility for safety to the only people who have real control in any meaningful sense — the operators and parents.

The style of a licensed home may be limited by agency requirements. The "large family environment" style I describe in this book is not legal under current regulations in some states. Most regulations limit enrollment to six children. It seems to me unwise to limit the styles of day care available to the public, especially when the demand for alternatives is growing, partly in response to the conservative swing to "basics" and partly because parents are questioning the highly structured environments of day care centers.

The second myth is that licensed homes can charge higher fees as a measure of their greater professionalism. This myth is doubly misleading. Fees are negotiable in most states, and in some, fees for families receiving federal or state aid are set by statute. It is in the interest of some state agencies to keep fees low, since recipients of aid are limited by the state in the amount they can spend for day care. These agencies will not authorize payments to unlicensed homes and will not accept rates higher than what is set by law or by agency policy. Licensing should not affect the rates you choose to charge parents nor the children you choose to accept.

The third myth is that state and local agencies have strict standards for the provider. In most states the provider's day care home need only meet minimum standards, as established by the agency; anyone who applies for a license and qualifies by law must be granted a license. A license does not guarantee quality care by the provider; it implies only that there is no health reason to deny the provider a license.

The fourth myth is that most day care services are licensed. In fact, the great majority of children being cared for by someone other than a parent are cared for in unlicensed homes. It is obvious that licensing is not and cannot be enforced. Those who provide day care but never contact the relevant state or local agency about licensing are almost never known. Those who come to the attention of the agencies are usually charged with a specific complaint and therefore may need assistance. There remain many thousands of homes where children are cared for to the satisfaction of their parents without any association with an official agency.

Advantage of a License

In some states, the advantages of qualifying for a formal license to offer day care services may not outweigh the effort you expend in qualifying, but you should consider them before you make a final decision. In some states a license will make you eligible for

1. low-cost insurance offered through the local day care association
2. referrals from the state or local agency
3. payment of fees by the state for qualified children
4. supplemental funds from the Department of Agriculture on a per-meal basis
5. membership in the local day care association

In my experience, only (1) and (5) were distinct advantages. The local day care association provides a growing network of support for providers that may be an important consideration for anyone who feels isolated in the day care business.

The other advantages generally are mixed blessings. The licensing agency will often keep a list of registered or licensed providers who are willing to have their name given to anyone seeking day care. There is no assurance that these individuals will be interested in your style of day care. Applicants receiving state funds for day care will usually only be able to pay according to state guidelines or statutes on fees and may not be able to afford your services. Finally, the paperwork required for funds from the Department of Agriculture requires time and effort and the rates are low; the funds for this program are now being cut back considerably.

The only other advantage to be considered is a psychological one: you will not be pressed by a caseworker or other government official to apply for a license if you already have one, and you will not have to listen to persuasions or threats if you refuse to comply with the agency.

Advantages of No License

The advantages of operating a day care service without a license in some states are the specific areas in which you can exercise your freedom and judgment. If you choose not to apply for a license, you will be free to exercise your judgment in the following areas:

1. definition of proper child care
2. ages of children accepted for care
3. number of children accepted for care
4. fees

A provider who does not seek a license will not be visited by a caseworker. The number and ages of children are determined by the provider. This provider will negotiate fees independent of state day care contracts.

The unlicensed provider in many states should expect the state or local agency to make an effort to persuade her to apply for a license. In general, however, unlicensed homes in many areas are left alone because the government agencies recognize the importance of their service to the community.

Making Your Decision

To determine whether you should seek a license, ask yourself the following questions:

Are you extremely well organized?

Do you have enough money to pay for required changes in your home to meet requirements (fire alarms, extinguisher, screens on some windows, fence, stair railings, repairs)?

Do complaints worry you?

Do you want official approval?

Do you want to limit your group to six children, including your own and not including more than two children under the age of two?

Do you want to be eligible for payment from families receiving day care money from the state?

Do you want to be eligible for some food money on a per-child basis from the Department of Agriculture?

Do you want to be eligible for low-cost insurance for the children while they are at your home in day care?

Do you want to be listed on the state's day care referral list?

If you answered yes to all or most of the above, then you probably should apply for a license. If you answered no, ask yourself the following questions:

Do you feel you can safely care for more than six children, including your own, with possibly more than two under the age of two?

Have you checked the regulations for your own information and implemented those that you consider important to the safety and health of the children?

Do you intend to charge more than the payment allowed to recipients of public assistance?

Do you feel secure in your mind that you are providing safe and healthy care according to your standards and those of your clientele?

Are you willing to take the risk of providing child care without special insurance, or are you willing to pay high fees to provide accident insurance for children in care?

Do you have strong support and confidence from *all* of your families?

Is an association with government agencies a low priority?

If you answered yes to all or most of the above, then you probably do not want a license and do want to be independent.

Process of Licensing

The process of applying and qualifying for a license can be as simple or as complicated as a government agency chooses to make it, and requirements may vary from state to state and even within a state. Requirements will also differ for day care homes and day care centers, and the licensing procedure will vary accordingly. To give you an idea of the most minimal and most standard requirements you are likely to face anywhere in the United States, I will lead you through a licensing procedure, step by step, for a day care home and a day care center.

Day Care Home

A day care home provides day care in the provider's living space to no more than six children, including your own, under the age of twelve (or another specific age); no more than two of the children may be under the age of two (or another specific age). To qualify to operate a day care home, an applicant must be eighteen years of age or older. Some states might have an additional minimum requirement that the provider have six months of experience with child care, by caring for either your own child or another person's child, or other specific experience or educational requirements.

    If you are eighteen years old and have a six-month-old baby, you can apply in some states to operate a day care home. Clearly, almost anyone can qualify to apply for a license. In most cases the health department will be able to identify the agency that will grant licenses for day care homes in your area; the relevant agency may be the health department, the state office for children, the state office for social services, or another agency. Contact this office and ask for the application forms and procedures. Usually the agency will send forms for a day care home to you, with instructions to return the application, possibly by a certain date.

When the application packet arrives, read it carefully to find out what requirements must be met before your home is examined by a caseworker or before you are interviewed. Other preliminary requirements *may* include the following:

signed approval of apartment or house owner if the prospective provider rents her home
signed approval of adjacent residents (neighbors) where zoning waiver is required
attendance at an orientation meeting sponsored by the agency granting the license

The purpose of the orientation meeting in some states is to direct the provider to a specific level of fees and clientele, specifically, those fees set by the state and those clients referred by the state. In some areas agency workers have not developed a clear perception of the importance of day care services as a form of employment and will refer to day care work as "something to do for a little extra money" or something to do at home "since you have to be there with your own kids anyway." Other agency workers are coming to realize that day care requires hard work, maturity, and intelligence and is not to be denigrated as "baby-sitting." Ignore any negative attitudes you encounter and concentrate on developing your business.

If you decide to continue with the application, fill out all the forms, which may include a history of the provider, biographical and medical; a written statement of child-rearing philosophy; schedule of activities for children; and a list of references from nonrelatives. In some states a biographical statement that includes any suggestion of medical problems that could be dangerous for children in care can be investigated by the caseworker; the caseworker may have the power under the law to gain access to any records deemed relevant in making a decision for a license.

If the application is accepted and the references give a good report of the applicant, the caseworker will then schedule a visit to the home to investigate the space to be used for child care; the investigation will cover the following areas of safety and play:

removal of all chemicals dangerous to children
locks on drawers with knives or other sharp objects
guard rails on stairs
gates on porches or leading to stairs to safeguard infants
places for individual children to keep their belongings (hats, coats, boots, shoes)
number and types of toys and other play equipment
yard area and its protection for children at play
fire extinguisher of a certain size
wiring that meets code
exits (two are required) from each floor on which children will play
individual sleeping arrangements for children who take naps

Some of the areas are dictated by electrical and plumbing codes; others are specifically described by state law; still others are investigated at the discretion of the caseworker.

In some states an applicant is required to pass two additional tests: a tuberculosis (TB) test, for a food handler's permit (granted by the Health Department), and a first aid to the injured test, given after completing a course offered by the American Red Cross. The TB test requires one hour, including the food handler's permit test, and approximately $2; the Red Cross test is administered after eight hours of classes, often given on two evenings, and requires a nominal fee.

In some states the caseworker will be able to issue a license immediately or within a few days of the first visit if he or she is satisfied. If she is not satisfied, she may make a request for specific changes and schedule a return visit. If the applicant complies satisfactorily with the requests, the license will be issued after the second visit. The license can be either provisional or full.

A provisional or temporary license is usually in force for a limited period of time, such as six months; unless there are serious complaints, it will be replaced by a full license.

Not every state will require every one of the steps or requirements listed above; some states may have even more requirements and a longer process of investigation. The least you can expect is that you will be required to be at least eighteen years old, to provide a history, and to receive a full license. The most you can expect depends on the attitude of the agency workers, although most caseworkers will attempt to be reasonable and helpful.

Once you receive a license from the state or city agency, you will be expected to comply with its basic rules governing home care. These can include maintenance of records for each child and direct supervision of all children at all times. The child's record will include name and address of parents, individual to be notified in case of emergency, child's doctor, permission for provider to administer medication, record of medications given, record of immunizations, and permission to take the child away from day care home, for instance on a field trip (see the form on the following page, *New Child Information*).

After the provider has been licensed and accepted the terms of the license, the caseworker will periodically monitor the home through drop-in and announced visits. Drop-in visits are used in some states to make sure that the provider maintains an acceptable day care environment at all times. Some states require that visits be announced as a courtesy to the provider. If the caseworker is satisfied for two years, the provider will receive a license-renewal visit.

The life of a licensed provider can be fairly uncomplicated after the license has been obtained, as long as there are no complaints. If a complaint is filed by anyone — parent, visitor, neighbor, complete stranger — the caseworker will make another visit to the home to determine whether there is a problem and if so to resolve it.

In addition to the requirements of the state or local licensing agency, the licensing requirements of some states may include a visit from the fire department, the health department, the building inspector, and the city or town electrician. Again, the requirements vary from state to state for day care homes, but each de-

New Child Information

Name of child _____ Birth date of child _____

Child's address _____

Mother's name _____ Father's name _____

Home phone _____ Home phone _____

Address _____ Address _____

Work phone _____ Work phone _____

Work address_____ Work address _____

Who else can be notified in case of emergency?

_____ Phone _____

_____ Phone _____

Child's doctor _____

Address _____ Phone _____

Emergency plan:

I hereby give _____ permission to authorize emergency care,

including emergency surgery, for _____. I understand that

every effort will be made to contact me prior to this procedure.

Parent's signature _____ Date _____

Immunization record:

	Date			Date
Polio	_____		Measles	_____
DPT	_____		Mumps	_____
DT	_____		Rubella	_____
TB skin test	_____		Smallpox	_____

Other health information you think significant, including past diseases or hospitalizations or trauma: _____

_____

_____

_____

_____

I give permission for _____ to go by car or foot on field trips with

the day care group. I require seat belt _____ I do not require seat belt _____.

Date _____ Parent's signature _____

Day care agreement: Care will be provided between the hours of ___A.M.

and ___P.M. on _____ each week for the fee

of _____ per _____. [Add late-fee agreement here if you use it.]

Provider's Signature _____ Parent's Signature _____

Date _____   Date _____

partment will usually inspect only those areas in which it specializes: the fire department will look for the safety of exits in case of fire; the health department will examine food-preparation areas; the building inspector will check to see that the home is generally of safe construction; and the electrician will look for electrical code violations.

The procedure of obtaining a license for a day care home may seem intimidating, but few states will require every step outlined above. These steps and requirements are presented to illustrate to you the areas of concern of licensing agencies and the direction of current government regulation. Before you finally decide whether or not you want a license for a day care home, go over the specific requirements in your area and discuss the procedures, if possible, with a licensed operator in your area.

Day Care Center

A day care center provides day care either in a space separate from the provider's living space or to ten or more children with more than one adult, or both. If you live in a two-apartment building and want to offer day care on the first floor while you live in the apartment on the second floor, you would be considered a day care center in some states. If you want to offer day care to seven or more children in your living space, you would again be considered a day care center in some states, while others set the number of children at ten or higher, depending on the ages of the children involved and the hours they are in care.

In some states the licensing requirements for a center can be far more stringent than those for a day care home; the procedure might be carried out by the same or a different agency. The minimum requirements for a license for a day care center can be the same as those for a day care home, but they generally involve stricter inspection of building or location of the proposed center, a required number of adults per child (usually two adults for ten children), and inspection of food handling and sanitation. In the government's eyes, a day care center approaches a school and therefore may be closely regulated. Anyone considering opening a day care center rather than a day care home should expect to face most if not all of the requirements listed under day care home inspection. In addition, the state or local agency may require monthly visits by the health department and regular but unannounced visits by nurses and sanitation inspectors.

If you choose to open a day care center in a garage apartment for three preschool children, you may receive more lenient treatment than the person who operates a center for twenty children in a small building with two or three assistants. Visit some day care centers in your area, observe their schedules and practices, and discuss the licensing procedures the provider went through.

Some states may not distinguish between day care homes and centers; some may recognize only homes and schools; others may have categories I have not thought of. Learn as much as you can about the laws and procedures in your area before initiating the licensing application.

Obtaining a license can be a time-consuming practice, as you should now realize. Regardless of your decision in this area, you should investigate the possibility of obtaining a city or town business license for conducting business in your home. Any regulation for any license worth considering will be designed to ensure the safety of the customers (children and parents in the case of day care services) and the maintenance of fair business practices.

Complaints — Licensed or Unlicensed

Whether you are licensed or independent, you must consider the possibility that a formal complaint will be filed with the licensing agency or any agency responsible for the welfare of children in your state. If you choose to run a very traditional protective and structured preschool environment in your home and you do it very well, you may never have a complaint — especially if you are a meticulous housekeeper. Though many parents would not choose this environment for their children, they also would not call a state agency and register a complaint that the environment was inadequate for the growth and development of their children because it was too rigid, even if they felt that it was. On the other hand, if you run almost any other style of day care home, you are likely to have at least one complaint in the course of several years of business. I had two in my five years of operation.

The first complaint came from a woman who visited with her mother (not with her child) and did not like the style. She expressed her disapproval and complained, not to me but to the Department of Social and Health Services, that "children were outside in the back yard without diapers on; there was grease dripping from the corner of the oven; the children were asleep on half-mattresses on the floor; the house was littered; and the children were dirty." The caseworker (I was licensed then) had been to my home several times in the past for her regularly scheduled checks, as required by the state. She was a reasonable woman but was required to investigate all complaints. She called and with an apology asked if she could make an appointment to discuss the complaint. I insisted that she come immediately and touched nothing until she arrived, an hour later. How could she be reassured about the condition of the house and children if she made an appointment for a week later? Of course, all the allegations were basically correct, with the exception of the half-mattresses — I use crib mattresses. But the worker was satisfied, as I was, that there was only an appropriate amount of toy litter, only an appropriate amount of food under the table — the amount you would expect after one lunch of six two- to four-year-olds — and there was only a little grease dripping from the corner of the oven. Though she did not personally approve of the bare-bottom toilet-training approach, she understood and accepted bare bottoms as an integral part of my method.

Though this worker was flexible and realistic and accepting of style differences, the department's questionnaire sent to my families as a result of the second complaint provided dramatic evidence of the values adopted by the department. The first and most important question, at the top of a list of about twenty questions, was, "Does [the day care provider] keep your child neat and clean?" The parents and I got a chuckle out of this, since "neat and clean" is quite low on the priority list for our children. To keep children neat and clean implies either preventing them from getting dirty or interrupting their activity continually to remove dirt and change clothes, and this is just not conducive to play and learning. I (and the parents I work with) prefer that the children are safe, happy, and exploratory rather than "neat and clean."

The second complaint came, years later, from a phoner who asked first if I was licensed and then how many children I cared for. Answering both truthfully (no license at this time and more than six children), she immediately hung up and registered a complaint with the licensing agency. This led to a visit from the second licensing worker assigned to my area, who told me, "Mrs. Murphy, you either have to stop caring for children or reapply for a license." I told her I would think about it, and from that point on simply did not pick up the registered letter at the post office (with day care from 8:00 A.M. to 8:30 P.M., how could I?). I had no further action or word from the department for the last three years of my day care business.

As a result of this encounter, I assume that my name was given to the attorney general's office, where it remains on file without action. (They would have taken action had there been repeated *serious* complaints of child abuse or neglect.) If the state should decide to pursue a case against you for failure to seek and obtain a license, the case will eventually end up in court. This course of action is generally rare, and for good reason. The state agency workers and others recognize the need for child day care services and will usually try to work out a reasonable solution for a provider with satisfied parents and happy children.

If you should receive a complaint from a parent, consider first whether it is the result of your style, and therefore whether the child and the child's parents would be happier with a different kind of day care. If it is not the result of your personal style, you will want to talk over the issue with the parents and settle any areas of misunderstanding or disagreement. One of the provider's greatest strengths in operating a day care home is the parents' support and agreement with the provider's approach, and this should be maintained whenever possible. If a parent ceases to trust the provider, the child will be better off in another environment.

To ensure a reasonably clear understanding between parent and provider, I ask my clients to sign a release form (see opposite page) that outlines the limits on my responsibility for the child during day care hours. This form alerts parents to an awareness of what anyone caring for a child can reasonably be held responsible for and perhaps some protection from the unscrupulous parent (rare). An accident is always possible, and both provider and parent should be alert to possible future issues.

Name, address, and phone number of day care provider _____

_____

Child's name _____ Age _____ Birth date _____

Parent's name _____

Address _____

City _____ State _____ Zip _____

Home phone _____ Work phone: Father _____ Mother _____

In case of emergency contact: _____ Phone: _____

DAY CARE RELEASE: I, the undersigned parent/guardian of _____, in enrolling my child at the _____ (day care name) _____ at ____ (address) ____, understand that he or she, in attending day care and using the day care facilities, does so at his or her own risk. The day care operator shall not be liable for any damage arising from personal injuries sustained by participating in or about the premises. Participant assumes full responsibility for all injuries and damage which may occur in or about premises.

In consideration of your acceptance of my child's entry, I, intending to be legally bound, do hereby waive, release, and forever discharge any and all rights and claims against ____ (day care provider's name) ____, assistants and substitutes, for damages or injury sustained by my child while participating in, or attending any day care activity related to _____ (day care name) _____, whether incident takes place on the premises or traveling to and from the premises.

In addition, I do hereby certify that my child is covered by insurance through

_____

Policy number _____

Subscriber   _____

CONSENT TO MEDICAL CARE: I, the undersigned parent/guardian of _____ do hereby grant authority to the staff of ____ (day care name) ____ to render a judgment concerning medical assistance or hospital care in the event of an injury or illness during my absence or if I am unable to be contacted.

Family doctor _____ Phone _____
Location_____

Date _____

Please list below any medicines that your child may be allergic to:

_____

3

Dollars and Sense

Day care is a business, and you must keep this principle firmly in mind if you are to receive fair compensation for the service you perform. If you consider yourself only a baby-sitter, you will probably feel frustrated, harassed, and used. This will not be good for you or the children you care for. Charge a fair rate for your services and do not underestimate your worth.

Defining Fair Compensation

Your rates should be based on the total income you would receive if you were taking the maximum number of children you feel you can handle. Specific examples of income options are discussed below; here I only want to give you a general rule of thumb. Establish a tentative fee schedule first, such as

Per Month	Age of Child
$120	age 6 and older (before and after school)
$200	age 5 (older children during summer)
$225	ages 4 to 5
$250	ages 2 to 4
$300	ages 1 to 2, or toilet trained
$350	up to age 1

These fees may have to be adjusted according to where you live. Consider the following questions in light of your fees:

1. Do many families in your area need child care? Is child care in demand?
2. What is the income of the neighborhood or larger community?

Are you near a hospital, university, shopping area, or industrial complex?

3. What is the preferred style of day care homes in your area? Does your style differ?

4. Do you need additional equipment? Will you purchase it immediately?

5. What materials will you buy on a regular basis?

6. Do you plan to serve meat or other expensive foods? Organic foods only?

7. Do you need a car for field trips? Seat belts? Gas?

8. Do you need a part-time or full-time assistant?

9. Will you include any special lessons or classes for which you will pay an outside teacher?

10. Will you buy insurance?

11. Will you provide diapers, baby food, etc.?

12. Do you need to add or improve safety measures such as new stairs, fences, and smoke alarms?

Your fees should reflect the cost of doing business, which includes materials, assistants, and insurance as well as your salary.

If you decide to run a licensed day care home, being licensed may have an effect on your rates. A license will limit the number and ages of the children, as discussed in Chapter 2. Licensed home and center care for infants was as high as $450 per month in Seattle in 1983. On the other hand, licensed care may mean a rate of $150 if a state agency pays. Much will depend on where the home is located and the style of care you offer. A license does not determine the quality of care; only the day care provider and children affect the quality of the environment. You will not, therefore, determine your fee by whether you are licensed, but by the clientele you choose to serve.

Determining fees in general is not difficult. The difficulty is in making the exceptions. Because a day care home is a very personal community service, you will necessarily give a great deal of individual consideration to determining fees for the care of a particular child. It may take several months for you to get an accurate idea of the market value of your service in your particular community. Today in general your service is very valuable. There is not enough good child care available anywhere in the country.

For children under the age of two, the situation is especially tight. If you are willing to provide infant care, you will have no trouble finding clients.

At times, one of your families' circumstances may change through divorce or illness, for example. Once a mother came to me saying that she would have to move her children because she could no longer afford my service. Because I really liked her children, I told her to find out what she would have to pay elsewhere and I would accept that amount. She was delighted, and I was glad not to lose her kids. She volunteered to provide compensation in other ways, and we have enjoyed her tickets to the theater, vegetables, and baby-sitting on occasion. Each child is different, and requires different effort and involvement. Why should the fee not be different as well?

Whenever you are discussing fees with a parent who is considering placing a child with you, consider the following questions; you may want to adjust your fees to accommodate this child. Do not feel that every family must pay the same rate.

1. Would you like to become involved with this family and have a long-term friendship with the parents?
2. Do you like the child? Will this child be a pleasure? Will the care of this child be a burden at any cost? Is there a potential or obvious personality conflict, or something you can't quite put your finger on?
3. What do you think the family can afford?
4. Does the family need only temporary care?
5. Would the family prefer to exchange services?
6. Does one or both parents have a service to exchange (for example, music lessons, evening or weekend child care, housework help, complimentary tickets of some kind)?
7. Is there a younger sibling coming along in the future?
8. Would you rather have this child's presence for a small amount of compensation, or not have the child as part of the group and have none of the compensation?

There is one final point to remember about fees. It is regrettable but true that people often value something more if it is expensive, and day care is no exception. I try to avoid people who react according to this rule. Generally, these families are much happier with a more structured situation that emphasizes what is becoming known as the fundamental approach. They are willing to pay a great deal but also want to see something tangible in exchange for their money. For some reason they feel that children should be closely supervised and led into fundamental learning in letters and numbers as early as possible. They believe that the learning accomplished through peer play and mixed-age interaction is not important or will just happen on its own. Unfortunately, many children these days do not have enough time in situations in which their social development can "happen on its own." Children spend many hours away from home in organized activities or watching television — learning something entirely different. Nevertheless, there are parents who value what I teach and the environment I provide and are willing to pay well for it; they understand its importance for the child and the personal sacrifice the provider makes in choosing this day care style. Those are the families you are probably looking for. Resist the temptation to accept a child just because the family is willing to pay your highest fee. It may not be worth it for any of you.

Income Options

The total gross income you will earn from a day care business will vary up to a certain point according to the number and ages of the children you accept. From the gross income you will have to deduct state and federal taxes after calculating your expenses; taxes and expenses are discussed separately, below. Here I will outline six sample day care homes or centers that provide a gross annual income ranging from $12,000 to $30,000. All fees are paid regardless of attendance; there is no late fee.

Plan 1: $12,000 Per Year

Plan 1 is the simplest option and is probably where most day care providers will begin. After a few months or a year in the day care business, you will find yourself moving into other plans with higher gross incomes.

Plan 1 assumes that a provider has four children unrelated to her under the age of five, and charges a flat fee of $250 per month per child. If the home is licensed, she can also have two children of her own; the state may have restrictions on the age range of the six children. The provider therefore earns $1000 per month (four children × $250 per month = $1000), or $12,000 per year. From the annual gross income of $12,000 the provider will deduct expenses and taxes (see below).

The plan assumes that children are present in the day care home for a full six-hour or eight-hour day, or that the families are paying for a full day regardless of the actual rate of attendance.

Plan 2: $19,200 Per Year

Plan 2 assumes a licensed home with six children unrelated to the provider; the fees are $250 per month per child over two years of age and $300 per child under two years of age. There are four children over the age of two ($1000 per month) and two children under the age of two ($600 per month), for a gross income of $1600 per month, or $19,200 per year. If the home is licensed, you probably cannot have any other children present during day care hours (the restrictions may vary from state to state).

In this plan children are, again, present during a full eight-hour day, or the family is paying for a full eight-hour day regardless of the child's actual rate of attendance. If you have a child of your own who will be present during day care hours, you must exclude one child and the cost of that child. For example, if your child is one year old and the fee for a child of this age is $300 per month, your monthly income will therefore be reduced to $1300 and your annual income to $15,600 — the total income from five, rather than six, children.

If your children are of school age, the state law regulating day care homes may require that you reduce the number of day care children in your home when your own children are present after school. Again, the number of children acceptable under state law may depend on the ages of the children; some states will allow two or more children after school if the other six children are over two and a half years old or are toilet trained.

Plan 3: $22,080 Per Year

Plan 3 assumes a licensed home with six day care children full-time and two day care children part-time, before and after school. For the six full-time day care children, the gross monthly income and annual income are the same as in Plan 2 ($1600 and $19,200, respectively). In addition, each part-time child is charged at the rate of $2 per hour for approximately three hours per day for five days per week (or $120 per month). Two part-time children will increase your monthly income by $240, to $1840, and your annual income by $2880, to $22,080. Again, as in Plan 2, the state licensing agency may impose restrictions on the number and ages of children.

Plan 4: $14,160 Per Year

Plan 4 is offered as an example of some of the variations possible in selecting children for your individual style. It assumes a licensed home with four preschool children part-time in the morning at $175 per month per child ($700 per month) and four school-age children part-time in the afternoon at $120 per month per child ($480 per month), for a gross monthly income of $1180, or a gross annual income of $14,160.

Plan 5: $23,760 Per Year

Plan 5 assumes a licensed home with a part-time assistant. In this plan there are a total of ten children; two children are under two and a half years of age, and four of the ten children are part-time (after-school children). The total monthly fees for these children are $600 for two infants ($300 per month per child), $900 for four full-time children over age two and a half ($225 per month per child), and $480 for four part-time after-school children ($120 per month per child), for a gross monthly income of $1980, or a gross annual income of $23,760.

The cost of the assistant is a deductible business expense and should not exceed the fees obtained from the additional children. If the cost of an assistant is greater than the fees you would receive from accepting additional children, then it is financially unwise to hire an assistant. On the other hand, you may take these additional children to support the salary of a second adult because you prefer working with a partner.

Plan 6: $31,860 Per Year

Plan 6 assumes an independent home (no license) and fourteen children. This plan was my personal choice for several years, because it offers the individual child the experience of a large home environment, an experience denied to most American children today. This environment offers the child a peer experience that used to be the norm in this country, through the family and the one-room schoolhouse. Regardless of the philosophy behind licensing efforts and modern educational theories, most, if not all, children will thrive in this environment.

In Plan 6 one full-time child is your own. Fees from other children are $600 for two infants ($300 per month per child), $1575 for seven full-time day care children between ages two and a half and five ($225 per month per child), and $480 for four part-time school-age children ($120 per month per child), for a gross monthly income of $2655, or a gross annual income of $31,860.

During the summer months, parents who are teachers will withdraw their children, but parents of the school-age children will want to send them to day care full time. This plan requires flexibility, but also an acceptance of the child's right to explore with peers without constant and excessive adult dominance. With more children full time in the summer, you will probably want to hire an assistant, at least during the summer months and perhaps part-time the rest of the year.

Expenses

From your gross annual income you will have to deduct expenses and taxes; expenses are the least of these, but can reduce your taxable income and therefore your taxes. If you choose to apply for reimbursement for meals from the United States Department of Agriculture, you will have to keep accurate attendance records to determine how many children were present for meals and snacks. Expenses also include the cost of equipment, materials, insurance, transportation for field trips, and the like. Plan to keep a record of all expenses incurred for the purpose of day care, including books for yourself (like this one) that will help you in your business. Save all receipts; a large envelope is all you need. Let's examine the standard expenses in running a day care home individually to give you an idea of where you can expect to spend money.

Food

Meals and snacks for day care children are the main expense you will incur. I was able to feed children a nutritious, tasty lunch and one snack of a raw vegetable or fruit and beverage for about $1.50 per day per child. For the four children in Plan 1, described above, the cost of meals should be calculated as follows:

4 children @ $1.50 per day = $6 per day, or $120 per month

Calculate an additional $.50 for the afternoon snack for each after-school child in Plans 3, 4, 5 and 6.

Each plan may include infants still eating baby food, and this cost can be borne by either the parent or the provider. It is unwise to have one child bring a separate lunch; the children are better off eating a meal prepared by the provider or all eating lunches brought from home.

The United States Department of Agriculture (USDA) currently has a food-cost reimbursement program that distributes funds to sponsoring organizations such as the state department of human resources. The amount of the reimbursement is determined by the number and ages of the children and which meals they eat. Here I use the amounts allowed by the program for preschool children: Breakfast is calculated at $.50 per day per child; snacks at $.29 per snack (twice a day, perhaps); and lunch and dinners are paid at the rate of $.98 per day per child. This money is available *only* to licensed homes through sponsoring agencies. In the past the provider's children were automatically eligible, but this rule has recently been changed; the provider's children can now be counted for reimbursement only if the provider's family qualifies for "free lunch," which is "low income." (Call the Department of Agriculture or the participating sponsoring agencies for exact income qualifications.) All of the children from other families are automatically eligible regardless of their family income.

If you apply for this program, you may be placed on a waiting list, as there is a maximum number of homes on this program at any one time under any particular sponsor. If you are persistent, you will eventually find a sponsoring agency that has room for your home under its sponsorship through the Department of Agriculture. After you apply and are accepted, a social worker will visit your home and explain the program and its requirements to you. To participate, you must keep records of what and how much of each food item you serve so that the sponsor can verify that you are serving foods from various categories according to minimum requirements. On your attendance records you should note the arrival and departure time of each child daily so that you can calculate the number of breakfasts, lunches, snacks, and dinners you have served. (See the Sample Attendance Record.) From this information you will calculate the amount due according to the amount paid for each type of meal. The sponsoring agency will supply you with forms that you must complete and return each month. The sponsor must receive the forms by a certain date each month, and you will receive confirmation of the amount you are to receive about a week after that date. The check will come about three weeks later. The social worker from the sponsoring agency will make two visits a year to check your bookkeeping and make sure that you are serving the amounts of each food per child per meal required. It all sounds quite complicated, but it is not — it's just time consuming.

Reimbursement Rates

Breakfast	$ .5026	each one served
Lunch or supper	$ .9850	each one served
Snack	$ .2950	each one served (sometimes two/day/child)
	$2.20	per day per child (rounded off), with two snacks

The added income from the USDA reimbursement program can be calculated for each of the plans described above. For one lunch ($.9850) and one snack ($.2950), the USDA will reimburse a day

Sample Attendance Record

Date		John 75/wk.		Jennifer 175/mo.		Erik 200/mo.		Kristi J. 5/day		Carl 6/day		Kristi B. 250/mo. 3-5:30		Paul 250/mo.		Naomi 300/mo.		Jamaica 200/mo.		March — Purchases & Expenses	
Mon.	1	8	5	8	5	8	4	/	/	8	4	10	5	10	4	3	5	3	5	Pens	$2.50
Tues.	2	8	5	8	5	8	4	9	1	8	5	10	5	10	4	3	5	3	5	Birthday candles	$1.50
Wed.	3	8	5	8	5	8	4	/	/	8	5	10	5	10	4	3	5	3	5		
Thurs.	4	8	5	8	5	8	5	9	1	8	5	10	5	10	4	3	5	3	5		
Fri.	5	sick		8	5	8	4	/	/	8	5	10	5	10	4	3	5	3	5		
Sat.	6									9	over										
Sun.	7									nite	6										
Mon.	8	8	5	8	5	8	3	/	/	8	5	10	5	10	4	3	5	3	5		
Tues.	9	8	5	8	5	8	6	9	1	8	5	10	5	10	4	3	5	3	5		
Wed.	10	8	5	sick		8	5	/	/	8	5	10	5	10	4	3	5	3	5		
Thurs.	11	8	5	sick		8	5	9	1	8	5	10	5	10	4	3	5	3	5		
Fri.	12	8	5	8	5	8	4	/	/	8	5	10	5	10	4	3	5	3	5		
Sat.	13																				
Sun.	14																				
Mon.	15	8	5	8	5	8	4	/	/	8	5	10	5	10	4	3	5	3	5		
Tues.	16	8	5	8	5	8	4	9	1	8	5	10	5	10	4	3	5	3	5	Used books	$2.00
Wed.	17	8	5	8	5	8	5	/	/	8	5	10	5	10	4	3	5	3	5	New bowls	$4.50
Thurs.	18	7⁰⁰	5	8	5	8	5	9	1	8	5	10	5	10	4	3	5	3	5		
Fri.	19	8	5	8	5	8	5	/	/	8	5	10	5	10	4	3	5	3	5		
Sat.	20																				
Sun.	21																				
Mon.	22	8	5	8	5	8	5	/	/	/	/	10	5	10	4	3	5	3	5		
Tues.	23	8	5	8	5	8	6	9	1	/	/	10	5	10	4	3	5	3	5		
Wed.	24	8	5	8	5	8	5	/	/	/	/	10	5	10	4	3	5	3	5		
Thurs.	25	8	5	8	5	8	5	9	1	/	/	10	5	10	5	3	5	3	5		
Fri.	26	8	5	8	5	8	5	/	/	/	/	10	5	10	6	3	5	3	5	Used kid's clothes	$1.50
Sat.	27																				
Sun.	28																				
Mon.	29	8	5	8	5	8	5	/	/	8	5	10	5	10	4	3	5	3	5		
Tues.	30	8	5	8	5	8	5	9	1	8	5	10	5	10	4	3	5	3	5		
Wed.	31	8	5	8	5	8	5	/	/	8	5	10	5	10	4	3	5	3	5		
Fee		250⁰⁰		250⁰⁰		300⁰⁰		200⁰⁰		265⁰⁰		175⁰⁰		200⁰⁰		115⁰⁰		138⁰⁰		= $1,893	$12.00

Paid Paid Paid Paid Paid Paid Paid Paid Paid
4/2 3/31 3/31 4/1 4/1 3/31 3/31 3/31 3/31

care home by $1.28 per day per child. For the children in Plan 1, for example, the reimbursement would be as follows:

4 children @ $1.28 per day = $5.12 per day, or $102.40 per month

The actual cost to you therefore is: $120.00 per month
                                        –102.40 per month (USDA
                                        ─────── reimbursement)
                                       $ 17.60 per month

At present, the total cost of the food before reimbursement ($120, in this example) is tax-deductible despite the USDA reimbursement.

In addition to the expenses of feeding day care children, you should calculate the cost of your own lunch. Generally $1 per day is acceptable ($20 per month).

Clothing

I bought no new clothing for work as a provider of day care; wear what you have.

Transportation

Transportation for day care children is optional. If you expect to take the older children on field trips, you may want to purchase a secondhand field-trip car — any large station wagon will do. You can salvage seat belts from a wrecking yard. Large old cars usually have very poor gas mileage and consume oil, but if you use them exclusively for day care children, the cost is minimal and deductible. The car need only be safe and reliable. The usual cost allotted per mile is fifteen cents. An average field trip will probably be not more than ten miles round trip (to a zoo, museum, park, beach). Average cost for a field trip may be $1.50 plus gas. The cost of maintaining a car exclusively for a day care business is also deductible.

Materials and Equipment

You may use day care as an excuse to buy your children every new and incredible toy and electronic thing and every piece of educational equipment that comes out, or you can keep your costs to a minimum by purchasing only art supplies and used toys. A minimum amount of $10 to $15 will cover felt-tipped pens, colored paper, paste, scissors, paint, material for making play dough, and a few used toys. I try to teach my day care children the importance of careful use of materials and of not wasting paper and other supplies. To do this I ask parents to contribute discarded office paper, such as computer printouts, to the day care home. Children thus learn to value the abundance in their lives and use it to better advantage. The annual cost for these materials is ($10 × 12) $120.

You can purchase large equipment exclusively for the day care home, but it should be attractive to children of all ages. A climber at $300 and a set of blocks at $200 will serve most age groups. The cost of these larger items can be deducted from your taxable income over a period of three or more years, depending on the accepted life span of the item. The cost of the climber and blocks may be deducted at a monthly rate for three years ($500 ÷ 36 months), at $13.88 per month, or $166.56 per year.

If the total cost of materials is $620 during the first year, the total deduction is $166.56 plus $120, or $286.56 for each of the first three years of business. Any purchases of other large items can also be prorated over three or more years.

Space

The portion of your home the day care children can enter and use is calculated as a business expense for federal tax purposes. If you live in a one-story, six-room house and allow the children to use three rooms (two play rooms and the kitchen) for eight hours (or more or less) per day for five days per week, you can deduct one-half of the cost of the home for one-third of the day for five days per week. The cost of the home includes all utilities, and it is best to calculate these separately. If you have a mortgage, the cost of the home is calculated on the basis of the taxes and interest, not principal. Assume your taxes and interest on a mortgage are $400 per month, or $4800 per year. The daily cost is $13.15 ($4800 ÷ 365); the cost for one-third (eight hours) of the day is $4.38. Since the children use only half of the house each day of day care, the daily cost is $2.19, or (on the basis of 260 working days in a year) $569.40 per year.

You may deduct the same percentage of the cost of utilities. If the total cost of all utilities (electricity, heat, gas, water, telephone) is $140 per month, or $1680 per year, the daily cost is $4.60 ($1680 ÷ 365). The cost for eight hours per day is $1.53 ($4.60 × ⅓). The cost per year (on the basis of 260 working days in a year) is $397.80.

The annual cost of running a day care home in your own home is a major tax deduction. In addition, the IRS allows other deductions related to your business. If you add a new roof, the cost of the portion over the area used for day care can be prorated for an annual deduction, as can a new bathroom for use by the children.

Assistant(s)

If you hire someone to assist you at any time during day care hours for the purpose of running your day care business, any salary or payment you make to that person is tax-deductible. Assume you hire an assistant for $3 per hour for three hours per day, five days a week, for two months during the summer. The total cost to you is $360 ($3/hr × 3 hrs/day = 9 × 5 days/wk = $45 × 8 wks = $360).

Other Expenses

Any other expenses you incur for the purpose of running your business are tax-deductible: tickets to a zoo or museum, books on child care to improve your understanding of day care matters, a first aid medical kit, and the like. Keep your receipts for tax purposes.

I have not included insurance in this list because insurance policies for an unlicensed home raise several questions. You may very well be able to get insurance if you are unlicensed, but you may not be able to make a successful claim against the policy for the simple reason that most policies include clauses about the insured party's meeting all local standards and so on. Local standards may be interpreted to mean licensing. This is not an area I have personal experience with. The Association of Day Care

Homes or its local affiliate offers reasonably priced insurance to licensed providers.

Taxes

You must pay state and federal taxes on your day care business income. This process is not as painful or as confusing as you may expect; after you have done it once or twice, you will wonder why you worried so much. Federal and state tax offices will supply you with the necessary forms for paying quarterly business taxes.

Federal Taxes

The federal government requires every business to file quarterly business taxes on estimated income, on April 15, June 15, September 15, and January 15. Let us assume you start your business in January and follow Plan 1; your monthly income is $1000. By April 1 you have earned (and received) $3000. Your expenses so far are the cost of space ($2.19 per day × 65 working days in three months = $142.35), materials ($10 per month, or $30.00 for three months), and food ($6 per day × 65 working days = $390). To determine your taxable income (the amount of money you must pay taxes on), you deduct your total expenses from your total income.

$3000.00 income for three months
−562.35 expenses
= $2437.65 taxable income

Assuming that your income and expenses remain the same throughout the year, your total annual taxable income will be $9750.60. The annual tax on this amount (in 1982) for an unmarried woman with one dependent is $750; the quarterly tax is therefore $187.50. A married person filing jointly would owe $431 for the year and $107.75 for the quarter, claiming a nonworking husband and child as dependents.

For tax purposes, expenses such as mortgages, utilities, and food should be calculated on a daily rather than a weekly or monthly basis. I have assumed 260 working days in a year (a five-

•

day work week); if you take a vacation for a week and do not offer day care in your home, you must reduce the number of days you do not offer day care. This is one reason for keeping accurate attendance records. Every quarter you can add up the number of days your day care home was open and multiply that by the daily cost of each expense. That figure is the cost for that quarter for that expense. The quarterly tax is filed on federal form 1040 ES, with a check for the amount of the estimated tax. By April 15 of the following year you must file a final tax return on Schedule C.

The added complications in this process are two: funds set aside in an IRA or Keogh account, and a change in the gross income. First, you must deposit money in a retirement account before you can deduct it, unless you are very self-disciplined and know you will not spend it before the deadline for depositing it. This is a good tax deduction and a wise investment in your own future; the amount deposited is a straight deduction, up to a certain limit, from your gross income. Second, if your income changes over the year, going up or down, you must recalculate at the quarterly deadline according to the change of income. If by July you are earning $1600 per month, you must assume you will do so for the remaining months of the year and calculate your tax on the basis of $1000 for six months and $1600 for six months. Obviously, the tax you owe will increase. You will also have to recalculate if your income decreases, for example, from $1000 to $800 per month.

State Taxes

Most states have income tax and require the same procedure as that followed by the federal government. You will be expected to file quarterly and pay an estimated tax. For a provider following Plan 1 the estimated annual tax will probably be no more than $400 per year, or $100 per quarter. In some states the tax due will be considerably less.

City Taxes

Some cities have income taxes, which often take the form of a once-a-year license fee if your business earnings are less than

$50,000 or some other amount larger than you expect to earn. The fee may be about $25 and the license may require minimal paperwork, filling out one or two pages of forms. Other cities will charge a very small quarterly percentage of your gross earnings or a minimum of perhaps $5 per quarter, whichever is larger.

Bookkeeping

Record-keeping should be simple so that you can find what you want when you want it. Keep your receipts in an envelope and keep a list of all payments from parents, showing person, date, and amount. If you have a calendar record showing when children arrived and departed, you can easily calculate the number of lunches and snacks you served. The IRS has its own figures on how much it will allow per meal per child, and you may find that you spend more than the acceptable amount.

When it is time to pay your quarterly taxes and file your annual return, organize your bills and receipts into straight deductions and prorated deductions. Do the calculations and then put away your records until the next quarter. The sample attendance sheet includes a column for listing monthly expenses as you incur them. Put this form with your receipts every month; it will make the task of doing quarterly business taxes much easier.

A Final Word

For many people a chapter on taxes and business costs can be intimidating, but this matter requires your attention only a few days of the year. The true purpose of this chapter is to show you how to calculate and manage a reasonable personal income. You can vary the six plans that have been described to earn an income that meets your needs. Experiment with different numbers and ages of children until you arrive at your desired personal income. Draw up a list of reasonable expenses — all you can think of that are relevant to your business. Call the state and federal tax information numbers and ask what your tax liability would be. Deduct the taxes from your hypothetical income. Can you live at this level? If you can, are you satisfied to earn at this level? If you are, then you can now consider finding the parents who will get your business started and make your projected income a reality.

4

Choosing Your Families

The individual children you care for and their families are the most crucial element determining the satisfaction you derive from your business and your self-esteem as a day care provider. A carefully selected group of children will respond positively to your day care style and benefit from their time with you. You will establish close professional and personal relationships with their parents, and find your business stable and thriving. The adverse is, unfortunately, equally true. A child you cannot work with and parents you cannot agree with will frustrate you and undermine your personal satisfaction and ability to work with the other children and their families. Choosing the individual children for your day care home therefore should be given as much thought and attention as choosing your style, managing your income and taxes, or any other facet of the day care business. The steps to be followed in selecting children are deceptively simple: they require judgment and sometimes financial sacrifice. If your only reason for accepting a child is that the parents will pay the fees, you may be facing a difficult child and family for which there is no adequate compensation. It is better to refer the family to another day care service and keep your eye on your long-term goals for your day care children and your business.

The steps you should follow are five: finding day care children, conducting the inquiry, preparing for the interview, holding the interview, and making the decision. In the event of an error in judgment — either yours or the parents' — a sixth step, handling a mismatch, is discussed.

Finding Day Care Children

Where do the first children come from? That depends upon how you go about beginning day care. In my case, I let one day care

63

center director know that I was *considering* opening a day care home, and parents began to inquire about my services. This is the tried and true "word of mouth" method. I recommend it highly. Explain your style and general plan to the day care providers in your area and ask them to refer suitable families to you. Be clear about the kinds of children you are interested in and speak first to day care providers you like or agree with on general principles. Those who refer families to you will probably have faith in you and your style and will instinctively only refer families they feel will be suited to your style. These referrals are the backbone of a beginning business and word of mouth to friends of your families will insure your future business.

If you do not receive referrals from other providers or there are few or no other providers in your area, you will have to use a more aggressive and less personal approach. Post small notices describing your day care home in places where parents are most likely to see them or to expect to find them: bulletin boards in grocery stores, laundromats, schools, day care centers, church and community centers, and city and town halls. Put a sign in your window. Put a sign in the window of your car. Run a one-line advertisement in the school newspaper or parent newsletter. When all else fails, run ads in the community and city newspapers and weekly newspapers. These advertisements are not very successful, in my experience. Generally, the more public the exposure, the less acceptable to you the response will be, but every now and then you will receive an inquiry from a family that works out well. The less personal your advertising method, generally, the more you will have to clarify your style of day care to an inquiring parent. You may receive many responses to newspaper advertisements, but you will probably want to pursue relatively few of them.

The Inquiry

What can you tell from a person's voice over the telephone? If you have learned that you can identify kindred spirits by phone, make use of this gift by all means and do not invite trouble by setting up an interview with someone who will probably not understand or value your day care home. If you are uncertain about a particular inquiry, the match is probably not a good one; if you need children badly, you may arrange an interview to make sure one way or the other. But again, be wary of accepting any child solely for the fees.

How much information you give over the phone is up to you. Some providers give no information on the phone, insisting instead that the caller bring the child for a visit before any details are discussed. This implies that rates and hours may be negotiable. If they are not, it is only fair to say so whenever the question is raised. In my case, I found that my hours were not flexible, so I always gave my hours on the phone; my rates were somewhat flexible, so I preferred to talk to the parent and see the child before setting a rate, and certainly before making even a tentative arrangement with the family. Occasionally a parent will want to make all arrangements by phone and begin full-time permanent day care the next day, with no visit or adjustment period for the child. I do not recommend this for you or the child.

If the parent and child seem suited to your style, make an appointment for a visit. If possible, both parents and their child should visit your home. Caution the parents not to bring the child with the expectation that this might be his or her new day care place; this is just a visit for the parents to learn what this home is like. The first visit should be scheduled for the middle of the morning when all the children have arrived and are playing together and you are relatively free to talk to the family and introduce them to your home. If you are making lunch, putting children down for a nap, or resting while the children sleep, the visitors will not see how children feel and what they do in this day care home — and seeing your home in operation is the main purpose of the visit. There will probably be times when you cannot arrange the visit during the morning or afternoon play, and you will have to do the best you can to explain what day care in your home is like.

Preparing for the Interview

In many people's eyes, my housekeeping standards leave a lot to be desired. But the parents with whom I am involved are glad to find a place where their children can make a mess and learn about cleaning it up without being made to feel guilty. These parents recognize the need for a relaxed attitude about mess and cleanliness in the day care home. Many have told me that they ruled out other day care homes because they were "too neat and clean," that is, too restrictive for children and unaccepting of the activity and chaos that accompany a group of busy children.

Nevertheless, I make it a policy to clean up just before a parent and child come to visit for the first time. Many people who will come to understand your "messy" house later will not stay long enough to find out what you offer if they walk in at the end of a whole week of day care before the floor is washed. I make an attempt to sort toys into small containers, arrange books neatly, wash the woodwork from four feet down, and scrub the kitchen sink and bathroom. I make sure the dishes are done, the laundry put away, and the shoes in the closet. I do not do this to deceive the parents. I am absolutely candid with prospective parents about my everyday goals, attitude, and behavior.

Because your time may be limited by the demands of the current day care children and the parents' time by other responsibilities, you may have to cover a great many subjects in what seems like a short amount of time. You should have written statements on your child-rearing philosophy and the children's activities ready to hand over. Make up a list of specific items you want to mention or questions you want to ask. At the end of this chapter are copies of handouts I give parents at the interview.

The Interview

The interview should enable both you and the parents to decide if your day care home fits in with what they are seeking for their child. Generally, only one interview is necessary, with some time afterward for parents and provider to make a decision. If a second interview seems necessary for either the provider or the parents, the home is probably not suited to the child and the parents. Because my style is so distinctive and open to the natural inclinations of children, parents either like it or dislike it, and a second interview is not necessary. During the interview the provider and parents should cover the basic topics: housekeeping, children's schedule, and the physical care of the day care home; the provider should also observe the parent-child interaction and explain the role she assumes as day care provider. I also present the parents with a questionnaire designed to clarify their goals in day care in comparison with a written statement of my philosophy. If fees are not negotiable, you should state this at the outset; if they are negotiable, the fee should be determined after you have decided whether or not to accept the child.

Housekeeping

The first thing I tell parents when we sit down to talk for the first time is, "You may never see this house as clean again as it is right now. I cleaned it up especially for you and I can't keep it this way for long." It is good to get the housekeeping issue out in the open immediately, as it seems to be an important factor in the decision-making process for many families. My house was under construction for four years; we added a second floor. Although construction did not directly interfere with activity on the first floor, there was some disruption. We took off the roof during the summer, when it rained for twelve days; as a result, the paint started to peel and there was considerable water damage to the ceiling and walls. When parents saw that this superficial state of disrepair had little effect on the children, the peeling paint and stained ceiling receded from view. Even the most extreme situation does not need to deter parents who are clear about what they value. One parent recently confided to me, "When I came here for the first time three years ago, I came in the front door, looked around at the leaky ceiling and plastic-covered floors, and asked myself if I was really going to leave Jenny here. Then I thought, 'Well, I like the woman, so I guess it will be okay.'" She and Jennifer have been very happy with my day care ever since, though I must admit she came for an interview on the worst possible day — the day it rained through the ceiling and we had to scatter buckets around the living room to catch the leaks. The children were the only ones who really enjoyed the experience. The people you want to serve are precisely those who can see through whatever superficial circumstances exist, right to the heart of your home.

Do not pretend that you might be willing to adjust your house-keeping standards (or any others) to please a prospective parent: you will both be disappointed when you find that your house-keeping standards are a reflection of your philosophy and your child care style. Parents who are overly concerned with neatness should probably be referred to a day care center, where there is far less opportunity for children to be messy and the physical environment is strictly monitored. If you follow my child care style, you will probably not encounter parents who think you are too neat.

Children's Schedule

Parents usually want to know the schedule for children in a day care home. The schedule can be posted and a copy distributed to parents during the interview. Schedules vary according to the interests of the provider and the needs of the children. My schedule was simple:

8:00 A.M. — Day care opens
8:45 A.M. — School-age children leave for school
8:00 to 11:30 A.M. — Children play, inside or out
11:30 A.M. — Clean-up time
11:45 A.M. — Lunch
1:00 P.M. to 3:30 P.M. — Nap time for children under four
3:30 P.M. — Schoolchildren arrive
3:30 to 5:15 P.M. — Children play, inside or out
5:15 P.M. — Clean-up time
5:30 P.M. — Day care closes

At no time during the day do I allow children to watch television, unless I am desperate for silence, or near silence. Children select their own activities.

Physical Area of Day Care Home

Parents will want to know where the children play and what areas are off-limits to them. Take the parents and their child on a tour of your home, pointing out the areas for play, napping, and meals, as well as the equipment and material available. Explain to the parents your policy on naps. I state clearly that I have not yet seen a child under four years old who does not need a nap after a full morning of play in day care, even though the child may not need one at home. After a few days of day care, any child is undoubtedly more tired because of the increased level of activity and will nap without protest. The bathroom may prompt a discussion about toilet training (see Chapter 8). Point out the locked medicine closet and any other special safety features of the day care area. Show the parents the outside play area or areas, and explain which children can play in the fenced area and which ones can play outside that area. Generally, I do not allow a child to play outside a fenced area unless I, the parents, and the child agree that the child is ready for this greater responsibility. I use specific telephone poles on our street as boundaries marking the limits of the outside play area. Explain also the kind of outside play you allow. Will you allow children to dig in the dirt? In the mud? Will you allow them to play in a small plastic pool? Ask the parents how they feel about picking up a wet or dirty child. If you want parents to send children in play clothes and to leave an extra set of clothing, say so.

If you have given over most of your home to day care children and their activities, point this out. Parents will want to know if their children will be able to play freely without worrying about breaking an adult's delicate lamps or china collection. How you have arranged your home to accommodate day care children will indicate your philosophy about children and their activities, and parents will ask the questions most relevant to their concerns for the child in this environment.

Parent-Child Interaction

During the tour, observe the way the parents treat their child; their manner toward the child will give you a reasonable idea of how the child will behave in your home and how the parents will respond to your style of handling children.

How much freedom to explore the environment do the parents allow their child? How consistent are they when they set limits? Do they follow through? How reasonable are the limits? What kind of enforcement do they use? Major clues to the ease or difficulty of your relationship with this child are to be found in how realistic the parents are in their expectations and, even more important, in how consistent they are in following through on what they say to the child.

If a parent shows appropriate disapproval to the child but the child ignores it and the parent drops the subject, you may be in for big trouble with this child. If the parent makes picky and inappropriate demands on the child and the child ignores them but responds to more serious demands, you will probably fare better. The child probably senses that the parent is being especially picky because of the situation, and may be demonstrating his or her own common sense about appropriate limitations. But you may have problems with the parent in this case. Generally, a child under six who does not respect limits set by a parent will be very demanding of your time and slow in adjusting to the day care group. It takes time to convince a child that some adults mean what they say when the first years of experience have taught the child otherwise. Even so, I would accept some children regardless of this additional demand. You will have to use your intuition to decide which children will respond to your efforts.

What does the tone of the parent's voice convey? How do the parents respond to the interaction of their child with other day care children? Is the visiting child more aggressive or less? Is he or she intimidated or fearful? Does he cling to his parents? Does she seem overwhelmed by the choice of equipment? Does he have an obvious interest in one particular kind of toy? Does she have sophisticated social skills for her age? On the basis of these observations and evaluations I decide whether the child will be happy and adjust easily and whether the parents will be supportive. The more similar your style to the style of the family, the greater the likelihood that the match is a good one and the day care relationship will be successful.

The Role of the Provider

At some point during the interview, parents will usually ask about what I do with the children. I reply candidly that I do not "do" anything with them; this reply inevitably leads to an explanation of my philosophy of "attentive noninterference."

Attentive noninterference means paying close attention to children and their activity but not interfering with their exploration and self-development. I teach children to do what they can for themselves and to rely on their peers and older children for assistance; I am available to assist in more serious disputes or in situations in which new skills need to be taught. Anyone who listens carefully will understand that doing nothing with the children actually entails quite a bit of effort and careful attention while *appearing* to be uninvolved. Unfortunately, many people do not want their children to be taught to be independent at a young age. I was once told by an interviewing parent that she had visited a day care center and was appalled that the three-year-olds were putting on their own coats. I assured her that the children took great joy in this new skill and awareness of their capabilities, and I ushered her out as fast as possible. What would she think of my two-year-olds flipping on their coats? You will not spend enough time with parents to change their basic attitudes. When you discover that there are fundamental philosophical differences between you and a family, state this immediately and encourage the family to look at other homes. If you can do so, refer the family to a home you think would match the family's style more closely than yours does. It is not worth your time to try to change the parent's child-rearing philosophy. If theirs does not roughly match yours, accepting the child will only cause disagreement and heartache somewhere down the road.

Although I do not "do" anything with the children, I do teach them. Some day care providers put coats on *for* children, put shoes on *for* children, open doors *for* children. This takes time and energy. I use my time and energy teaching the children to do these things for themselves and each other. Some people believe that it is important to give children help and protection in order to give them a feeling of security and safety. I believe that knowing one's real abilities and limits provides one with security and safety in a more meaningful way — even if that person is a child. It may be pleasant to be doted on, but taking pride in accomplishments and independence and seeing a child's pride can be healthier and more productive for everyone.

Independent children are often thought to be difficult to deal with, because they do not blindly follow authority. They test limits

conscientiously. They continually try to do things that are just
beyond their current abilities. They make terrible messes and often
increase the mess by trying to clean it up. But independent children
are less fussy and more cooperative than dependent ones, and
make fewer demands on an adult for simple things like dressing,
washing, project assistance, food preparation, and feeding. They
are happier because they feel they have more control over their
own lives. They are excited at the realization of their increasing
competence. The kind of help they ask for is often a pleasure to
provide because it involves imagination and more teaching rather
than repetition. A parent who needs a dependent child to fulfill
his or her own needs will see my child care style as a threat. This
parent cannot accept the new role that would be required. Such
a parent usually recognizes the attitudinal differences between his
or her child and that of the more independent day care children.
The parent may express this awareness by such comments as, "My
child needs individual affection, individual attention"; "He is
shy"; "She takes a long time to adjust to new situations"; "He
is used to being at home with me"; "She needs help with things";
"He hasn't been around other children much." Though these
statements may all be true, there is often little recognition from
the parent that he or she has fostered these characteristics to meet
his or her own needs. If a parent is very apprehensive about the
lack of help her child will receive, refer her to another home. She
will not understand or accept the attentive-noninterference
approach to children. She will have reservations about the quality
of your care and the safety of her child. These feelings will be
transferred to the child, who may in turn feel unsafe, or may at
the very least experience confusion and conflict. How can the child
feel happy and loving toward a provider whom her own mother
feels is inadequate? The child's loyalty is divided.

Occasionally, overprotective parents will recognize the unnecessary limitations they have imposed on the child and will be looking
for someone who can change the pattern of adult–child interaction. These parents usually are able to verbalize this awareness
and they will see your methods as essential for the healthy development of their child. Such a parent will not feel threatened but
relieved that he has found a way to interrupt and change an
unhealthy pattern of development in the child. He may even learn

new ways of relating to his child. He will see you as a resource and will come to you for suggestions. He will expect support from you in his efforts to improve his parenting methods. This parent will be pleased to find his child struggling with a sock at 5:00 P.M. and will not object when you lead the child who has begun to whine or fuss to the other room to finish putting on the sock. This family is a joy to work with! There is satisfaction in seeing the child grow stronger and more confident and happier, just as there is joy in seeing the parent begin to relax and become less protective and more confident and thus able to enjoy the child more.

This kind of positive experience should be kept in mind as you develop your own personal philosophy about caring for children. The purpose of running a business may be to earn an income, but the purpose of running a day care business must also be to enable children to grow and develop according to their own needs, personalities, and instincts. However you define your philosophy, it must benefit the child as a child.

The Questionnaire

The purpose of the interview is to enable you and the parents to determine whether your views on child care are compatible. If after the tour and general discussion you are still undecided about a family or do not want to rely solely on your conversation with them, you may ask them to answer a questionnaire on expectations and priorities (see the sample questionnaire at the end of this chapter). Their answers should indicate to you more clearly whether their views are in agreement with yours. Rephrase the questions to suit your particular concerns and circumstances, adding to or subtracting from the list as seems necessary.

After the parents have answered the questionnaire, go over it with them to define areas of agreement and disagreement. There will undoubtedly be areas where you differ. Both you and the parents will have reasons for specific choices, which you can discuss. If an important, unsolvable difference remains, then I suggest that you try not to alter your style to fit the family; let the parents make the adjustment if they still want to place their child with you.

It is important for you to explain during this discussion that day care is a very taxing, demanding occupation. You will not have the energy to be totally consistent and fully alert every minute of every day. There will be times when basic maintenance will be all that the provider can accomplish. Beyond this, you strive to implement your particular ideas and goals to the best of your ability.

Statement of Philosophy

If at this point you want to take care of this particular child, you should offer some written information to the parents. They may want to read it there or take it home and call you with questions. This information should include your expectations and goals for children at different ages and your policy on discipline. In addition, you may add statements on other subjects of interest to you. The statement I give parents is long enough to answer most questions parents have. Parents generally find this statement helpful in bringing their expectations into line with your practices (see the Statement of Philosophy at the end of this chapter). It also gives them some idea about your stability, maturity, and self-confidence in the management of children and your business. At this point I also give the parents a copy of the Child Information Sheet and a formal agreement on liability. I may also decide on a fee, or at this point I ask them to think over the discussion and to call me later with their decision or any further questions.

Acceptance

If the parents decide to send their child to your day care home, you can clarify any remaining questions on the fee and payment schedule. Request a completed Child Information Sheet. In addition, I generally suggest a trial period of approximately two weeks, during which either parent or provider may withdraw from the agreement without giving a reason. Withdrawal during this period should not be a common occurrence; the option is made available to both parent and provider in the event of unusual or unforeseeable circumstances. If you accept a child for day care, you should be comfortable with the prospect of having this child.

A Mistake

At some point in your day care business you may find you have accepted a child and family that do not adjust to your style, for whatever reason. I have on occasion interviewed families desperate for child care. In one case I recognized immediately that this family was not a good match and therefore not a good risk. Their socioeconomic background was very different from mine, and the way the parents related to the child and their expectations for their daughter were very different from mine. The parents made an obvious effort to cover up negative feelings about my lifestyle: they were desperate. The family was living in the neighborhood with the father's parents. I felt it difficult to refuse them, so I agreed to take the child (aged two) on a temporary basis, until they could find a home better suited to their needs. The mother's working hours were 7:30 A.M. to 6:00 P.M., which meant she had to make other arrangements for picking up and dropping off the child. Finally, after about four months of care, the family moved the child, leaving a debt and complaining that I did not discipline their child severely enough. Without the confidence and respect of the parents, though, I could do little to change their attitudes and treatment of their child. Unless there are repeated signs of physical abuse, a state agency will not become involved with such a family. The best I and the child could hope for is that another provider, one who did have the confidence and trust of the family, would become concerned for the child's welfare.

When you accept a child from such a family, you are taking a risk. Financial loss is the most frequent and obvious but certainly the least important. The risk I am referring to is the trouble a hostile family can cause you by formal complaints or anonymous calls to the licensing agency. Some licensing workers are aware of this kind of problem, but many are not. The licensing worker may treat the day care home operator as a child, imposing limits, supervision, punishment. Harassment from such a worker is annoying and may cause you anxiety, but is otherwise usually harmless. Nevertheless, you can eliminate virtually all complaints if you follow your judgment and only take families you judge to be a good match for your style.

Following are five handouts that I usually give prospective parents — a parent questionnaire, two handouts that cover my philosophy and discipline policy, a handout outlining the equipment available in my day care home, and an important handout on children's special training.

Parent Questionnaire

Expectations and Priorities

Please indicate in the space provided your agreement or disagreement with the priorities and expectations listed below. If you agree with the statement, place a + in the space provided; if you disagree with the item, place a − in the space. Not all of these questions and statements reflect my philosophy. In fact, some are in direct opposition to others. They are simply a tool for us to find out to what degree we hold similar expectations.

Children should

_____ not have to share toys and things brought from home.
_____ keep their shoes and socks on except for nap time.
_____ not put on other children's clothing.
_____ be expected, taught, and encouraged to dress themselves to the level of their developmental potential at any age.
_____ learn to accept aggression and express aggression.
_____ learn to sit quietly and pay attention to instructions given by an adult.
_____ be allowed to play "doctor" and other games designed by them to explore the body.
_____ be expected to eat foods they don't like.
_____ play outside at least part of every day, whether they want to or not (weather permitting).
_____ be allowed to express their feelings freely.
_____ learn to accept authority from adults without argument.
_____ be toilet trained by age two.

I would like my children to learn to

_____ solve problems with other children through negotiation and listening.
_____ share and take turns with personal as well as day care property.
_____ be motivated through enjoyment of an activity or accomplishment (intrinsic) rather than through reward (extrinsic).
_____ verbalize their feelings and needs.
_____ become independent as much as possible.

_____ stay clean.

_____ respect adults.

_____ accept individual differences.

_____ be free to explore their bodies and learn to think of their bodies as nice, pleasurable, and under their personal control.

_____ feel self-confident and good about themselves.

_____ value the environment and all forms of life.

_____ fear and believe in God.

_____ recognize the letters and numbers and progress as quickly as possible in the academic area in preparation for school.

_____ enjoy a wide range of activities.

_____ develop a sense of internal authority.

_____ use self-control in their behavior.

_____ eat a greater variety of foods.

_____ finish the food they ask for.

_____ use good table manners.

_____ discern the natural consequences of their actions.

_____ participate in making decisions.

_____ ask questions freely.

_____ consider the needs of peers.

_____ ask for help when really needed.

_____ offer help to others when they are in need.

The day care provider should

_____ provide a choice of activities for the children at all times.

_____ see that the children are involved in an offered activity.

_____ allow children to make up their own games and activities and interfere as little as possible.

_____ be very involved in helping the children and give them close supervision.

_____ keep the children neat and clean.

_____ settle disputes between children.

_____ decide who is right and who is wrong.

_____ provide hot lunches.

_____ eliminate sugar and preservatives from the diet.

_____ treat day care children like her own (i.e., use same disciplinary methods).

_____ never spank children.

_____ remove children to another room when they misbehave.

_____ be consistent.

_____ give the children lots of love and affection.

_____ recognize and consider individual differences between children.

_____ communicate freely with parents about their children.

_____ keep children in groups of peers.

_____ answer questions honestly and with concern for the understanding of the child.

Parent Handout

General Philosophy and Goals for the New Child

This is the first group experience for most of the children that begin day care here. Until now they have spent most of their time with adults or with one other child with an adult present. Many have learned that when adults are in view, they will immediately solve all the problems that arise, from buttoning a coat to getting the desired toy from another child. I have found that when adults do not jump to "help," children are very capable of solving or learning to solve most of the small problems that come up during the day. I give children credit for being capable, and I have found that the joy children express when they realize they *can* do so many things for themselves that they thought they could not do is extraordinary!

Two-year-olds can be taught to put on their own clothing, including socks and shoes, and four- or five-year-olds to tie shoes. They can open doors for themselves, can put on their own coats by the "flip method," and can work out agreements over toys.

Through the natural concern we all feel as parents, children are often reinforced for extended crying during times of "small ouchies" (as opposed to severe injuries). I try hard to teach children to express their feelings in these cases as surprise or anger or fear of being seriously hurt — which I think is actually the case — rather than great pain. My results have been good, and I encourage parents to try hard not to make a big deal out of small hurts.

When during the first few days, a child is understandably angered by being left, I practice active listening — expressing for the child in words the anger or fear he is expressing in crying or tantrums. After the child has had time to express these feelings and after he has been reassured about what is going to happen and when, if he continues the tantrum and can't go to other activity, I explain that if he needs to cry he can cry in the other room and return to play with us as soon as he feels better and wants to come out. This usually causes initial anger (no audience and no more sympathy), but in less than five minutes the child will emerge to test this out. When crying begins again, immediately it is back to the other room. This time, in three minutes or less the child will come out, ready to involve himself in something else. There are some children, of course, who do not adjust this quickly and easily, but I have found that without exception, after five consecutive days or less the trauma decreases for children over one year old, and by the end of the first week the child is part of the gang and having a good time without having to be removed from the group. A child who comes on an irregular basis or for less than three consecutive days has a very difficult time anticipating what will happen and often has the subconscious impression that if she does not enjoy herself — that is, cries loud enough and long enough — her parents will surely change their minds and keep her home. When children come on a nonconsecutive schedule, they may believe that their parents are undecided about their attendance. This leads to a drastic increase in the time and effort the child will spend in trying to convince the parent and herself and the day care provider that she should be kept home where everything is known, understood, safe, etc. I think children see their role as trying by any means possible to eliminate transitions and changes, as these *do* cause stress. Not allowing the child to continue manipulative behavior helps relieve the child of this role or responsibility, and enables him or her to get on with behavior and activities that are more intrinsically rewarding.

Parent Handout

Discipline Policy

A. Positive reinforcement
   I use positive reinforcement to encourage constructive, thoughtful behavior and cooperation. (Not food, but attention, physical affection, eye contact, smiles, etc.)
B. Recognition of feelings
   Usually there are feelings behind negative behavior; I use active listening to get to the cause and feelings behind negative behavior. Often verbalizing these feelings is enough to give the child the control to stop the behavior. If not, I apply the rules.
C. Statement of the rules
   1. no hurting (physically or emotionally; intentionally)
   2. no malicious teasing
   3. all equipment is for everyone to use; take turns, sharing is stressed
   4. no throwing or abuse of equipment
   5. no inappropriate tantrums
D. Inappropriate behavior leads to
   1. a statement of my feelings about the behavior
   2. perhaps an active listening session concerning possible causes and feelings
   3. discussion of the natural consequences of the behavior
   4. reminder of the rule and the reason for the rule
   5. removal of the thing involved
   6. "time out" — isolation from other children for short time
   7. parent conference if behavior continues
E. Examples
   1. Infant: Reinforce with physical and verbal reward for favorable behavior, remove the cause of problem when possible, remove the infant from the situation by distraction or redirection to another

activity. Couple "No" only with harmful behavior or as a warning of danger.

2. Toddlers: Reinforce desired behavior with extra physical and verbal attention. After stating my objection, ignore as much undesirable behavior as possible — when not possible to ignore, discuss while removing cause of problem and/or the child. Redirect activity — isolate when necessary (not often or for long at this age).

3. Ages 3–4: Reinforce desired behavior with praise, physical attention, and privileges. Stress child's new ability to make appropriate decisions. When undesirable behavior occurs, give the child a chance to change his own behavior without being told by simply stating my feelings about the situation. Talk out feelings and possible causes of the behavior to dissipate the negative feelings causing the problem. If change does not occur, state the possible natural consequences of the behavior, then remind about the rule and the reason for it, take away if things involved, "time out" when appropriate for short times.

4. Ages 4–6: Reinforce desired behavior as above, stressing the child's maturity and ability to make good decisions and to find appropriate ways of dealing with problems and difficulties with other children. When intervention is necessary, encourage children to discuss their problems with one another, possible role playing, try out compromises, try out rules which they help to construct. If all else fails, "time out," restriction of privileges, etc.

5. I do not believe in spanking as a frequent form of discipline, although I occasionally resort to a slap on the bottom with my own children.

In general, I believe in helping the children to develop their communication skills, to get in conscious touch with their feelings and to solve their own problems with one another through working it out verbally as much as possible.

Parent Handout

Equipment List

Each day offers opportunities for use of equipment and activity in each of the following categories. The schedule is very flexible, if not nonexistent. Lunch and naps are constant, that is about all. Equipment is rotated to some extent, offering continued interest in "new" materials. Children sometimes bring games or toys from home with the understanding that everything that is brought is to be shared.

Large-Muscle Development
1 big wheel
1 large trike
3 small trikes
4 sit-push and ride toys
2 tire swings, 3 other small
    swings for 2+ yrs.
    balls, bats
1 large waterbed

1 house gym with slide
2 infant rocking horses
2 wonder horses
1 pair stilts
1 pair roller skates
1 scooter
2 splash pools, hoses,
    sprinkler

Small-Muscle Development (hand–eye coordination)
blocks
hammer and nails
hammer and workbench
"sewing"
meshing cans
Tinker Toys
sandpaper letter blocks

stringing beads
Lincoln Logs
Lego
cards
many puzzles, age-appropriate
nuts and bolts
shape and color work

Imagination
dress-up for male and female
lots of various small people
    and animal toys
farm
school
kaleidoscopes
lots of cars, trucks, planes,
    trains of various sizes
musical instruments and
    noisemakers

empty food containers — play
    store
electric train
large teepee, room for five
    children
Big Toy — back-yard climbing
    and play toy
puppets
dolls
stuffed animals

Creative
play dough
crayons
scissors
paper
paste
stapler
hole punch
watercolors

finger paint
cutter toys for play dough
clay
rolling pins
felt pens
colored pencils
pens and pencils and erasers
fabric pieces

Books and records, ages 1–9
records for the children to
    manipulate

records for children to listen to
    on adult-operated machine

Infant equipment
Jack-be-nimble jumping seat
crib, protective playpen
stroller

infant rocking horse
General Motors car seat for
    sitting in around the house

Home Equipment
>   stove   cradle
>   cupboard   small chairs
>   fridge   small tables

Table Games
>   TRADE   Water Works
>   Checkers   Connect
>   Chinese checkers   UNO
>   dominoes   canasta deck of cards
>   MAD   Trouble
>   backgammon   Sorry
>   chess

Emergency Substitute

Neighbors are available in emergency; occasionally I have a substitute for medical appointments or needed time out. Occasionally a parent is trading day care work hours for child care, and that parent will take over for me.

Parent Handout

Special Things

Often parents feel uncomfortable or guilty about sending their children to day care. They want the child to feel comforted and often believe that a blanket or pacifier or special toy will ensure the child's comfort and happiness. Quite the contrary, though children use these special things at home to give them comfort, especially when a parent is angered, in the day care setting special things often cause problems for the child. Blankets and toys interfere with the child's ability to become involved in other activities; a pacifier interferes with communication; special things that are very personal and important cause the child to feel that he or she must defend and protect them.

I have found that most children have no urgent need for these special things in a new setting. They are able to understand, after the age of one and a half or so, that this is a different place from home and that they will meet different expectations regarding behavior and those special things that are a part of their life at home.

Probably the most important factor in the child's adjustment to a new day care situation, mine or any other, is the parent's attitude about the time that the child spends in day care and about the day care home. Children are very sensitive to their parents' feelings and attitudes and quickly pick up anxiety, uncertainty, hesitation, and reservation on the part of the parents.

If you do not support my philosophy and goals, this is not a good place for your child. The child will be in constant conflict — how can a child have a good time and adjust if her parents don't really want her to? If my lifestyle or philosophy do not mesh with what you think is good for your child, then you will hope that the child will not adjust to it, and in fact the child will not. There will be unhappiness for all involved. I cannot change the basis on which I have built this environment, so it is important that parents feel real support and enthusiasm, giving their child the freedom to invest himself or herself in this peer group and in this day care home.

5

You and the New Child: Getting Through the First Days

Deciding to put a child in day care can be difficult for parents. Knowing that the child will have other children to play with and other adults to rely on does not ease their discomfort. The child's tears at drop-off time obscure all other considerations. The day care provider must prepare both parents and child for the drop-off trauma, explaining to the parents that the child's tears and resistance are normal and will soon pass. For most children the drop-off trauma will last about one hour on the first full day, one-half hour on the second day, one-quarter hour on the third day, and three minutes on the fourth day. On the following Monday, the trauma will last perhaps one hour, but it will decline substantially to a few minutes per day for the rest of the week. By the middle of the second week of full-time day care most children have adjusted to the new schedule and new environment. If you follow the specific suggestions outlined in this chapter, the adjustment process will be comparatively painless and swift for both the child and the parents. If they do not make a concentrated effort to help the child adjust, the provider and parents will be faced with a long period of adjustment and a perpetually unhappy child. This is hardly fair to anyone.

Full-Time Day Care Children

Most children seem to feel it is necessary to do everything in their power to prevent separation from a parent. They will use any and all means at their disposal to avoid a painful transition to this first separation. Parents and providers who are prepared for this resistance will be able to limit it to a reasonable period of time. The steps in preparing a child are simple but can be crucial; if for some reason parents cannot go through the steps of preparation discussed below, the provider will just have to do the best she can, beginning on the first full day of care.

Preparation

The preparation actually begins with the child's first visit to the day care home, for the interview. The child should see that the home is not very different from any other home, except that there are probably more children and more equipment. Additional preparation should include two or three more visits to the day care home, each designed to familiarize the child with the new place and new children. When you arrange these visits with the parents, remind them of your policy on special things or toys: the child should not bring to day care any toy, special or otherwise, that cannot be shared with the other children (with rare exceptions).

The second visit. During the second visit, the parent should plan to remain and observe the children and the provider as they go about their regular business. The parent may play with the child and explore the environment with him, but should allow him to get involved with the other children and equipment independently as much as possible. If the child is shy, he or she may spend the second visit sitting on the parent's lap. This is acceptable. The child is taking inventory of mom's or dad's feelings and evaluating the situation. There will be plenty of time to explore later.

Although this second visit is considered as an adjustment visit, it is still appropriate for either you or the parent to cancel your agreement. If you feel for any reason — even a reason you cannot put your finger on — that either the parents or the child will not be happy with what you offer, or if you sense a personality conflict with the child or parents, this is the time to make your feelings known, as tactfully as possible. An acceptable approach might be to say, "I sense that you are not entirely comfortable with my lifestyle (housekeeping standards, this group of kids, amount of supervision, educational philosophy). My experience tells me that when a parent is not completely comfortable with the day care setting, the child picks up this ambivalence and does not adjust

well. I would like to give you a referral to another home that might
meet your needs better and be more appropriate for you." You
can also say, "You know, I can't quite put my finger on it, but
I have the feeling that this is not the right place for Kevin. I don't
want to set your child up for a failure or an unnecessary change,
so I don't think it would be fair for me to take him here. I think
he might be happier at Mary's. She lives just about a mile from
here." If the parent is desperate for immediate care and has
exhausted other possibilities for the moment, you might take the
child temporarily. Temporary care, however, is difficult for the
child and should be avoided if possible. In addition, I can almost
guarantee that you will have problems with a family that uses your
home as a stop-gap measure. You cannot expect, and will not get,
the support and cooperation from these parents that you will get
from your other families, and you will probably have behavior
problems with the child. If parents and the child have reservations
about the commitment to your day care home, they will reserve
their emotional investment in order to protect themselves from
feeling loss in the future.

During the second visit parent and child should begin to feel
comfortable in your home, interested in the various activities sur-
rounding them, and comfortable with the prospect of full-time
care. This visit can last a half-day or less, but should be at least
one or two hours long.

The third visit. During the third visit, the child is left at the day
care home for one hour or more in the morning, during play time.
The parent should prepare the child for this visit by telling her
that mom or dad will leave her for one hour (or however long
is decided on) and will pick her up and take her home for lunch.
Usually one hour is long enough for the child to overcome the
separation and have fun with the other children. The child should
be picked up before he or she becomes overly tired or hungry.

The fourth visit. The fourth visit should be made the day after
the third visit. The child should be brought to the home for half
a day, including lunch. The child may not eat the first few days,
but will watch the lunch routine closely, getting a better idea of
the rules and attitudes in the environment. If a child is slow to
adjust, these short visits can be extended until the child seems
willing to spend a full day; most children understand after three

visits or fewer that they are expected to settle into day care until a parent picks them up. Like any adult, a child will resist being deposited in a strange situation with no preparation; short visits of gradually increasing duration allow the child to look over the environment and accept it.

Full-Time Day Care

As soon as the child begins full-time day care, you should present him or her and the parents with the basic practices that make your home run smoothly. The first few days of full-time care will prompt a number of emotions in children, and these and related problems should be handled immediately and consistently. Especially on the first day you should expect to deal with the following points, and your policy on each should be clear to the parents and child: the drop-off procedure, the child's special things, tantrums, the "poor me" syndrome, minor hurts, naps, and the pick-up procedure. Go over your policy on these questions with the parent before the first full day. In addition, you should have on file a completed Child Information Sheet.

The drop-off procedure. On the first full day, the parent should stay for a few minutes to give the child an opportunity to see that he or she is comfortable with this environment and this day care provider. You and the parents may have met before, but this might be the first opportunity for the child to observe the relationship between you and the parent. Perhaps the child was too busy with the other children or things to watch you and Mom. There should be no question in the child's mind about the parent's departure. Mother is leaving *soon,* in three minutes, and she should not stay longer than it takes to accomplish the purpose. There is inevitably a negative anticipation of separation, and this anxiety is hard for the child. Do not give the child the power to determine when the parent leaves. Once the child knows that Mom approves of the place and will be back at a predetermined time, Mom should leave. The quicker the departure, the less upsetting it will be for the child. Do not belittle the child or forbid his attempts to waylay his mother; simply proceed with the drop-off in spite of these attempts.

After the parent has left, listen closely to the child to determine what he is expressing. Is he afraid? Is he angry? Are his feelings hurt by being left (excluded from his parent's activity)? You will probably be able to tell by observation. Most children do not want to be comforted in this situation, but you can try. If your approach is rebuffed, kneel down and say, "It is really hard to be left in a new place. You might be afraid because you don't know me yet. You sound angry because your mother didn't take you with her." Or you may say, "You sound like your feelings are hurt. You can cry if you want to. I think most people feel the same way when they are left in a new place. I am glad to see you, though, and I really think you will have a good time here with the other kids when you are no longer upset."

Be sure there is a clean departure. The parent should say, "Goodbye, I will be back later." Be sure the child sees the parent go out the door. Often it is helpful for the child to watch the parent walk from the house and drive off in the car. When a parent leaves secretly, the child will play happily for a minute and then realize she has been tricked, deserted, deceived. She is justifiably angry and hurt, at not being able to have her say, at not getting that goodbye kiss, most of all at not being trusted with the departure information. I have seen a very young child spend a lot of his day looking for the disappearing parent, not believing that the parent has gone to work. The child believed that the parent was lurking about the yard or in a closet, when actually the parent took him to the back yard and waited for him to become involved in play, then jumped over the fence and left without telling me or the child. Insecurity is the result of such parental cowardice. The fits and yelling upon separation are short-lived, usually ending a minute after the parent has left in the car. After one to two weeks of daily attendance, there will probably be no separation trauma at all. My day care children, without exception, happily kiss their parents goodbye and move on to their own plan for the morning.

If you feel that the drop-off experience is more difficult for the parent than for the child, you may call the parent at work or at home and reassure him or her by reporting how long the child was unhappy and what the child is doing now. Explain to the parent that children somehow feel obligated to do all they can to keep the parent close to them. Children feel it is their role to be unhappy when being left. To help a child overcome this stage, the parent must cooperate in a simple, clear drop-off. A good drop-off runs as follows: The parent brings in the child. The parent may take off the child's coat and hang it up, kiss the child goodbye, and promise to be back after work to pick him or her up. Then the parent goes out the door quickly, waves to the child in the window, and drives away. Now the child can get on with the day.

After the parent leaves. The first few days, when a child is angered by being left, I help her express and accept her anger by actively listening for and naming her feelings. Usually five minutes or so is enough time for most children between one and three years old to get over these feelings and get on to something more interesting. I hold the child and sympathize with the unhappiness for this short time, if I am accepted. Then I begin to talk about the enjoyable things there are to do, and try to draw the child into an appropriate activity. Often, though, a child will not want to be held, will not want sympathy, and will have nothing to do with my efforts to draw her away from her current feelings. In this case, on the first two days I allow the child to hold back and watch, ignoring her most of the time if she is fairly quiet after the first ten minutes. After a couple of days I begin to express some expectations for her joining the group. I might say, "Come to the table now and try the play dough. It's lunch time, please sit here. This book is for you. Here are some cars for the parking lot." If the child persists in being withdrawn, I have been known to say, "It is against the rules to sulk after the third day. Now you have to play and have fun." Believe it or not, this works and the child begins to join in.

The only two children who refused all my efforts to draw them into the play group were two three-year-olds, a boy and a girl, from two families who did not have any firm schedule for day care. Both sets of parents were newly separated. The fathers were the culprits in these particular cases. Each father was ambivalent about the environment; each felt that his child needed a more structured, traditional, school-preparation, learning environment — more "challenge." Each enrolled his child for full-time summer day care but said he would pick up the child for special trips during the day, to grandma's, to the office, and so on. These pick-ups were not planned in advance, and the children came to believe that these surprise pick-ups were in response to their prolonged drop-off unhappiness. Neither child was able to adjust and become part of the group, and neither father was able to accomplish a clean quick drop-off routine. The children seemed to believe that if they held out long enough and were unhappy enough, Dad would surely come and rescue them. The children also seemed afraid to become part of the group for fear of losing friends when they were taken away at the end of the summer, and also to be disdainful of children in favor of adult activity, such as sitting at the office with a coloring book until Dad was through work.

These families were unaware of the conflicting messages received by their children until I discussed the problem with them. Even then they were unable to adjust their attitudes to ease the situation, but rather felt threatened and criticized. The kids were afraid that if they became involved and happy here, they would somehow be disloyal to their parents and would lose those "special" surprise pick-ups, those special times with their fathers given as atonement for leaving the children in day care. These excursions eased the guilt of the fathers, who continued to feel that their children should be in school or at home. The pattern of reinforcing the child's unhappy behavior through sympathy and surprise pick-ups led to a very difficult time for these children in day care. In the end, both families refused to recognize the emotional problems the children were having, removed their children, and placed them in a very structured and traditional day care environment which advertised a formal school-like curriculum. Both fathers had successfully convinced themselves that their children were not having a good time and were not joining in because they were beyond learning about peer play and social interaction, that they were in need of more intellectual stimulation.

There is little you or any other adult can do if the child's parent is unable to make the adjustment to a child in day care, is unwilling to establish a schedule, or accomplish a clean drop-off. Regardless of a child's interest in a new and intriguing environment, he or she is too young to understand the conflicts a parent must suffer at this time. The child feels he or she must reject the day care home in order to remain loyal to the parent. If after repeated efforts you cannot convince the parent of the wisdom of your drop-off policy and first-days policy, advise the parent to find other day care facilities.

Tantrums. What is a tantrum? Either controlled or uncontrolled yelling, crying, or flailing, with the motivating factor being anger or an effort to control the adult. A child may throw a tantrum when he or she is dropped off, when another child will not give up a desired toy, or when he or she is not allowed to play outside the yard or go on a field trip. Tantrums are especially common during the first few days of full-time child care, and are more common among children between one and two years old. The method I describe is designed to minimize the tantrum and related stress for the child, the provider, and the other children.

When a child has a tantrum, I allow about one-half minute before asking the child in a friendly voice to stop, please. I suggest an alternate activity, such as blocks, play dough, or play with a friend. If this is unsuccessful, as it always is, I explain in a cordial voice that we have a place where children can cry or carry on as much as they like. I lead the child to the nap room, where there are no toys or other children. I explain to the child that the other childen sometimes get upset when someone is making so much unhappy noise: "We are glad you have come to play. I hope you will be finished crying pretty soon so you can come out and play with the kids." Depending on the disciplinary methods used at the child's own home, the child may not understand or believe that you actually intend for him to stay in there until he is finished. Any child who has been in my day care home for more than two weeks knows that I am serious, and most do not get as far as the nap room before they spontaneously stop their crying, sometimes saying "I'm done." The child usually stops at the mere suggestion that he must go into the other room to cry, where there is no audience.

The new child may expect a spanking when an adult is serious. If the child will not stay in the nap room, it may be necessary to accommodate him with one swift swat to the bottom as you walk him back into the room. (As a rule I do not spank children; spanking is a last resort, after repeated efforts with the other methods I describe.) Often the child will test your limits by coming out before he finishes or by starting again as soon as he crosses the threshold of the room. This time I put the child back immediately saying, "No, you have to stay in here until you are finished. *Then* you can come out and play." I close the door and wait for a brief break in the crying, perhaps while the child is catching his breath. When this break comes, I quickly open the door and say, "Are you finished? Would you like to come out now?" Many times the child will take this opportunity to stop and come out. Usually this is the end of the tantrum and the child quickly becomes involved in other activity. If, however, the tantrum begins again, either immediately or a little later, I take him right back to the room with the same explanation and invitation. Children do not enjoy crying; they do not enjoy being alone in an uninteresting room. They are glad to have someone forbid this unpleasant pastime by eliminating the choice for them so they can resume pleasurable activity. Some children have enjoyed the attention that excessive crying often brings. When denied that attention, they quickly overcome this behavior. A swat on the bottom is usually not necessary if you are determined to work this through. If the child seems to expect a spanking, ask the parent about the method used at home.

I use this method with children beginning at the age of ten months, depending on the child. Children at ten months understand most of what you say. They understand the intonation and intent of your voice and action and recognize the connection between yelling and the time-out room almost immediately. You should use whatever term the baby is familiar with, such as fussing, crying, or yelling. If you do not know which term the parent uses, use them all to make sure the child understands. If the child's crying changes — begins to become hysterical — she is afraid; be sure to leave the door wide open, or stay in the room with the child without giving her any attention. As soon as you have even a brief opportunity to invite the child out (a pause in the crying), pick her up and say, "Good, you can come out when you stop crying." Of course, some children are not able to stop crying voluntarily at this age. You have to use your judgment. It may take three or four visits to the nap room for children between ten months and one year of age to realize you are serious, but they will learn very quickly that there are better things to do than "carry on."

By one year children understand all of what is going on and all of what you say. Only if you are inconsistent will you have trouble with this method. Children seem to have an amazing amount of control over the expression of their emotions — or perhaps my process itself becomes the focus of their attention and they forget about their anger. For whatever reason, this method works like a miracle, and I recommend it for the sanity of the other kids. To maintain self-control in a situation that can make you angry, it is important for you to feel that you can eliminate this behavior. For the sake of the child who needs help to get out of the corner he or she is in, give the child an option simply to give up a tantrum for something else.

"Poor me" syndrome. Some children become different kids as soon as Mom walks in the door at 5:30 P.M. They immediately become martyrs, digging up long-buried disagreements and complaints in hopes of gaining the complete attention of the parent. It is especially important that the parent not reinforce the child's role of "poor me." There is no reason to pity a child who spends the day playing with friends in a good day care home. If the parent is sorry to leave the child at my home, he or she must make clear the reason for that sorrow. He can say, "I would like to spend more time with you," and then add a supporting statement about the day care, such as "I'm sure you will have a good day. You and I like your friends and there is so much to do here that you enjoy." Without this kind of explanation, children easily get the impression that they, not the parent, should be unhappy and sorry to be left. When children understand that their parent actually regrets leaving them in day care, they will continue to feel unhappy and victimized all day, waiting to show the parent that he or she is right. The child fulfills the parent's expectation of being unhappy. At other times, the child will change her attitude as soon as the parent is gone, enjoy the day, and then immediately adopt the role of the victimized child as soon as the parent reappears. Parents of these childrren often never believe that their child is really happy and occupied during the day. Perhaps that idea is too threatening. You should discuss this problem with the parent, but keep in mind that the attitudes of most parents are not easily changed.

Small hurts. Children who expect attention for crying and for enduring the rigors of separation will undoubtedly expect special attention for small hurts. They have been given this attention by their parents and will expect it from the provider during the first few days of care. These children believe that small hurts and transition anxiety are major tragedies. They have been taught that they are victims of a cruel world, and have learned that they will get attention from adults when they express hurt or fear, so they do on the slightest excuse.

By contrast, other children learn that small hurts are to be minimized, briefly acknowledged, or ignored. Transitions are accepted as a normal part of life, difficult for everyone but negotiable and temporary. These children seem to take the normal bumps and scratches of play quite nonchalantly. They recover from transition trauma quickly and move on to other activity.

I am not advising you to ignore children who are hurt or afraid; I am suggesting that you ignore children who pretend to be but are not really hurt or afraid. When a child approaches you for sympathy for a minor hurt, try a brief explanation, such as "Everyone gets little hurts now and then. I'm glad you are not hurt. You don't have to worry about little hurts." Avoid the use of phrases such as "poor little boy" or "poor little Jane." Redirect the child's focus to legitimate feelings by saying, "That fall scared you, didn't it? You thought you might really get hurt because you couldn't stop yourself, and that is scary. Now that you know you are all right, you can stop crying." When children learn that they will not get attention for the small inconveniences of life, they begin to ignore them too. Sometimes two children who are accustomed to "ouch attention" will get together and see who has the biggest "ouch." Sometimes this can seem amusing to an adult, but it should be disturbing to see children depend on this as a way of getting attention. If a child spends lots of time and energy on being hurt, you should discuss this with the parents. This kind of behavior is not too difficult to change if parents are aware of the power they have in this area and realize that magnified attention to these complaints is not necessary to prove to the child that they care. There are other, healthier ways to show caring.

Naps. Some children never take a nap until they enter day care. You may have to remind some parents that all children take naps in day care, regardless of their practice at home. Because of the lower level of activity and absence of other children in the private home, a child may not really need one. But children need one at my home. The new child will probably resist taking a nap for the first few days, until he or she realizes that every child under four years old takes a nap, without exception. In Chapter 6 I describe techniques for making the child sleep. Make no exceptions to the napping rule. No child can be happy in day care if he or she is too tired to play.

The pick-up procedure. When parents arrive, often exactly at closing time, they may be tired, hurried, worried, thinking about dinner, and yet full of questions. The new parent especially will want to know how the child's day went. In my home children are not ready and waiting to go. I do not make an effort to prepare them except by announcing the 5:15 P.M. toy pick-up and telling them it is time to put on shoes and socks. Usually a parent will walk in, find his or her child, check to make sure the child's shoes and socks are on or help find them, get the child's jacket, and call a goodbye as they fight the bottleneck at the front door.

When the child is ready and waiting at the window with drawings in hand, the parent may be relieved just to motion the child to the car and drive off, but there are many serious drawbacks to this ready-and-waiting approach. First, it is better for the children to be having a good time when parents arrive than to be waiting restlessly. After clean-up time kids are free to use toys and materials. I want the kids to be anxious to return, possibly to resume an interrupted game. Children seem to lose their enthusiasm for day care when their day ends in a period of waiting, while they watch other children get picked up.

Second, when children have been waiting to go home, there is no opportunity for parents to talk with the provider while the child is occupied with playing. If a parent insists that the child wait while she talks with the provider, the adults have no privacy and the child quickly slides into an impatient stance, often ending in a scene that is embarrassing for the parent and unfair to the child.

Third, when children are ready and waiting or even just ready, parents have no opportunity to see firsthand how their children behave in the day care home environment. It is *very* important for parents to see their children at play, even though they may view the interruption as a negative responsibility. I ask children not to alert other children when a parent arrives, so that the parent has a chance to see the day care experience. In some cases, a young Dr. Jekyll turns into Mr. Hyde, giving the parent the impression that his child is not only unhappy in day care but also a monster. Most children have no difficulty with the transition from play to pick-up, but other children will fall apart if there is family discord or insecurity at home.

Fourth, some parents would never cross the threshold of my home if not forced to do so to collect their children. This forced exposure increases the commitment of a reluctant parent and allows the parent to interact with the children, who often give hugs and kisses to their friends' parents. Who can resist the innocent, even conniving, affection of a child? Increasing the number and the strength of connections to the day care home through this kind of exposure will enhance the day care experience as a whole as well as for that particular family.

Fifth, sometimes a child will make gifts for his or her parents. If the parent does not come in to collect the child, these gifts may be forgotten or never presented. Although the process of the child's art may be more important than the finished product, it is still important to the child. Furthermore, the parent may need help in accepting gifts with appropriate appreciation. If parents have difficulty expressing delight or appreciation, you can help them learn to express gratitude for the child's effort without commenting on the work itself. The parent might say, "Thank you. I missed you too. Thank you for thinking about me today." This is an appropriate reception for a gift that obviously involved little effort or inspiration but is an expression of love. When it is evident that a child has invested some effort, the child should be able to hear the difference in the parent's acceptance. The parent might say, "I can tell that you really enjoyed making this and that you put a lot of thought and effort into it. Thank you. Shall we put this up at home?"

The pick-up procedure should be much easier than the drop-off: parent and child are glad to see each other after a long day. But even though it is easier, it is no less important for the child. Advise the new parent about your procedure and see that it is followed during the first few days, until it becomes a habit. The child will leave happy and be less anxious when he or she returns the next day.

Late parents. Many other day care operators have complained to me that several parents are frequently late in picking up children, even when the provider charges an extra late pick-up fee. My experience is that a late fee legitimizes late pick-ups and does not solve the problem for a provider who is serious about her closing time. There will undoubtedly be real emergencies, when a parent is unavoidably detained though making every effort to arrive on time. With these few exceptions, parents will pick up their children promptly if you follow these steps.

First, be sure in your initial interview that you make your closing time very clear. Not "about 5:30" but "I close at exactly 5:30."

Second, if a parent is even five minutes late, point this out immediately and explain to the parent that your time with your children as a family is very limited. I tell my parents, "My children won't have anything to do with me when other children are here. It is very important to me that all the day care kids be picked up on time."

Third, if this is not enough, you may add, "When you pick up your child on time, I feel that you respect my needs and my life. When parents are late, it reflects a lack of understanding or caring for my family. If you are not able to get here at closing time, you should look for a provider who is open later." With this explanation and expectation, I have not had parents show up late.

Part-Time Day Care Children

Preparing a child for regular part-time day care requires the same steps described for children entering full-time day care, but the adjustment period will probably be longer. For this reason the schedule should take into consideration the needs of the child as much as possible.

The best part-time schedule for a child is every weekday for a minimum of two hours during the morning play time — from 9:00 A.M. to 11:00 A.M. The school children are gone, lunch is not an issue, and the child will have enough time to develop important peer relationships and to experience belonging as well as play.

A second option is three consecutive mornings. Although there will be some difficulty in separation and transition at the beginning of the first day every week, alternating days cause even greater difficulty. Morning schedules can be easily extended to incorporate lunch or nap time when needed.

A third choice is an all-afternoon schedule. In general I do not recommend afternoon day care for preschool-age children. If the child is dropped off shortly before or after lunch and is picked up by 4:00 P.M., he or she does not become an integral part of the group and does not experience any period of satisfying play. The first half-hour of any play period is spent in planning, negotiation, and preparation by the children. The rest of this afternoon time is taken up by lunch and a nap. Though napping is not usually a problem in day care, there are few satisfactions for the child on an afternoon schedule. If an afternoon schedule is absolutely necessary, the time should be extended to 5:00 or 5:30, so the late afternoon hours provide the child with more time to become involved in play and to participate in the day care experience. The child will also get a better sense of the rules and roles of other children by contributing to the clean-up procedure.

If a child feels like less than a full member of the day care group, his or her experience of day care will not be positive or pleasurable, and the values you are teaching the other children about fairness to all members will be undermined.

Drop-In Day Care Children

A "drop-in" day care schedule is anything less than three half-days per week. The term *drop-in* makes the arrangement sound casual, but it is not. The drop-in day care child requires special preparation. This child will experience stronger feelings of separation and develop little feelings of belonging to the group unless the arrangement continues for a long time. The younger the child, the longer it will take him or her to grasp that visits to the day care home will happen at different times, and hence the longer it will take him or her to feel secure in the visits and to be able to predict when they will occur. Adjustment will take longer and be more difficult, and may not take place at all if the parent is not completely supportive.

Bringing a child occasionally for a nap will work out well if the child has been with you in day care before or is younger than one or older than two. (For reasons mysterious to me, toddlers between one and two find drop-in child care very difficult.) There are, of course, exceptional children who accept drop-in child care easily and happily, but they are rare, and you are gambling with the atmosphere of the whole day when you accept drop-in children. I do not advise it.

Preparation for drop-in child care is crucial if the child is to experience any pleasure in day care and if the other children are to be able to continue their regular activities. No day care provider should tolerate any parent who simply deposits an unprepared child in the confusion and uncertainty of a strange environment. Every parent and child should make preliminary visits to the day care home before any final arrangements are made. After these visits, I urge the parents to follow five steps in preparing the child for drop-in day care.

First, the parent should talk about the drop-in time with the child the day before and again before leaving the house, possibly while dressing or at breakfast. Relate the time that the child will go to day care to daily events in the child's life, such as after lunch, before or after a nap, or before dinner.

Second, the parent should describe in detail what the child can expect. Who will be there? Will the child be there for lunch, nap, a snack? Will school children arrive?

Third, if the child does not have a choice, the parent must make this clear. Going to day care should be presented as a plan and a fact. The parent should explain, "I am going to spend the morning with Aunt Marilyn. You are going to spend the morning with Karen and your friends. You will stay for lunch and I will pick you up after your nap, just before snack time."

Fourth, the child should be reminded of some of his or her favorite activities at day care: "You can play with the orange play dough or the car puzzle. You can play doctor with Brianna and Paul, and you can think up new things to do. You might like to make a picture to send to Grandpa this morning."

Fifth, if the child shows anxiety or resistance to the plan, the parent should clarify his or her feelings: "It is sometimes hard to be left in a place where you haven't been very much. I feel that way sometimes when I go to a meeting or to a party. But I usually have a good time after I get used to being there. I think you will enjoy yourself too. I will miss you too, but we will have some time together this evening after dinner.'' Once the child understands that the day care visit is inevitable and his or her feelings are not unusual, adjustment will usually follow.

I warn parents not to try to ease their own conscience or the child's anxiety with a bribe. The parent should not say, ''I will bring you something special when I come to pick you up.'' If the parent makes such a promise, the child will spend all day waiting to be picked up, looking forward to the special something. But no treat can live up to the child's expectation. Furthermore, the parent is implying that there is something negative about day care that must be atoned for by a gift. If the child senses the parent's ambivalence about day care, he cannot enjoy himself. He must hold back from involvement in order to justify the gift and in order to be loyal to the parent. If the parent relies on a gift in this situation, the child will come to expect gifts every time he must do something he does not want to do.

Because of the problems involved with drop-in day care, I not only advise you, the future day care provider, against it, I also advise parents to consider a baby-sitter at home. The day care environment is the delicate world of childhood, in which children explore their abilities and interests. A child who is regularly made unhappy by confusing emotions and uncertain parental response will affect all other children in the day care home.

The first days in child care should enable the child to deal with his or her conflicting feelings and move into the regular day care world, but the child needs the support of both provider and parent to do so. The methods of preparation I have described are designed primarily to ease the transition of the child, not the parent, although they may help the parent also. With cooperation and understanding between parent and provider, the child's transition to day care can be accomplished smoothly and pleasantly.

6

Infants in Day Care

Infants seem to have fewer problems than older children in adapting to day care. I do not find infants any more demanding of my energy or time than older children, but they do require a different kind of time. I love babies and have thoroughly enjoyed every baby in my home. The older children love babies too, and a new baby immediately becomes the center of attention, until a younger one comes along a year or so later. Infants so quickly show their individuality and personality that they soon become a part of the group, and their participation extends far beyond their superficial role as "the baby." I strongly recommend taking at least one baby; I have found babies to be a great addition to my large family environment.

What does infant care entail in the day care home? The same things that infant care requires at home. The only difference might be in the amount of attention given by older children in a large family environment day care home. This substitutes for some adult attention. We have become accustomed to thinking that only adult attention is suitable for babies. Actually, I think babies prefer the attention of children to that of adults.

The youngest child I have accepted for day care was a two-month-old boy, Stephen, a healthy and good-natured baby. He received almost constant attention and play in the morning and evenings when he was with his parents. During his time in my home he seemed content to sit in a well-padded child's car seat on a table, out of easy reach of the children but still able to see them. Much of the time a child was standing on a chair next to him, talking and touching him gently, keeping him company. I did not spend much time with him aside from his changing and feeding periods. I enjoyed holding and cuddling him during bottle feedings. I paid close attention to his physical needs by changing him promptly when necessary and feeding upon demand. Like my own first child, he really only cried when he needed changing, food, or sleep, and I offered these remedies until the complaint stopped. Of course, many babies are not as relaxed and generally satisfied as were Stephen and my son, Sean. Such babies undoubtedly require more energy and attention. But children like Stephen and Sean seemed to do very well with the little time I actually gave them. They seemed to know that they were loved and would be taken care of as needed. They enjoyed being moved around the house and being in the center of the activity. The caring and attention from the other children probably added to their security.

The main problem for babies is communication. They are much more active internally than adults perceive. Babies arrive in this world with more sophisticated abilities and greater awareness than we previously thought; the problem is that adults have not been able to perceive and interpret signals and communication from infants. As a result, parents have underestimated their children from birth. This problem continues throughout life to various degrees. I have certainly had problems convincing people that their children are capable of mastering a certain skill or understanding adult communication. Only with concrete demonstration (such as a baby's first nap, described later in this chapter), am I able to convince parents that very young children accurately interpret adult vocal tone, body language, and other clues to grasp the message we think they are too young to understand. This attitude may also lead parents to think that you are "too hard" on their child, that you expect too much. After all, "she is only a baby."

The second problem for most babies is boredom. There is simply not enough going on around them to keep them interested. This is the reason for most fussiness that is not caused by wetness, hunger, or fatigue. Perhaps because the day care home environment is more stimulating and exciting, these babies are less fussy than are babies who stay at home without other children. Before infants develop a great deal of manual dexterity and hand-eye coordination, their chief means of exploration is their mouth, so do not hesitate to offer items for oral exploration as long as they are not sharp, breakable, too dirty, or too small. Move the baby frequently in the infant car seat to provide a change of scenery.

Babies usually like to spend some time on the floor, sometimes on their stomachs and sometimes on their backs. Limit floor time to the periods of the day when the fewest children are present. Babies learn to flip over quite early, so they usually take care of their own position. Some babies move around early, and some sit right where you put them until they can get up and walk. Those who sit early have a tendency to push with their legs suddenly and flip themselves back on their heads from a sitting position. A foam pad or pillows in back can prevent painful head bumps. The Johnny Jump-Up seat is great for children as soon as they can keep themselves upright. I stuff towels around them to keep them from falling to one side or flipping upside down. Always use the tie in the seat, and suspend the seat so the infant's toes touch the floor, enabling the child to push and bounce up and down. As soon as the baby can crawl or use a rolling walker, the jumper will be too limiting. The infant of about ten or eleven months will move around the room, using furniture to maintain balance. There is a wide age range for the first steps, but from ten months (for very petite, wiry, strong babies) to fifteen months (for large, heavy, soft babies) is normal.

Drop-off Procedure

The drop-off procedure is the same for infants as for older children. Young infants do not seem to have problems being left in a new day care home after the first day, and some do not even have problems the first day. After the age of six or seven months, the adjustment to a new place and new people is much harder and the drop-off trauma may be extended. Handle this with as much patience as you can. You may just have to live with it for a while. Holding and gentle talk might or might not be helpful. Try it. If the infant is ten months old or older, you can use minimal separation in another room and reintegration into the group as described in Chapter 5 for tantrums.

Sometimes an infant will be unusually difficult. Naomi began day care at ten months. Her parents went through the steps of short visits with her before beginning full-time day care, and understood the necessity for a clean break in the morning. They strongly supported my philosophy and style, and had confidence in me. Naomi clearly enjoyed the love and security of a good family. She was an exceptionally bright and strong-willed child and seemed to know exactly what the adults were up to. She understood the entire day care arrangement from the very first moment she came in — and she didn't like it one bit. She had never had a nap and didn't think she needed one. She had never been left with anyone and saw no reason to start now. After twelve days of six hours of screaming a day, regardless of my efforts, the parents and I decided to seek counseling. I made an appointment for all of us for the following Wednesday afternoon. Two days before the appointment, Naomi's dad dropped her off as usual, and instead of instantly yelling, she crawled from the door with a very straight face, giving me a stoic look as she passed, and began exploring the toys strewn around the floor. She had finally accepted the fact that she was going to be here every day all day whether she yelled or not. She never cried again at drop-off time.

Naomi was not emotionally needy; she was angry. A needy child should be held, loved, and comforted during this transition. Children who are not needy or particularly stubborn or angry will fuss for a while, then forget their complaint and move on to other things. These children can usually be distracted by your toy offerings.

The Mouth

Young infants learn about their world and the things in it by testing things in their mouth. They lick, bite, suck, taste, and generally get a feel for things through their mouths. You will want to have a number of things within reaching distance of the infant so the child can explore from the car seat. I suggest hand-sized balls of various colors and materials, pieces of cloth, small toys that are too large to be swallowed, and anything else the child can chew or throw without doing harm to himself or others. Avoid printed material, as many inks contain lead.

When the infant is old enough to spend time on the floor, you will have to be more careful about small things that can be swallowed — pieces of a puzzle, wheels from a small truck, loose buttons — and larger toys or household articles that could injure the infant. If you accept a baby for a large family day care home, you will have to keep the child near you while he or she is in the mouth-testing stage. Occasionally a child will continue to put things in his or her mouth long after this stage should have passed. Most infants do not forget the item in their mouth and do not swallow things that adults might consider to be of hazardous size, but some children seem more prone to accidental swallowing. Discuss this with the parents and come to an understanding about what you will allow to go into the child's mouth and what things will be lying around on the floor. A child who continues to put things in the mouth cannot progress to more independent play with other children without close supervision.

Naps

If the baby is accustomed to sleeping at home during the day, you will probably not have any problems with naps in day care. Babies who roll around in their sleep need a confined space, corner, or playpen to sleep in. Others can nap on pillows or small mattresses. Infants who are not accustomed to napping at home and resist napping at day care are often able to relax and fall asleep if they are put on a pillow and covered with a blanket in a room where they can be near you. It may be necessary to tell the baby in a firm voice that he *has* to stay on the pillow and keep his head down. You may have to illustrate the point by physically putting his head down on the pillow when you deliver the edict. In Naomi's case, I began with a pillow directly at my feet as I sat at my desk and typed during nap time. I made her stay there with her head down. She went to sleep and woke an hour later crying. Putting my hand on her head, I made her go back to sleep. She awoke an hour later happy, so I felt she was ready to get up. Two weeks later I moved the pillow to a far corner of the room. Two weeks after that I moved her into the nap room. She protested at each stage, but realized she had to take the nap as I directed.

A friend, Debby, and her one-year-old baby, Corina, visited my home one afternoon. Corina became crabby and fussy shortly after lunch and had to be carried around for a couple of hours.

When I suggested that the baby take a nap, Debbie replied that Corina would not nap. I said, "Sure she will. Would you like me to show you?" I carried Corina to the corner where I had placed two pillows and a blanket. I put Corina face down on the pillows and firmly said, "Corina, you are going to take a nap now. It is time for you to sleep. You are tired and fussy. You have to stay here on the pillows. You have to keep your head down." She looked at me with indignation and wonder, and proceeded to back off the pillows, sit up, and stare at me. I responded by immediately picking her up, putting her back on the pillows, and saying, "No. You have to stay here. You have to keep your head down." Again I showed her what I wanted. With a sudden cry she looked at me with disbelief. I said, "No fussing, Corina. It is time to sleep. Be quiet now and go to sleep." I then gently but firmly pushed her head down on the pillow once more, covered her with the blanket, and turned away. She stopped crying and promptly went to sleep. Corina has had a nap at home every day since. Her mother learned from watching me and now confidently insists on the nap. As long as babies are tired, they will go to sleep if they understand that there is no alternative.

In early infancy, my oldest child seemed to need to be wrapped tightly in a blanket to feel secure enough to fall asleep. He would cry until I wrapped him up, then suddenly stop and quickly go to sleep. I tried this technique with my second child, Brianna, but she could not stand to have her arms confined. She would fight and cry until her arms were free, then fall asleep. You can try either method, and you will know immediately which one is appropriate for a particular child.

Self-Feeding

When should a baby feed itself? The answer to this question depends in part on how much mess you can tolerate. I gave my children a spoon to grasp while I spoonfed them at four months. Some of my day care children began to feed themselves with a spoon at ten months. Finger food and bite-sized pieces of food can precede spoon use by several months. My rule of thumb is that as soon as babies can sit up in a high chair (about 7 months), they can participate in their feeding. It is unwise to let infants feed themselves entirely at an early age; they may need more then an hour actually to get the entire meal into their mouths. A joint effort is usually best: give the child his or her own spoon with food on it and give bites from another spoon. The child will alternately choose between your spoon and his, but will get a full lunch in a reasonable amount of time.

Baby Supplies

Who will take responsibility for providing food and diapers? The decision is up to the operator. If you have an infant of your own, it may be no problem to pick up more diapers and baby food at the store. You can estimate the cost and add it to the cost of care for that child. If you have no other infants, you may not want to be bothered with shopping for special provisions. In this case you may arrange with the parent to provide these items on a weekly basis.

After having used cloth diapers for my own two babies and disposables for many day care babies over the past five years, I strongly recommend disposables. Disposable diapers with elastic legs are best for children who frequently have loose stools, whereas those without elastic are best for children prone to rashes, as this type allows more air circulation. Keep A & D ointment on hand for rashes. If you apply a liberal coat of A & D to a gently cleaned blistered bottom, the blisters will be nearly gone in a few hours. The petroleum base protects the skin from further irritation and the vitamin content promotes fast healing.

Either the parent or the provider can make the infant's food. When my first child, Sean, was old enough for baby food, I enjoyed cooking and blending healthy combinations of vegetables and meats, fruits and vegetables, and fruits and meats. I froze these purees in ice-cube trays, then packaged the cubes in individual plastic bags. I made enough for a month at a time. There is no doubt in my mind that the general quality and nutritional value of homemade baby food is higher than that of commercial baby food. It is easier, of course, to use food brought by parents for their child. I did this also.

Some mothers graduate their babies from purees to finely chopped foods that have been put through a food mill. This enables the child to eat any food that is served to the rest of the family. I skipped this step, and my kids and day care kids went from purees to finger and bite-sized food. When children have teeth early, at seven or eight months, there is no need for the middle step; if their teeth come in late, at one year or later, milled food may be preferable.

Bottle-fed infants will be happiest using the same kind of nipple both at home and in day care. Usually parents prefer to bring the formula to day care rather than leave the choice up to the day care provider. Both powdered and liquid formulas are easy to use. Occasionally a mother may bring frozen breast milk, which can be stored in the freezer in an ice-cube tray or baby bottle. This may be supplemented with milk or formula of the mother's choice.

Weaning from the Bottle

There is no need to take a bottle away from a child. If tap water is put in the bottle, the child will lose interest on her own. When the child asks for milk or juice, you should give it to her in a small glass, about one-quarter full at first. If you are completely consistent about offering only water in the bottle and other beverages in cups and glasses, the child will quickly wean herself. If you are not consistent, it will take forever and the child will stubbornly demand beverages in the bottle and reject drinking from cups or glasses.

Pacifiers

Weaning a child from a pacifier is more difficult than weaning a child from a bottle. I do not feel that this issue is important enough to prompt a struggle with the child. My daughter, Brianna, was a two-pacifier child — one in the mouth and one in the hand. Occasionally she experimented with two in the mouth and two in the hand. At age three she developed a sore, chapped ring around her lips in the winter. I told her that it was from the moisture under the pacifiers and would heal if she stopped using them. She collected them and threw them in the garbage, and that was that.

Helping a child to stop sucking his or her thumb is more difficult. Brianna did not suck her thumb after infancy until she saw a seven-year-old sucking her thumb. A light went on in Brianna's head and the thumb went into her mouth. At age eight and a half she limits her sucking to bedtime and is trying to stop, but it is difficult for her. Thumb-sucking by a school-age child during waking hours would probably be embarrassing and therefore more of a problem. I have no solution.

Teething

Children get their first teeth at different times. Some get their first two soon after birth, and others not until after one year. Sometimes the teeth appear four at a time, with no noticeable irritation to the child; for other children, each tooth takes weeks to come in and causes swelling, inflammation, and general discomfort. I cannot recommend any of the commercial products for teething problems, since I have never used any of them and none has ever been recommended to me by other parents. I have found frozen teething rings to be helpful to the child. These are made of soft plastic and filled with a jellylike substance that will freeze and remain frozen for some time. I keep four in the freezer at all times, to be available when needed. Homemade frozen popsicles are also soothing, but drippy and filling.

Common Infant Medical Problems

Diarrhea. In my experience, the most common recurring problem is diarrhea or very soft stool. If you use disposable diapers with elastic around the legs and change the baby immediately, protecting the baby's bottom with A & D ointment, the child will have little or no problem with painful rashes or infection. If the diarrhea persists beyond one day, you should advise the parents to consult a doctor. You may also put the child on a special diet. That requires clear liquids for twenty-four hours — clear juices, diluted Jell-o, ginger ale, Gatorade. After the first twenty-four hours, add ripe bananas, cooked carrots, and rice products. As the child's condition improves, I add soft, bland foods, avoiding dairy and wheat products for several days. If the diarrhea returns, I go back to clear liquids. The child should drink a lot of liquids, as dehydration is a major problem with diarrhea. If the diarrhea continues or does not respond to this treatment, or if the infant has a fever or other sign of illness, consult a doctor. The parents will probably be aware of the child's condition and symptoms; if not, inform them. Unless the doctor advises against it, they should continue the diet at home for it to be effective.

Ear infections. The second most common problem among infants is ear infections. Generally, the child becomes a little irritable with a slight fever, then gets a higher fever and rubs the infected ear occasionally. My daughter had an ear infection when she was two weeks old, and continued to have one at two-week intervals for about three years. The infection lasted two weeks, and the medication lasted two weeks. When she was three and a half years old, the infections suddenly disappeared, and now she has not had one for five years. The medical explanation is that the eustachian tube is very small in some young children and is quickly blocked by the mucous accompanying a cold. This blocking causes the environment suitable for ear infection, which then causes the fever. In very young children, ear infections and high fevers can be dangerous; ear infections that are not treated may lead to permanent hearing loss, and high fevers may progress to dangerous levels, possibly resulting in brain damage or diseases leading to heart damage. For this reason it is very important for you to monitor the child's temperature and call the parent to take the child for a medical examination as soon as the temperature rises. Whatever medication is prescribed should be administered completely.

Conjunctivitis. Another common and very contagious problem is conjunctivitis, or pinkeye. It is very uncomfortable. One or both eyes may become infected and emit a discharge that is transmitted to other children by hands and fingers. If you notice cloudiness or mucous in the eye of a child or infant, require the parent to seek treatment and to keep the child at home until at least twenty-four hours after treatment has begun. You will have to continue giving eyedrops when the child returns to day care; be sure to put the drops in both eyes, and treat the child until you have seen no evidence of the condition for two days. Children resist eyedrops because they sting. The best method I have found is to have the child lie down with his or her head in my lap. I put the drops in the inside corner of each closed eye and hold the child's head gently until he or she opens the eyes. If the drops are wiped away, you have to start over. The child will accept the medication if you are persistent, and will cooperate after a couple of treatments.

Rashes. Skin rashes are also common among infants and young children. Some children seem to be much more sensitive to skin rashes than others and will have an incredible variety of sizes, textures, and shades of welts, bumps, and splotches. Most are not treatable or problematic for the child, but parents may want to have their child examined by a doctor until they learn to identify the different rashes. Some spots indicate sickness, such as chicken pox or Fifth's disease, and have no treatment. Others indicate parasites, such as ringworm, scabies, or chiggers. These need immediate treatment. Until you recognize which rashes need treatment, all should be examined by a doctor. Usually a baby's rashes do not need treatment but reflect a sensitivity to food, soap, or a chemical in a fabric or detergent. Sometimes these splotches disappear, never to reappear, before anyone is able to determine their cause. If the spots appear where there is close contact with clothing, then investigate the clothing and laundry soap first. If the rash appears to follow the weather, it might indeed be related to cold, wind, or heat. If the rash is on the child's bottom, it probably means that his or her stool or urine is very strong and that something in the diet is causing this condition.

Vaginal yeast infection. Occasionally you will come across an infant or toddler with vaginal yeast infection. This needs treatment immediately, as it is very irritating and uncomfortable.

Cradle cap. Cradle cap is a fungus growth on the scalp; if not removed, the growth may become very thick, injuring the skin and possibly becoming infected and requiring medical attention. You can prevent the advancement of this growth by massaging baby oil into the scalp and allowing it to sit until it becomes cheesy.

Teaching Eating Habits in Day Care

The day care provider is in an excellent position to expand the tastes of young children, something parents often would love to do but do not have the time or energy for. New day care children will seldom offer a nonparent the same kind of stubborn resistance they present to their parents — that is, not at first. For this reason, it is important that you use your position as a new authority figure to set new expectations for a child. At home, parents can wait for a child to become really hungry before introducing new foods. In day care, you cannot wait. Children become crabby and irritable when hungry. Often they do not know they are hungry and do not see the relationship between their ill temper and hunger. Ill temper may make it even more difficult for a child to try new foods that he or she has decided in advance are inedible. I quickly learned that it is a mistake to allow children to skip lunch — everyone pays later in the day, when a picky eater turns into an unbearable, irritable child who even more staunchly refuses to eat. You could, of course, give in to the "banana cure." In the long run, however, this is not to the child's benefit and puts you in an impossible position. Before long, none of the children will eat previously acceptable but unpopular raw vegetable salad.

I subscribe to the theory that children will choose a well-balanced healthy diet if allowed to choose from a variety of nutritious foods. I very quickly learned, however, that I cannot offer a smorgasbord daily. If I did, many children would choose to subsist on one favorite food regardless of the other foods available, because parents often do not offer variety but rely on known, easy foods. As a rule, I require all children to eat the food I serve. They must finish their first serving and then may have unlimited servings of food of their own choice. The only stipulation is that the child must finish any food he or she asks for.

It is important to serve portions of food appropriate to the appetite of each child. Some children cannot be expected to eat more than two bites of each food served — even if they like it and are hungry. Others will eat at least seconds of everything even though they are served adult portions to begin with. Children will rarely eat with their normal appetite the first week in day care. By the end of the second week, you will probably know how much food a child seems to need and what the child likes. Most of my day care children had good eating habits and seemed to enjoy the food I served; they were willing to eat all foods when told they had to. Some children, however, had very poor eating habits initially and refused to eat most of the food I served, holding out for bananas or peanut-butter sandwiches, which they believed would eventually be substituted. Depending on the child's age, I solved the problem by using one of the methods described below.

The USDA requires day care operators to serve meat, peanut butter, or eggs as the protein food, rather than tofu or combinations of other high-protein food. There have been several vegetarians in my day care groups, meat prices are high, and peanut butter contains a high quantity of oil; for these reasons I often substitute other high-protein foods for those preferred by the government. Among my families, parents who prefer meat over bean curd eat traditional meat-heavy dinners in the evening and encourage me to concentrate on vegetables during day care hours.

Only in the case of a special diet should a family be allowed to send food. Since I do not serve sugar, red meat, or foods with additives or preservatives, there is very little to which any family can reasonably object. Occasionally I may care for a child who cannot eat dairy products (milk, yogurt, cheese), or a child who is allergic to a particular food, such as tomatoes or citrus fruits. In these cases, children may bring food sometimes to supplement the meals in the day care home.

Lunch

Lunch can be a reasonably orderly period, but you should not expect small children to behave as agreeably or as quietly as a group of adults would. If you can accept the normal amount of wiggling, dawdling, and joking of children placed close together, you will have relatively little trouble with lunch time.

Note where the children are sitting. Certain children will play if seated next to each other and will not finish eating before nap time. Others — siblings, or rivals of the same age — will quarrel. Others may prefer to sit next to a child who is willing to act as a receptacle for unwanted food. Arrange the children so that they will eat lunch with a minimum of upsets and distractions. If they are seated at the table while you prepare food, invite them to play a table game such as Telegraph. (One child begins by whispering a phrase into the ear of her neighbor, the second repeats what he thinks he heard in the ear of the next child, and so on until the message has been around the table and the last child repeats it aloud.) "What am I?" is another favorite table game. They can also sing songs, tell stories or adventures, or compare old "ouches."

Make sure the food is not too hot. Serve well-balanced, carefully prepared, attractive foods. (Menus and recipes can be found at the end of this chapter.) Serve a portion of each food for each child based on that individual's appetite. It is better to serve too little than too much; the child can always ask for more. Do not give a child more food than he or she would normally eat. Serve the slowest eater first, then the next slowest, and so forth.

When food is greeted with enthusiasm, make a positive comment such as, "I'm glad you like the lunch. I try to serve food that will make you strong and that you will like." If food is greeted with "Ugh, I hate this stuff," invite the child to take his food into the other room and eat alone. Tell him that you try to serve food that is tasty and nutritious. If he does not like it, he can keep his comments to himself or leave the table. His comments affect the attitude of younger children, who will probably like whatever is served if not prejudiced by the negative comments of the other children.

When a child is very slow or refuses to eat, consider the possibility of sickness, pending sickness, or a late breakfast. New children will usually not eat the first few days, preferring to watch. If you decide that the child may be sick or is simply not hungry, excuse her from lunch. If she is not new to day care, remind her that she may not leave the table until she has finished her lunch.

As children finish, excuse them from the table to play in another room or outside until lunch is over. If a child sits over lunch eating very slowly, allow him to continue until 1:00 P.M. (nap time), then set aside the rest to be offered at snack time.

Snacks

Snacks are served once or twice a day, depending on the day care hours and when the children eat breakfast. Most of the time I do not serve a morning snack, because children eat breakfast just before arriving between 8:00 A.M. and 9:00 A.M. and I serve lunch at 11:30 A.M. Early in my day care career I followed the licensing agency's rules, which require morning snacks, and found that the children then did not eat lunch. Later in the day, perhaps at 4:00 P.M., they wanted a very large snack, and then were not hungry for dinner. As a result, I ignored the rules and skipped the morning snack; the children ate a good lunch and a snack at 4:00 P.M. Usually a snack consists of juice, milk, or juice popsicles, and apple quarters, banana halves, carrot slices, pieces of raw cauliflower, or raw frozen peas. USDA regulations require only bread or crackers and milk. When children have bread and milk for lunch in any quantity, I serve a vegetable at snack time — usually one that is hard to serve successfully at meals when other food is available. The reasons for the USDA's food requirements are political, not nutritional, so I have no qualms about using my own judgment. I urge you to do the same. In my day care home no child is allowed to bring any sugared foods or junk foods such as chips or cupcakes for snacks. I explain to each family that many of the parents are very concerned about the sugar content and quality of the food their children eat. Because one child eating junk food will cause problems with the others, none of the children can bring these foods to day care. (Sugar-coated cereal qualifies as a junk food and sometimes is the only food that a parent will want to send in the morning when a child has missed breakfast.)

There is one exception to these rules — the birthday party. Sometimes the parent will bring cupcakes and ice cream, balloons, hats, and little gifts. If the parent does not provide a party, I make a cake with candles and we sing and play birthday games or see a movie from the library. In a large family environment you cannot allow any child to go without a birthday party with day care friends, unless the parent tells you that there will be a party on the weekend to which the day care children will be invited. This is usually the case.

Problem Eaters

New children are usually the problem eaters, but not always. Sometimes a child has been in day care part-time and will not have learned the rules for eating. If you follow the methods described below from the second through the fourth weeks, you will be able to change limited eating preferences and will not have to devote much energy or attention to the new child's eating after this time. An occasional direction to take another bite will be sufficient.

Infants Four to Eighteen Months

If you care for a baby from early infancy, you will probably never have a "problem eater," because the child will be accustomed to a variety of foods from the beginning and will accept it as a normal part of his or her experience. If, on the other hand, a child enters day care after eight months, he will probably have some preferences already established, depending on the food he has been offered at home. If the child has been offered a variety of healthy table foods, cut or mashed to appropriate size, you will face few problems. Only seasonings or some mixtures may be new. If, on the other hand, the child has been given only "standard" infant foods such as fruits, pudding, custard, potatoes, and macaroni and cheese, he will initially refuse unsweetened foods such as vegetables, meats, and unusual fruits. Infants will usually accept any new food if they are very hungry. Do not allow the baby to snack on crackers, teething biscuits, bottles, or bananas if he has refused a balanced array of foods. Find out from the parents what they feed him and balance the diet during day care hours.

When offering new or unpopular foods, put a very small

amount — four peas, a one-inch cube of squash, one beet slice, or two string beans — in a dish in front of the infant. Just leave the food and ignore the child. If she eats the food, casually ask if she would like more. Try one more bite. Also offer another new food, perhaps along with an old, accepted food. Sometimes you will not know what is new, just what is preferred. The child may smash the food or play with it; as long as she keeps it on the table, I ignore this behavior in a young infant. Try again later when she is hungrier, after a nap.

Throwing food. If the infant completely rejects the food by throwing it on the floor, I immediately pick him up from the table and put him down on the floor, saying, "When you throw food on the floor, I will take you from the table. Food belongs in your dish or in your mouth." Often the infant will want to rejoin the group at the table and will begin fussing and signaling to be put back in his chair. I explain clearly, "No food on the floor. If you throw food on the floor I will put you down. Next time you will stay down." I then put him back in his chair. Often the infant will want to test what I have said. If so, I put him down and leave him down. After everyone else is finished eating, he may be ready to try again. Do not try again while other children are at the table, because the infant loves the audience and will continue testing. If he throws food down again, put him down, saying, "Lunch time is over." Do nothing more until snack time, when you should offer him his *lunch* food again.

Camouflage. If it is obvious that a child can wait longer than you can, use the camouflage method. Hide small bits of new or unpopular food behind, under, or mixed with other food on the spoon. Concentrate on introducing new tastes gradually, rather than on getting the child to eat a quantity at one sitting. With children of any age, getting the food past clenched teeth is usually the problem. Often one taste is enough to persuade a child to eat a new food, but not always. Just seeing other children eat the same food enthusiastically may persuade the child.

Children Aged One and One-Half to Four Years

Many children have learned by a very early age that if they are very patient or very stubborn, they will get their way — with eating or anything else. Because I lose my patience much sooner than most children in this contest of wills, I make a move to convince the child that he or she is supposed to eat differently in day care, according to a new set of expectations. What parents do at home is up to them, but parents are usually delighted to hear about the progress of their children in accepting new foods. They then change their expectations for their children as well, leading to new eating behavior at home.

If a child refuses to try a new food after being invited and cajoled, I move to the pinch-and-poke method — *before* I get angry. I used this method quite successfully with Joel, a three-year-old. Joel began day care with a dull look in his eyes, a low level of activity, and the habit of vomiting all foods except peanut butter and bananas. The first day I thought he might be sick, so I allowed him to leave the table. But his mother later told me that he often vomited food he disliked. The next day, when Joel vomited again, I said, "Joel, vomiting won't work here. You have to eat this food and keep it in your stomach, even if you have to eat it ten times until five o'clock." With this I removed the vomited food and replaced it with new food. He refused to eat, so I firmly squeezed his cheeks with two fingers until his mouth opened, and put a small bite in with the other hand. He spit it out and I repeated the maneuver with a larger bite. This time I said, "You have to eat it. If you don't want me to feed you this way, then you eat it by yourself." He swallowed the bite and sat. "Take another bite." He put the food on a spoon and held it in midair. "Now." He put the food into his mouth, and held it there. I said, "You have to chew the food and swallow it. You have to eat all the food on your plate before you can leave the table. Chew it." Nothing happened. I worked his jaw two or three times firmly but carefully with my hands. My voice was full of determination but not anger. Joel continued chewing and eventually swallowed it — gagging, but not vomiting. Very slowly and with continual instruction from me, he then ate his food. The next day it was not necessary for me to put a bite in his mouth, and Joel never vomited food at my home again, and rarely at his home. He was occasionally left sitting alone, chewing slowly long after the other children had left the table. But after the first month Joel was eating everything I served him, liking most of it, and looking and acting more lively.

Children Aged Four and Over

In the summer, school-age children may join day care for the full day, including lunch. Most of them will be children you have cared for at a younger age and will already know your expectations. The pinch-and-poke method is not appropriate for older children. I have found that just requiring children to eat their food before leaving the table is enough. Start with very small portions of all foods so you do not create an impossible situation. The child may have seconds on favored foods when firsts are gone. Then — stick to your word, if it takes all afternoon. The second day will require less effort and time, and by the end of the week new children will be finishing lunch along with the others and you can increase portions to the normal size for that child.

The methods I have described are generally low-keyed; I try to avoid a contest of wills, which may seem like a game to the child but can turn to anger after a morning of play. The point of each method is to get the food into the child if possible. The child who prefers to go hungry until snack time quickly learns that lunch time in my day care home is for eating lunch, and if lunch is not eaten, it reappears at snack time.

Recipes

Mackerel Casserole for 10

3 c egg noodles   1 can mushroom soup
1 lb. frozen peas   1 or 2 cans drained mackerel
1 lb. grated cheese

Cook noodles in boiling water, adding peas just as noodles are done.
  Let sit for about a minute before draining.
Mix remaining ingredients together and stir into the cooked noodles and
  peas. If you make it ahead, put in baking pan and heat in the oven;
  if you make it at the last minute, you can serve it as soon as cheese
  melts (about 3–5 minutes on low).

Spinach Soufflé for 10

1 large can drained and
   squeezed spinach
1½ pounds shredded cheese

chopped olives (optional)
8 eggs

Mix all ingredients together in a baking dish, bake in preheated oven
   at 350° for about 30–45 minutes until center is done.
Cut into squares and serve hot or cold. Some kids will prefer this with
   catsup.

Chicken Chili for 12

stewed chicken and its juice
2 or 3 cans of tomatoes
assortment of cooked beans
   (garbanzo, navy, chili, pinto,

etc.) cooked in chicken stock
   or water
chili powder
onions, celery (optional)

Combine cooked, boned chicken, broth, beans, tomatoes, and chili
   powder to taste and simmer together for at least an hour before serving.
   I like it better with additional tomato sauce and simmered several hours,
   with lots of spices.

Scrambled Standby for 12

6 eggs
2 c leftover rice
1 lb. grated cheese
1 c peas

1 c beans
½ c onions
garlic to taste

Mix ingredients together, then cook in skillet till somewhat dry.

Zucchini-Spaghetti for 10 (freezes well)

tomato sauce
stewed tomatoes
canned tomatoes   } total 6 cups
tomato paste
2 onions, diced
2 stalks celery, chopped

2 medium zucchini or other
   summer squashes, shredded or
   finely chopped
sweet basil, garlic, salt and
   pepper, bay leaf
other "Italian" spices

Combine tomato products in whatever proportion you prefer, ending with
   a thick mixture.
Add vegetables and cook for at least 3 hours in an iron pot, if you have
   one. This will bring iron out of the pot and add it to the sauce, which
   in combination with the vitamin C from the tomatoes is a very usable
   source of iron. Serve on noodles or vegetables.

Squash Pie — Crustless for 10

2–3 cups baked yellow squash
3 eggs
½ c honey
2 tsp cinnamon

1 tsp ginger
1 tsp cloves
2 c evaporated milk
    (1 can for a dryer pie)

Mix all ingredients; a blender works well. Pour into a very large pie tin or two small ones, or rectangular baking dish. Cook at 350° for about 1 hour.

Whole-Wheat Pancake with Fruit Topping

Use any whole-wheat pancake mix, adding about ½ egg per child. Add apple juice instead of milk or water. Batter should be quite thin. Cook in a little hot oil.

FRUIT TOPPING
2 bananas
1 apple

¼ c honey
2 tsp cinnamon

Chop fruit, mix in honey and cinnamon.

Mackerel Salad for 10

1 can drained mackerel
½ c salad dressing
1 c shredded cheddar cheese

1 c frozen peas
¼ c lemon juice

Mix these ingredients and add lettuce, celery, etc.

Vegetable Salad

purple and green cabbage
carrots
frozen peas

cauliflower
broccoli
pineapple

Grate vegetables. For a dressing, use salad dressing mixed with pineapple juice.

Rice Plus

steamed rice in broth and
   tomatoes
peas

onions
garlic, cumin
grated jack or swiss cheese

Refry rice, adding other ingredients. Reserve cheese to melt over the top
   before serving.

Chow Yumm for 10

2 T oil
bite-size pieces of pork, chicken,
   beef (optional) (½ pound is
   plenty)
1 onion, chopped
2 cloves garlic (optional)
⅛ tsp powdered ginger
2 stalks celery, chopped
2 broccoli stalks, chopped

2 small zucchini, diced
3 c nappa (Chinese cabbage),
   chopped
5 c mung bean sprouts
small amount of soy sauce
broccoli tops from the stalks
   added earlier (add 2 minutes
   before serving)

Stir-fry meat, adding chopped vegetables in order listed. Cook until bean
   sprouts are clear and almost limp. Cook broccoli tops only 2 minutes,
   then serve on steamed rice.

Egg-Foo Yumm

6 eggs
1 c leftover rice

2 c leftover chow yumm,
   drained

Drain leftover vegetables, mix with egg, fry in oil on medium high heat
   until bottom is cooked and holds together. Flip like a large pancake
   or divide and turn in pieces. Cook other side until fairly dry throughout.

Welsh Rabbit

WHITE SAUCE
2 c milk
3 T flour
salt and pepper

2 tsp dry mustard
1 or 2 eggs

2-2½ pounds shredded cheddar
   cheese

½ can tomato soup

Add milk to flour slowly, while stirring constantly with a whisk. Cook
   on high and continue stirring till it begins to thicken. Remove from
   heat, add eggs, stirring briskly, and cook again until thick. Add grated
   cheese gradually until melted.
Add tomato soup, stir. Serve over soda crackers.

Carrot Salad

4 c grated carrots	1 c peanuts
½ c raisins	1 c diced pineapple

DRESSING
½ c salad dressing	1 T peanut butter
½ c pineapple juice	½ tsp curry powder (optional)

Fruit Yogurt Salad

bananas	apple	orange	pear
peach .	pineapple	plum	raisins

Use whatever combination you have, mostly bananas. I use strawberry or vanilla yogurt as dressing. Yogurt flavored with fruit rather than with syrup and sugar added is preferred.

Burritos for 10

12 tortillas, frozen	1 c frozen peas
3 c refried beans and/or rice	1 lb shredded cheddar cheese
("vegetarian" refried canned	1 head shredded lettuce, or more
beans do not have lard added	
and are preferred)	

Reheat tortillas laid out on a cookie sheet in the oven until warm. Spread with cheese and broil until cheese is just melted.
Add warmed beans with peas and lettuce and serve folded.

Peanut Butter Candy

½ c peanut butter	½ c honey
1 c powdered milk (not instant)	

Mix and knead until no longer sticky but smooth and firm. Add powdered milk as needed. Roll into balls and refrigerate.

Spiced Apple Snackin' Squares

4 envelopes unflavored gelatin	¾ c boiling water
2 c unsweetened applesauce	¼ tsp ground cinnamon

Sprinkle gelatin over ½ cup applesauce. Add boiling water and stir thoroughly until gelatin is dissolved; stir in cinnamon and remaining applesauce.
Pour into 8- or 9-inch square pan and chill till firm. Cut into squares.

8

Toilet Training and
Sexual Awareness

Parents of toddlers will want to know your views and methods concerning toilet training. They may not associate sexual awareness in children with toilet training, but you will find that when you begin the toilet-training phase, children's interest in their bodies will increase. Your views on both should be clear in your mind and perhaps even described in the handouts you give parents at their first interview. This is not a subject you should be vague about; the children will ask questions and identify your attitude even if you have not clarified your feelings for yourself. In general, I believe in being honest with children. Neither subject should pose any difficulties if you settle on a method or an approach and follow it, letting the child know what is expected and accepted.

Toilet Training

Changing diapers — especially disposables with elastic legs — is simply not much trouble, certainly not enough to fight about with a child. There is no reason not to wait for a sign that the child is ready for toilet training, as long as that sign comes by age three. Unfortunately, many parents are impatient to toilet train, or rather to *have* their children toilet trained. Parents have heard that children should be trained by a certain age, and become concerned about the intelligence or normality of their child if he or she is not trained by that age. They may be concerned about their own adequacy and success as parents. With these pressures, the child is unwittingly given an unusual amount of power to elicit positive or negative responses from parents.

Beginning to toilet train before the child is ready sets her up for failure. If she is going through the stage in which she wants exactly the opposite of what the parent wants, no matter what it is, do not begin training. It's not worth it. Children from twenty-four to about twenty-eight months seem to be especially fascinated with determining and testing their power over adults, especially their parents. Because the child is much less involved with the day care provider, it may be much easier for that person to train her. If you can do this, the child may not realize that toilet training is a weapon that can be used to enrage parents.

If the child is under two and a half and is already using elimination to manipulate a parent, it is best to continue with diapers and wait until she reaches a new stage of development. I prefer to avoid a power struggle during this period in child development; I have found that the toilet issue is much easier to deal with either a few months later, at age three, or before age two, if the child shows motivation and interest. At these ages children are more willing to cooperate, to give up this expression of personal power, and may even realize that diaper changing interferes with their activity. The child realizes it is more convenient for *her* to use the toilet, and doing so makes a favorable impression on other children in the same age group. Toilet training thus becomes an accomplishment the child can be proud of.

Trying to train a child who is expressing anger for any reason — a disturbance at home, a change in the day care situation, the arrival of a new sibling — is not wise. The child may cooperate during day care but refuse at home, causing even greater problems for the parents. When this happens, parents should revert to diapers for home use, unless the child is three or older. After age three they should require the child to participate in cleaning up "accidents," require toilet use if their child is to wear pants, and offer rewards for cooperation. If the child seems angry, the parents should find the cause of that anger and deal with that problem. The toilet training will solve itself in this case.

Children Between One and One-Half and Two Years

Each child is different; one will respond to bribes, others to threats, and others to appeals for cooperation and maturity. I do not use any of these methods. I use the bare-bottom-and-clear-expectation approach. So far I have not met a child between one and two and a half years who balked at a bare bottom. Children seem quite pleased to have their bodies available for their inspection.

I usually begin toilet training when the parent has seen evidence of interest from the child. If a potty chair is available, children will usually try using it at about one and a half to two years. This is a sign of interest. If the child tells the parent he needs to "go," this is also a sign. Staying dry for three hours at a time is a sign of physical control and readiness. When the parent and child express interest and readiness, the day care provider should start toilet training. I often encourage the parent to begin on a weekend. The child should do well at home before beginning training in day care, because there is so much more activity in day care that it is harder for a child to remember the new toileting expectation.

When you decide to begin toilet training, tell the child clearly about your expectation for him to use the toilet. Do not ask the child to tell you when he needs to go. In day care it is much harder to remember to tell than simply to keep the child bare-bottomed, inviting the child to use the toilet every hour or so the first week. When you invite the child to use the toilet on the first day, walk with him. Invite the child to go alone the second day. If the child balks or refuses the invitational approach, drop it immediately. At the next interval, perhaps half an hour later, tell the child it is "time to try to go pee." Take him to the potty chair, or if necessary pick him up and place him on the chair. You are not demanding results, just going through the motions of trying. By the third day he will probably run off to the bathroom when you say, "Time to go pee." Use a diaper at nap time only. When the child makes trips to the bathroom on his own, usually during the second week, he is trained.

When a child is able to get to the bathroom for a week without once being reminded and has no "accidents," you may let him wear pants in the car for short trips, making sure that he uses the toilet immediately before the trip and every hour or so thereafter. It is hard at first for a child to remember that pants are not the same as a diaper. Some children are very attentive to their toileting and are pleased with their progress. Others are not and will need several months with bare bottoms before they are able to wear pants without wetting. In my day care home there are usually a couple of bare bottoms, so a child who is absent-minded about toileting can go bare bottomed longer without feeling conspicuous. There is no limit to the number of children who can be trained at one time with this approach.

Parents often begin toilet training with pants on before the age of two, expecting the training period to last several months — and it does, until the child is about two and a half or three, when he or she suddenly becomes "trained." Actually, the child has grown out of the oppositional stage and has finally come to remember that the pants are not diapers. You can start early and have the child trained by two and a half, or you can wait until two and a half and, using the bare-bottom approach, have the child trained in only 2 or 3 days. Since I have had total success with this method, I have no advice to offer if you run into problems except to extend the bare-bottom period. If the child has the physical control and is emotionally secure and you are conscientious in following the method described here, I guarantee you will both be successful.

If the parent wants to begin training before you think the child is ready, or before the child is one and a half, you can remind the parent that day care involves so much activity and involvement that it is much more difficult for a child to remember toileting than it might be at home. If the parent insists, and if the child is consistently successful for ten consecutive days at home without accident, you may try training in day care. Often, though, children who are successful at home at this age cannot remember on their own amid the activity. As long as you are willing to remind the child every hour or so, the training will probably succeed, but this is an unnecessary interruption for you both, and training is much easier later. It is better to avoid this very early training if possible.

Training methods that avoid the bare bottom seem to require several weeks, during which the child brings home a bag of wet pants. If you believe that diapers, not pants, are for wetting, then you and the parent should not put the child in a position where he will probably wet his pants. This can cause guilt, even when you excuse the wetting by using the term *accident*. I think it is unfair to put children in an almost impossible situation by expecting them to pay attention to toileting before the age of two. At two and a half the transition to pants is usually made easily, and it is even easier at age three.

I have known parents and day care workers who object to the bare-bottom approach on hygienic grounds. After consulting with my pediatrician, however, I found support for my beliefs that germs in a day care home are much like family germs, and that covering the child's bottom does not prevent disease, just as baring it does not cause disease. The pediatrician also informed me that airing the genital area helps prevent the rashes, irritations, and discomfort experienced by many children from contact with clothing washed in detergents and soap additives and with synthetic clothing itself. Armed with this professional information, I continue to use and recommend bare bottoms for toilet trainees.

Girls who are unaccustomed to being bare-bottomed or who seem uncomfortable may wear short dresses or skirts during training without interference. Boys can wear adult-sized T-shirts and sweaters reaching to the knees.

Children Between Three and Four Years

Occasionally a child three years or older will enter day care without having been toilet trained. If the child has been examined by a doctor and has no physical problem, she should be trained in day care. After a grace period of one or two weeks — time to adjust, to get to know what to expect from me and this new place — I use all means of friendly persuasion in the morning. If there are still wet pants in the afternoon, I state my expectations clearly to the child: "Starting now, I expect you to use the toilet. I am not going to put diapers on you anymore. If you want to keep your pants on, you be sure to keep them dry and clean. No accidents allowed." I do not like to use the word *accident* with children of this age, because wetting or soiling is *not* an accident at this age, except during sickness. But children understand the term *accident* without question. I explain simply, "Pants are not for soiling or wetting; diapers are. You are too old for diapers, so now you use the toilet." I invite the child to use the toilet approximately every two hours so there will be no opportunity for a *real* accident.

If on the second day the child has an "accident," which is usually reported with a grin, I may apply two or three good spanks to the bare bottom and explain, "You are too old to pee on the floor. I expect you to use the toilet. I do not want to clean up after you. You get some paper from the bathroom and clean it up yourself. Put it in the toilet where it belongs and don't do it again." I insist that the child clean it up, or at least help. This has never failed with three-year-olds.

Sexual Awareness

If you use my bare-bottom toilet-training method, you will see the otherwise often invisible sexual awareness and interest of children under the age of two and a half. They explore themselves and show some limited interest in the genitals of their friends. This interest does not disappear after children are toilet trained.

Children who are allowed to express their interest in their sexuality and bodies fully at this young age often play thinly disguised sexual exploration games or express completely undisguised interest. Games consist of playing "doctor" or "baby," which requires that clothing be removed. Children are very absorbed in these games for one or two months, then lose interest for a while and move on to another game, such as Monster or Chase. Later the interest reappears, perhaps sparked by the appearance of a new bare bottom in training.

This early experimentation and the way in which it is viewed by adults can have an enormous effect upon the immediate and future attitudes of the child. There is a growing body of information today on the sexual behavior and attitudes of our male and female population. In the day care situation you are in a position to prompt parents to reexamine their feelings and values about sex. When parents realize that their child is aware of and learning about his or her body, they become interested in the child's sexual behavior. A parent may hear from the child about a game or incident of a sexual nature that happened in day care, and this will give the parent and the provider the opportunity to discuss their attitudes about the child's curiosity and discoveries. I consider this kind of opportunity a definite advantage of the day care home. Day care centers do not provide the privacy necessary for children to play doctor; instead, children often hide in a bathroom to explore the body, which results in feelings of guilt and being "dirty."

If you feel unprepared for or uncomfortable with the questions and concerns of parents about their children's interests, you may organize a meeting and request a speaker from Planned Parenthood, a nearby college or university, or a local group interested in helping the public clarify their sexual attitudes and values. I have found that parents are very interested and concerned about the normal development of their children in all areas, and respond enthusiastically to a meeting on sexual development. (Appendix A contains materials for parents about sexuality. This material was very well received by and useful to parents of my day care children.) When parents are offered an opportunity to discuss in a group their own early impressions, information, training, behavior, and values, they gain personal insight and are much more comfortable with their feelings and attitudes. They also get factual information about what they can expect normal children to understand at different ages and what kind of sexual behavior they can expect at different ages. Bringing together families whose children are involved with one another will ease the anxious feelings that occasionally accompany this stage of childhood.

Is there disagreement over what behavior is acceptable for children in your day care? If so, you must come to an understanding with the parent on how the situation will be handled. I once agreed to tell a child, "Your mother is not comfortable with this game and she doesn't want you to play it here." I said to my own child, "Joseph's mother is not comfortable with this game. She doesn't want him to play it. Her feelings about the body are different from ours, and we respect her ideas for her family." That was all that was necessary. The children learned an important lesson: they learned to respect different values of different people.

Sexual values and attitudes are so basic and so indicative of other values that it is not likely that families who differ seriously on this topic will leave their children together. If a parent disagrees with your philosophy and that of the other parents, the parent will usually withdraw the child and seek a day care environment that agrees more closely with his or her philosophy.

To clarify my position on this issue, I have adopted a set of rules that I feel are appropriate for children who are playing exploratory sexual games in a day care setting:

1. Activity is limited to consenting children.
2. Children must be in the same age range.
3. No tools or instruments or toys should be put in any holes.
4. Body exploration games are private; they are not to take place in the living room, where an unexpected adult might be embarrassed when intruding.

These limitations allow maximum freedom while providing for physical safety, eliminating relationships that might lead to one child being victimized by another, and teaching the child that sexual activity is a personal matter. I outline these four rules to children as I notice an interest in sexual games. In a specific instance, I might remove an older or younger child who did not qualify in years or maturity as a peer of the others. Once the rules are understood by all the children, there seems to be no problem with enforcement. Kids seem to understand on some level that this is serious stuff, and they respect adult judgment in this area without question. For this reason, after making sure all the children know the restrictions, I will allow two or three or even four kids (I have never seen a larger group here) to go off by themselves and close the door. They usually tell me not to come in. They might say they are playing a "private game." I do not interrupt unless lunch time or another activity is scheduled.

Children over four years old either become self-conscious or lose interest, I don't know which. Perhaps their curiosity has been satisfied and other interests take over. Perhaps they are participating in sexual games somewhere else. For whatever reason, their interest is no longer obvious in the day care setting. They may express new attitudes, however. The older child may suddenly be concerned about the propriety of what the younger ones are doing in the private room. This is an opportunity to introduce children older than five to related ideas.

At age five and older, it is important to begin educating children in the sexual norm and expectations of the society at large and in the reactions that may arise from children and adults with different values and attitudes about sex and their bodies. Children who are not warned about the generally restrictive attitude of society regarding sexual behavior are vulnerable to humiliation and social ostracism by their peers. This experience is not useful or positive in any way. Since day care children are usually under ten years old, you will not have to handle more complicated issues and questions regarding appropriate behavior for the adolescent and teenager.

When a child asks a question, I take the opportunity to introduce new information and ideas appropriate to his or her age. I also keep several sex-education books designed for children on the bookshelves. (These are included in the book list in Appendix B.) It is not necessary to initiate sexuality explanations if good books are available. The children will seek them out and read them together, or ask you to read them aloud. The child's overt interest in sex is not constant. It will pop up occasionally, and disappear just as quickly as it came.

The only result of a child's sexual game that could possibly be considered a side effect is an occasional irritation of a girl's labia. I keep A & D ointment on hand for this. For more persistent irritation, you may apply Mycolog cream very sparingly. This cream is a prescription medication, but has been very helpful with the little girls in my home. I do not recommend stressing the connection between sexual games or masturbation and labial irritation. Rather, I just handle the problem as routinely as possible.

9

What Do You Teach 'Em, Anyway?

Parents often want to know exactly what you will be teaching their child; most often they expect you to reply by listing the traditional subjects that are "taught": letters and numbers, songs and stories, games and rules, colors and shapes. I do not teach these things, and I quickly hand parents a list of the things I do teach — a description of values and attitudes that I believe children must learn if they are to grow fully as individuals and as members of a community. (I have included a copy of this handout at the end of this chapter.) I urge parents to take it home and read it, usually after their first visit or interview, along with the other handouts or statements of my child-rearing philosophy. Teaching the values and attitudes in this handout may seem an ambitious, if not impossible goal. Yet my day care children learn these values and more; they accept the implicit sense I have of their self-worth and in turn extend this to the other children and adults they encounter. Some of what the children learn is the result of practical experience; some is the result of more thoughtful moments.

I have referred throughout this book to a philosophy I call attentive noninterference. As I have said before, it is hard to define, though easier to describe in practice. It is my personal choice, made after seeing the consequences of the alternative — parental or other adult interference. After a child has learned a certain skill, such as putting on a pair of shoes, he or she needs to perfect the skill. For many children, practicing leads to an intense, concentrated effort; for others, practicing leads to an adult stepping in and speeding up the chore of tying shoelaces or buttoning a coat. When this happens, the child learns one or more of the following things:

1. The adult does not think the child is capable of accomplishing the task.

2. Adults know more than children and therefore the child is incapable or inept.
3. Adults enjoy helping or doing things for children that children can do for themselves, as well as those things children cannot do for themselves.
4. The child can give the adult pleasure, and the child will receive a reward for allowing the adult to "help."
5. The adult will take over the activity of the child if the child indicates that he cannot — or will not — do it himself.
6. The adult will step in and do the task for the child if the child does nothing.
7. The adult will take over to stop the child from fussing.

None of these seven options reinforces the child's sense of his self-worth or competence.

It is very difficult for both the adult and the child to change this pattern of interference. Yet experience has taught me that it is less difficult for the child to change his or her behavior when the adult is not readily available. If the adult can refrain from interrupting the child, I call this behavior attentive noninterference. Attentive noninterference means to be *aware* of a situation but to take no action. This attitude does not come easily to most concerned adults. It is difficult to refrain from "helping" a child who needs to practice, but it is better for the child. Attentive non-interference is also valuable when children are capable of working out disagreements, giving comfort to another child, negotiating for a desirable role in a game, or working out their own problems and developing the skills to solve these problems efficiently and effectively.

I am not advocating neglect. In fact, it would be more accurate to describe the adult's overbearing interference as neglect, for it neglects the child's need to mature through his or her own effort and experimentation. By contrast, my approach of active noninterference requires that the adult do something that is more difficult than preempting the effort of one who is less skilled.

First, the adult must observe the child's present level of accomplishment regarding any particular activity or skill.

Second, the adult must teach the necessary skills by using demonstration, hands-on assistance (that is, your hands on the child's), verbal instruction, verbal cues, and encouragement and reinforcement for the child's efforts and approximations.

Third, the adult must teach interpersonal dispute settlement by having kids talk through the problematic incident using active listening and questions; helping kids accept responsibility for their own actions; role-playing with kids to help them understand the consequences of their actions for others; and assisting in negotiations between children.

Fourth, the adult must provide the child with an opportunity to practice an activity or skill as soon as possible.

Fifth, and perhaps most difficult, the adult must stay out of the way.

Sixth, the adult must assist *only* if truly convinced that the child needs assistance and only to the degree really necessary.

If you follow these guidelines, you will be working at attentive noninterference most of the time.* It is too much to expect anyone to be consistent every minute of the day, but you must make up your mind to stick with it and do the best you can.

It was very difficult for me in the beginning not to interfere and interrupt children to praise or instruct or help them. It was difficult not to rush to their rescue in needless situations, difficult not to be dragged into disputes and tiny problems where I was not really needed. It does take a great deal of attention to make children work out their problems, to teach them to solve their

---

*The children I cared for during the five years of home day care were normal children with loving, caring, concerned parents, though many began adjustment to the divorce of their parents soon after beginning day care. None was the object of parental abuse or neglect. Troubled children with major unresolved family problems, children who are mistreated by loved ones, or children who have physical or mental handicaps undoubtedly require far more interaction with the day care provider and far more direct individual nurturing and demonstrative affection than that which I recommend for my normal, well-adjusted child population. The group of children I describe have their physiological, safety, and belonging and love needs met within their family. Their needs for self-esteem are being met in their homes and through peer interaction in day care. With this solid base, I feel the methods I describe will promote individual growth in all areas. Though I would recommend practicing the same principles with all children, implementation would surely require different emphasis with special populations. There is a great satisfaction in seeing disturbed children accomplish appropriate goals, as I experienced satisfaction in seeing my group accomplish its goals. Having no experience with severely disturbed children though, I would like to stress that the situations and children I describe can be generalized only to other secure and well-loved normal children of the same age range.

own problems at certain times, and to work through other problems with them at other times. When Maxine comes to me and says, "Larry hit me," I remind myself that we all know the rules, we all know *why* there should be no hitting, and there is probably no need to repeat that with these two children. Next I notice that no one is hurt and that Maxine does not offer any further information about the situation. This often means that there is much more to the situation than was reported, but Maxine knows all she needs to know to solve the problem. Often children just want to see if they can draw you in, not knowing exactly what they want you to do or how they want the situation to change. I begin by letting the child know that I heard her. I say, "Maxine, Larry hit you," or "He did?" This will often be all that is expected or required. If Maxine is not satisfied, I add, "You don't like hitting, do you? Did you tell Larry what you think about hitting and how you feel? It sounds like he is angry and wants to make you angry or sorry about something. I think you can go back and work this out with him if it is important to you." If Maxine prompted the hitting in some way, she will most likely return to the room saying, "I told Karen on you," and that will be the end of it.

Children between one and a half and three years will often engage in a tug of war over a toy. If I know which one showed the first interest, I try to make sure that this child has the first opportunity to use the toy. Another child may show interest only because the toy is interesting to the first. There may be competition between these two children over everything. When the struggle begins, I assess the source of the argument, then I try to ignore it. There will be pulling and sometimes fussing. If it appears that the child in the right is in danger of losing the tug of war, I encourage her verbally by saying, "Hold on tight, Kristi; don't let go just because she is bigger. She can have a turn when you're finished." "Maxine, you can have a turn when Kristi is finished; there are other things you can play with while you wait. The biggest person is not always the one who gets what she wants." Only when these efforts fail do I remove the second child to another spot of the room and offer a substitute toy. If this does not put an end to the controversy and the second child does not accept the situation, I take her to the nap room and tell her, "When Kristi is finished, she will give you a turn. You can come out and play when you are finished with this behavior." Usually before I have turned to leave, the crying or fussing is over. The child then leaves the nap room and goes on to another activity, or she might sit and wait with a protruding lip.

If I do not know who is in the right in a struggle, I say firmly, "Whoever had it first hold on tight, and whoever grabbed let go." Much to my amazement, when I first said this in jest, it was successful. But, alas, children sometimes forget who had it first, and all they are aware of is their own desire. Sometimes I do have to resort to confiscating the toy and explaining that since they cannot decide who should have the first turn, I must put the toy away, because it is causing too much unhappiness and noise. When children aged three and older are faced with losing a toy, they usually decide they would rather decide among themselves who had the first turn and for how long. You can use the timer on the kitchen stove as an impartial enforcer. The stove timer is a lifesaver — always fair, never biased, and never forgetful.

Attentive noninterference takes a great deal of teaching time and almost no doing time. In the long run, teaching *is* more efficient than doing. After you teach a child how to perform a task — open the door, buckle shoes, flip a coat — you need only leave him or her alone, forcing the child to practice.

It takes time for children to believe that they can do simple things, and after the first time it may still be several weeks before they perform the task without trying to convince you that they cannot do it. My trite response to a child saying "I can't" is "You can't unless you try; if you try you can. You did that yesterday." Then I may verbally lead the child through the steps of the task again. I have spent countless hours standing in the kitchen next to the back door giving verbal instructions to two-year-olds on how to open the door. If I help them with my hands on theirs, I then close the door so they have the opportunity to try it again immediately on their own. After the child has experienced the feeling of the task with your help, he is one step closer to performing it for himself. If you watch an older child and note her technique with a particular door (a sticky door requires that the right hand push against the jam while the left one turns the knob and pulls, for instance), you will learn from that child how to teach the younger ones to deal with that particular door. The older children become more competent and see the younger children being left on their own after the initial instruction. Since the children at first do not understand the noninterference philosophy, older children are usually delighted to help out a younger friend, enhancing that relationship. After the first few weeks, younger children have had enough experience in my day care home to know that I will not do something for them, and they turn instead for assistance to their older friends, which I believe they should.

It can be very difficult to refuse to help a small child who is bewildered by a pair of shoes or a sticky door, but that child will never learn to rely on his or her own abilities if not required to do so. Attentive noninterference may appear at first to demand more of children of all ages, but in fact it gives them more — more faith and trust in their abilities, more support for their efforts, no matter how limited, and more consideration for their need and desire to grow.

The philosophy of attentive noninterference is behind everything the children learn in my day care home, from learning to put on shoes and socks to the consequences of their actions. Each area reinforces another, until young children ultimately achieve a confidence and satisfaction in themselves.

Children Dressing Themselves

I teach children to dress themselves by following a basic pattern for each skill — putting on socks, shoes, pants, or whatever piece of clothing the child is dealing with. As soon as a child can understand the basic instruction, he or she is old enough to start learning. This is also an area in which children enjoy practicing; they seem to enjoy the control practice gives them over their clothing and the process of dressing. The basic pattern of instruction is designed to enable the child to understand how each skill is performed so that she can do it alone:

1. Demonstrate while describing the activity.
2. If the child cannot then follow the verbal instructions, put your hands on the child's hands and repeat the verbal instructions while your hands help as needed.

3. Each time the child begins, let her get as far as possible without coaching, then give needed cues, and finally hands-on-hands help when necessary. If the child's hands fall away, stop assistance and explain that you are only there to help with the job, not to do it. Replace the child's hands and continue.

4. If it is evident that the child is capable but has a case of the "I can'ts," take her into the nap room and say, "When you have your socks [pants, shoes, or whatever] on, you may come out and play." You must be sure the child is capable and you must be sure that you carry through with your statement. Send the child back if she comes out before the task is completed. A child may have the "I can'ts" only when parents appear, so it is important for parents to know your methods and the rationale behind them and to offer their support.

Socks

Beginning at the age of eighteen to twenty months, children can be taught to put on loose-fitting socks. Small, elastic, or long stockings are more difficult and should not be tried until the child is two years old. Instructions are the same for all types of stockings:

"Sit on the floor."

"Show me the edge of the hole of the sock." (If child is uncertain, show him the edge.)

"Use your eyes and your fingers together; if you watch me, you won't know what your fingers are doing, so watch your fingers."

"Pinch the two sides of the hole in the sock with both hands and pull it open to make the hole big enough for your toes."

"Pull the sock edge on both sides gently and slowly down over your toes. Now pull it down your foot and over your heel."

"Is your heel in the sock's heel? No? You can turn the sock around so that it is."

Shoes

Shoes with laces. Teach the child to tie shoes with laces by saying:
"Sit on the floor."

"Show me the laces. Now show me the tongue of the shoe."

"Loosen the laces to make room for your foot: pull on the string, first one and then the other."

"Pinch the tongue and pull it out and up to keep it out of your foot's way and to make room for your foot."

"Hold the bottom of your shoe at the heel."

"Put your foot into the hole using your eyes and hands together."

"Push with your foot and with the hands on the shoe's heel."

"Wiggle the shoe heel a little bit to help your foot in." (Adults may have to put hand on top of child's hand to assist in working in the foot if the shoe is not roomy.)

Tying shoes. Some children are ready to tie shoes at age three, but most are not ready until three and a half or four years. Be sure the laces are long and supple enough for a child to manipulate.

"When your shoe is on, lay both laces straight to one side of your foot. Take the lace coming from that side and cross it over the other lace and lay it down on the other side of the foot."

"Bring the end of that lace under the other lace and back up through the triangle hole."

"Pull on both laces in different directions."

"Make a loop with one lace holding the bottom of the loop near the shoe."

"Make a loop with the other lace holding it near the shoe also."

"Hold a loop with each hand like pinching, cross one loop on top of the other, push the one on top back and down to come through the little hole at the bottom."

"Grab the loop that is coming through the hole."

"Pull on both loops at the same time."

Taking off shoes. "Put your heel in your hand, push up with your hand till the shoe comes off." (This direction will not work with high-lacing or tight shoes.)

Shoes with straps. (age two and a half). "Sit on the floor."

"Show me the strap; show me the buckle."

"Hold the strap back with one hand to make room for your foot."

"Put your toes in the shoe."

"Hold the shoe with the heel in your hand and push on the heel and with your foot at the same time."

"Put the end of the strap through the buckle, and pull the strap back as hard as you can. See the little hole? This little metal stick goes into that hole. Hold the strap back with one hand and put the little stick into the hole with the other hand. Keep your finger on the stick while you let go of the strap and push it down over the holding finger. When you see the stick come through the hole, then put the tip of the strap through the rest of the buckle."

Pants

"Sit on the floor."

"Lay the pants flat on the floor with the front up." (Point out the difference between the front and back of the pants if the child does not know what to look for, using tags inside the pants, zippers, pockets, and so forth.)

"Hold the pants at the top with one hand at each side."

"Put a foot in the large hole and down into the leg hole on its own side." (Help the child by holding the pant's leg at the bottom so that the child can see what is happening.)

"Put the other foot in the big hole, then down into the leg on that side."

"Pull the pants up as far as you can from the waist."

"Pull up each pant leg one at a time by pulling the pant leg over your knee."

"Put your hands down at the bottom and work the bottom over your feet."

"Now stand up, grab the top of the pants with one hand at each side, and pull up."

"Reach around in the back. Can you feel where the elastic is in the back?" (Guide the child's hands to the elastic at the top.)

"Put your thumb inside the elastic and pull up with your thumb."

"Do the same on the other side, now the front, pulling on the elastic each time."

"Work back and front, taking turns until the pants are completely on."

Coats

This is the flip method, which can be used by children eighteen months old and older.

"Lay the coat on the floor with the inside facing up, arms stretched out to the sides."

"Stand at the hood or collar."

"Bend over and stick each hand in the closest arm hole."

"Stand up, raising your arms straight out and flipping the coat over your head as you stand."

"Presto, the coat slides on!"

Closures

Buttons. Some buttons are more difficult than others, depending on tightness, size, and shape. Two- and three-year-olds will need constant help with most buttons.

Point out which button goes in which hole. Choose a button to work on that the child can see and reach easily.

"Take the button with the fingers on the button side of you."

"Hold the coat at the buttonhole with the other hand."

"Push the button through the hole, grabbing it on the other side and pulling it through," or "Put your fingers through the buttonhole, grab the button, and pull it through."

Unbuttoning. "Grab the button and tip it down flat so you can see under it to push it through the hole."

"Help with the other hand by holding the edge of your coat by the buttonhole firm and tight, pulling down a little on the coat while putting the button in the hole."

Snaps. Point out the hole and the bump in the respective parts of the snap, explaining the goal of making them fit together and "snap" to stay that way. Remind the child to use eyes along with fingers.

"Put the bump over the hole, keep it there, move your fingers, and press hard."

Zippers in pants. Snap first, or button at top as needed.

"Use one hand to hold the pants at the bottom of the zipper."

"Pull up on the zipper while pulling down on the pants at the same time."

Zippers in jackets. Large zippers are much easier than small ones for children four years old and younger. Point out the parts of the zipper to the child, explaining the parts and where they go. Stress the importance of keeping the zipper down all the way while inserting the other piece.

You must have the idea by now. You only need to make sure the child knows the vocabulary you use as you describe every move his or her fingers will make in the task.

Visitors

Running a typing business simultaneously with day care has many advantages for the children, as well as for me. A constant stream of people we call "typees" is coming and going. The children quickly get over their awkwardness in front of strangers, and after a few weeks of brief exchanges with several typees per day, they begin to enjoy meeting new personalities. Most typees are interested in the day care home, since many have never been with a group of young children. The adults are delighted with the friendliness of the children and their efforts to draw them into conversation. They are barraged with questions and almost without exception become briefly involved with at least one or two of the children.

Some of these typees bring new information and experience into the house and occasionally initiate a very important learning experience. One client from Zambia, studying geography at the University of Washington, usually spent about an hour proofreading his material. One day Jennifer, aged four, watched him with amazement for several moments before placing herself squarely in front of him as he sat on the couch. She said with much curiosity, "What *is* that all over your face?" The student, with a puzzled look, responded, "You mean this water? I have been sweating from walking here." "No," said Jennifer, "what is that brown stuff all over your face?" A wide smile broke out on the face of the student. "I have it all over my hands and all over my body. Haven't you seen anyone like me before?" The student briefly described his country, where his family and most of the other people were the same color as he. Jennifer seemed quite pleased and satisfied with her discovery and chatted with him during every subsequent visit.

Sometimes a visitor will tell my day care children about his or her children in some other day care or at home. This is often a learning experience for the visitors as well as for the children. Visitors universally express great surprise that such a large number of children of such varying ages (one to five years) are so happily involved with each other without adult direction and management. My day care children matter-of-factly advise the visitors about their activities and daily schedule.

Feelings

When children and adults talk together about their feelings, when adults help children identify feelings, and when adults do not express ridicule or rejection when talking about these feelings, children come to acknowledge the wealth of emotion that is a part of the richness of experience. Once feelings are accepted as normal and important, the way is paved for children to treat each other with consideration and understanding.

Adults should also teach children that they can learn to control actions that might cause problems. We can help children ventilate and discuss their feelings, since expressing uncomfortable feelings can sometimes dissipate them. When an adult deals with a child's negative feelings, it is not necessary to inflict guilt; the adult only needs to point out that the victim, perpetrator, and friendship are damaged when one person hurts another. The child needs not to be made ashamed or punished but rather to be helped to understand the consequences of his action — how it affects others and himself. When children are too young for this approach (under age five), I use a very limited verbal discussion and a firm statement of the rule in question, such as, "We have all decided that there will be no hitting. I do not allow any children to hit you and I will not let you hit anyone else. If we let hitting go on, everyone would be unhappy and afraid. I want you to sit down here and think about what it might be like if we decided hitting was okay. How will it be better if there is no hitting?" This process is called taking time out, and is similar to the procedure described for handling tantrums (see Chapter 5).

Nonsexist Attitudes

Mothers are not servants, and helping boys and girls develop basic skills is always better for both mother and children. These skills will enable children to negotiate egalitarian relationships in later years and achieve greater personal satisfaction in their lives. I have found that boys enjoy learning cooking, sewing, grocery shopping, and washing, unless they have been taught that these activities are inappropriate.

In a day care setting with children under six years old, the most effective approach to teaching egalitarian attitudes is to encourage children to switch the roles of their characters during play; sometimes the boy, in the character of the father, will stay home and take care of the children while Mother runs the gas station in the next room. Kids also enjoy switching sex roles; several boys enjoy donning wig, long dress, and lipstick to be the guests at a tea party or be the mother. It is also important to avoid limiting other kinds of play to one or the other sex, since girls will want to play in the dirt and boys will want to play with the dolls and help in the kitchen. I believe there is some innate preference in children for certain kinds of activities and levels of activity. Certainly they need to and enjoy practicing their future roles in the family and in the larger world. But these predispositions should not be used to limit children or to discourage individuals who feel differently from the majority of children of the same sex. I strive to encourage each child to follow his or her personal inclination without regard for what others might think is appropriate for a young boy or girl. Both boys and girls need to be freed from limiting beliefs about themselves and their friends.

Encouraging a girl's independence and acquisition of a variety of skills, such as carpentry, plumbing, and car care, will lead to her self-confidence as a woman. She will be prepared to tackle problems and make her own decisions. She will also be capable in areas in which other women are dependent. Today it is popular and thus not too difficult for a girl to proclaim her liberation and unusual interests and skills. By contrast, it may be much harder to ask a nine-year-old boy to defend his liberated stance with his peers. It is enough that he understand and practice the principle of fairness and that he value the self-confidence and independence this principle gives him.

The long-range benefits of attentive noninterference and flexible sex roles give children experience in peer interdependence rather than adult dependence. These children will grow to be adults who look to their own intimate community to solve problems together rather than to a more distant and authoritarian parent figure. They will be able to make choices and take responsibility for their actions, and they will be self-confident and able both to give and to accept assistance when needed as caring members of their community.

Realistic Expectations

When children resolve their own problems and invent their own diversions, they develop realistic expectations. Each child is at some point confronted with certain questions, and how he or she answers them can determine how that child will fare in other relationships in later years. "How much leadership or bossing will my friends tolerate?" "Is it necessary to compromise to stay in the game?" "Will my friends give me sympathy and consolation when I am tired and crabby?" "If I admit that I am tired and crabby, will that help?" "Can I expect my friends to listen to me when I yell at them?" "Can I expect myself to tie my shoes yet?" "Should I like everyone all the time?" "If I don't like someone, how should I act?" "How would I feel if I knew that someone didn't like me?"

Expectations are a very important part of life at any age, and play a large role in the degree of satisfaction a person finds in activity and relationships. Developing realistic expectations can begin early and can be an important factor in day care parenting. You will decide when the child is demonstrating an unreasonable or unrealistic expectation. For example, if a ten-month-old continues to throw a toy over the fence and demand that it be retrieved, he is engaged in an experiment. The results of his experiment will be the basis for his future expectations in similar situations. I suggest that you do not retrieve the toy until the child is again in the house, thereby teaching the child that there are limits to what he can expect from others, and that when he rejects something, he may not have another immediate opportunity to regain it. The baby needs to learn what you want him to learn from his first experiment. If it is easier for you simply to retrieve the toy than to listen to the baby's cries, you will be teaching him to cry to get what he wants, and you and others will be retrieving toys and other things for months or years to come. Once the child establishes a pattern of behavior, you will find it much harder to teach a new pattern; in addition, you may be teaching the child that the rules of adults are arbitrary and without apparent order.

Helping a child develop realistic expectations for himself is more difficult than helping him develop his expectations of others. We all want our children to be happy, intelligent, beautiful, and we have been taught by various parenting guides different ways to help our children become what we want them to be. The suggestions given by experts may be very good, but it is often difficult to apply good advice to children who have very different personalities. What is appropriate for some children may not be appropriate for others. The message "You are a smart child" will often not have the positive effect we might expect it to have. It is hard to predict how children will react to adult comments and encouragement, even if it is well-intended. We want our children to participate in activity for the intrinsic pleasure and positive effect that activity brings, yet we may motivate them with material incentives. This material reward may quickly replace the other satisfactions if it is frequently coupled with desired behavior. Through their need to be loved and accepted, some children may be motivated by parental approval, and gain no personal satisfaction from a particular activity. Certainly there is a place for material reward and parental approval; the key is to maintain some balance among the motivational factors. If a child undertakes an activity because of parental urging or another factor not inherent in the activity, parents and others should reconsider pushing the child in that area. If the child senses no personal reward — pleasure, pride of accomplishment — in performing an activity, then only the adult's needs are being met, and the child is not discovering his or her capabilities or understanding the value of that particular activity. It is better to let the child follow his or her own inclinations into an activity that will be rewarding. Both parent and child must accept that the child is an individual, with specific talents, likes, and dislikes, who should not be made to match an artificial standard.

Our belief today that everyone can be self-sufficient in all ways, or that everyone's needs and wants will be fulfilled either through hard work or government assistance, inevitably leads to a failure to recognize the differences between individuals. We want our children to achieve, but we also seem to define achievement in adult terms. Leaving young children free to test their abilities also leaves them free to discover where they need assistance or when they can offer it. In a day care setting with children of various ages, children have an unusual opportunity to become interdependent in terms of fulfilling their community and individual needs. I teach children how to put on their own clothing, one piece at a time, as they gain the necessary coordination. The tasks they can do for themselves are supplemented with assistance from older children as much as possible in a supportive exchange. While I type these words, I see Paul (three years) buckling the sandal of Naomi (two and a half), who is in turn buckling the sandal of Jamaica (two and a half). Each girl put on her own sandal unaided, then struggled for about two minutes before being offered help by another child. None of the children expected or asked me to intervene. They are enjoying this opportunity to perfect their skill while helping a friend in need. This nurturing experience is important to the older children and develops in them a caring for others and the knowledge that they can afford to be generous with their skills and resources. When the children are intimately involved with a group of varying ages and abilities, they learn to accept differences and to appreciate others for individual personality and special qualities. They come to understand that each person has something personal and unique to contribute, and that not every group member can contribute in the same way. They come to respect and accept each person and themselves.

Dispute Settlement

You can teach children to settle disputes, then help them practice their new problem-solving skills by making them produce solutions and listening to their reports on the outcome. Problem-solving is a skill that becomes easier and more refined with practice, requiring less time and effort.

Children Aged Five and Older

The first goal in teaching dispute settlement is to help children realize that they are not satisfied with their old ways of settling problems. For example, if the children have been arguing over toys, they need to understand that "might does not make right," or that the youngest child should not always get her way by virtue of her age. When they see that their earlier solutions do not seem fair to all, they are ready to think about other possible solutions. An example might be that the person who had it first is entitled to the first turn. From these disputes children can establish general rules of behavior that they understand, such as no grabbing or everyone has the right to some time alone. When children develop their own values and standards of behavior — forming rules from them — the rules can be very powerful.

You can use the golden rule, "Do unto others as you would have them do unto you," to help a child determine what behavior is acceptable in general and to identify the source of a particular problem. With an adult maintaining order and fairness in the discussion, children will begin recalling what happened and who did what. Some role-playing with older children may be necessary to help them understand cause and effect in a hurtful situation. Each child can act out another child's role and practice alternative responses that might have ended the conflict.

In settling a dispute, it is not necessary to demand that children apologize. Usually the children will feel apologetic when they talk it out. You may say, "If you feel sorry that this happened, it would help your friendship to say how you feel." To the other child, "If you want to be friends and you can forgive him and yourself, you should tell him how you feel, too." It is important to remind children that angry feelings are to be expected; we all get angry. It is fine to express anger in some ways but not in others.

Children Under Five

First consider if the child is tired. If so, forget any grand schemes and give the child a nap.

At age three and a half to four or so, children will often respond to a direct and open approach that focuses first on the arguing. Coming upon two three-year-olds, Sean and Jonathan, pushing and shoving over a toy, I approached and said, "It doesn't look like you are having a good time. Sean, is fighting fun? Jonathan, do you feel good when you are fighting? I'm not going to stop you or settle your argument. I'm not going to decide who should have this toy, and I'm not going to take it away. You can fight if you want to, or you can stop and make an agreement. It's up to you." The two boys watched with wonder as I turned and walked away. Then they looked at each other. "I don't want to fight," said Jonathan. "Me too," said Sean.

I do not recommend this approach with children who are not closely matched. If the children differ greatly in age, strength, or social conscience, you will have to play a more active role, reasoning with the kids and working back through the problem with them. Do not allow the stronger child to learn that she will always win, or the smaller one that she must lose. Nor is it fair to insist that the younger child win because of her age or the older child always give way to the desires of the younger. At about this age children are usually beginning to internalize ideas about fairness and about how each person expects to be treated and therefore must treat others.

Before the age of three, children seem to be very preoccupied with "mine" and "I want." Children at this age are so straightforward that their problems seem easier to deal with. You can make direct statements and comments on such simplistic demands as "I want" that will readily solve the specific problem and also teach fair play. When Aggie says, "my chair," and Tim is sitting in it and has been sitting in it for some time, you can say simply, "You want that chair, Aggie, but it is for everyone to use and right now Tim is using it. Why don't you ask Tim if you can have a turn when he is finished?" If Tim knows his lines, he will say yes. If he says no, then you might say to him, "Tim, you don't like the way Aggie is acting about the chair, do you? She asked you, though, this time, and I think she should have a turn when you are finished." This will usually produce the desired result. If it does not, repeat the process of pointing out the fair use of things that must be shared.

The emphasis in settling any dispute should be on sharing and taking turns; the children I care for in this age group need no lessons in knowing their own rights. It may be too early to expect them to take on the role of the other child or to role-play, but they will be fascinated with your explanation just the same. If a young child balks at my explanation, I use the time-out method to enable the child to think quietly about what I have said; time out is very effective in convincing a young child that he or she must go by the rules. Children generally understand rules at this age, but you must back them up with action for a child to accept them.

Competition

Your acceptance of or enthusiasm for a child should not depend on his or her accomplishments or comparing favorably with others. Children will take pleasure in their abilities and skills and derive satisfaction from sharing them with other children if they do not feel that there is a danger of losing something in being surpassed in skill by another child. In an environment where children are not compared with one another or given labels such as "first," "best," or "better," they will strive to improve, to better their own record in areas that are important to them. The child who experiences satisfaction in self-improvement can be happy with another child's accomplishments. Many times a day my typing is pleasantly interrupted by a child who excitedly reports on the new accomplishment of another child in addition to her own. My experience has not shown me that children in direct competition with peers are more highly motivated to do better, but I have found that competition for approval or affection causes hurt feelings and drives firm wedges between peers.

Natural Consequences

Allowing a child to experience the natural consequences of his or her own action is probably the most effective teaching method. I use the term "natural consequences" to refer to physical limitations, potential dangers, and so on; I do not recommend this approach in interpersonal relations. I have seen parents leave a child to work out behavior problems without any guidance or problem-solving sessions, and the usual results are that other children simply refuse to play with this child and that the child is unaware that his behavior is unacceptable. After all, Mother seems to accept it. Letting a child discover the natural consequences for himself or herself is best limited to areas in which there can be little confusion between cause and effect but also little real danger to the child.

An adult is in a position to decide under which circumstances this method is safe and effective, but the day care provider must also consider the individual child and family involved. The incident I am about to relate illustrates the effectiveness of the method and also the importance of accurately judging the family. Foremost is the importance of the adult's invisible control of the situation to guard against mishap.

John entered my day care home when he was about three years old. Though quite tall for his age and very bright, John had never been taught or allowed to experience his limitations or abilities, because his parents were both extremely protective. He still crawled up and down stairs that the two-year-olds easily negotiated. His parents were apprehensive about circumstances most other parents see as the normal hazards of childhood; for instance, standing on a picnic bench at the park, John would be fenced in by the bodies of his parents, one at either side, their arms ready to reach out and stop him from falling. It is true that there is a very slight possibility that a child could be seriously hurt by falling fifteen inches from a picnic bench. But the possibility is so slight that the learning experience from such a fall far outweighs the hazards. John was both totally convinced of his inability to perform elementary physical tasks (such as navigating stairs) and totally unaware of real danger. Apparently he had never experienced falling or any frightening small accident, because at my house he seemed quite anxious to explore, even to the extent of climbing shelves, sinks, and counters, and was quite sure-footed. Yet he climbed stairs like an infant; he had clearly been given the message that he would surely fall if he tried walking.

During the summer my assistant and I often took the ten children to a nearby beach, where we could picnic and read stories.

On one early summer day I gathered the children around to tell them about the slope of the beach bottom, explaining to them that the slope was steep and that they should not go beyond their waists. Each child demonstrated his knowledge of "waist," and off they went. My assistant and I watched them carefully. All the children except John seemed to believe what I had told them: if they stepped beyond the waist levels they would be in water to the chest; one more step and it would be to the chin, and on the third it would be to the eyes. Only John did not grasp the connection. I watched him and reminded him to go only to his waist. He took two steps farther out and, with surprise in his eyes and his cheeks puffed with air, bobbed in the water. I immediately jumped in (I was prepared for this) and pulled him out. He was shaken. He had experienced for himself the consequences of going beyond the safe limits I had described. John sat beside me on the grass for about five minutes, then went back into the water. He did not need a second warning. He was now willing to listen to the limits I set up: he stayed at waist level or less the rest of the afternoon. This experience led to a new respect for the real dangers of water, which John had never before experienced. This knowledge and belief will make swimming a safer activity for him in the future. Being in the water with an adult supplies complete safety — while the adult's hand is held — but leaves the child open to danger some other time, when the adult is not there and the child has no fear based on reality. I misjudged the parents' ability to learn from this experience, for when I described the swimming incident John was pulled out of my home and enrolled in a very structured protective school.

Allowing children to learn about the natural consequences of their actions must be done within limits. I have learned that you can *never* prevent all accidents, even if you stand two feet from the child all day long. Some type of accident is bound to happen sometime. It is unrealistic for an adult continually to supervise a child's every move: the child must learn for herself in order to grow. But adults can provide a safe and secure environment in which children can learn about safety for themselves with a minimum of real danger — and this is something they must learn if they are even to progress beyond an infant stage. I make my day care home as safe as possible by eliminating sharp sticks from the outside play areas and using equipment designed for safety as well as enjoyment, but I let children fall from a bicycle or a box. Through learning the natural consequences of their actions, children learn to distinguish between a minor fall that might result in a bruise and a careless act that could be very dangerous for them.

Accidental Ethics

Your attitudes on specific matters will teach children all kinds of things you may or may not intend to teach. When a child reports with excitement that she has just found a huge spider, what is your reaction? What will this teach her about spiders? Your reaction will possibly teach her that:

1. Spiders are dangerous and yucky and should be killed or avoided at all costs.
2. Spiders are not important; nor are any other small or even not so small animals. People can do what they like about spiders.
3. Spiders eat garden pests and are harmless to humans. They are part of the web of all living things and should be protected from intentional harm.

Even if you have not clarified your own feelings to yourself, children will reflect your attitudes with surprising precision. While children sat at the lunch table one day, Paul spotted a huge brown spider scurrying toward the basement door. "Careful not to hurt him," he shouted. "Quick, open the basement door; he lives down there."

The simplest rules you establish for the use and maintenance of supplies and equipment will also transmit specific messages:

"Keep tops on felt pens": Resources — personal or public — can be maximized through proper care.
"Clean up messes with washcloths and rags, not with paper": Paper is made from trees, which take years to grow; resources are not limitless and must be preserved.
"No riding Big Wheels until after 10:00 A.M.": Children have the right to play and enjoy the Big Wheel, and the neighbors

have the right to sleep in the mornings; we establish a rule that satisfies both needs. Compromise and cooperation are part of adult life.

Most difficult for me, and a factor I believe to be most important in determining the content of "accidental ethics," is the tone of my voice. You will hear, as I do, your voice and your words coming from the children, either in response to you or with one another. It is most striking between an older and younger child. Above all, I want to teach children to respect one another. It is therefore most important that I speak with respect to them. It is not difficult to maintain adult authority. But maintaining a tone of respect for the children along with authority is more difficult than you may believe. But when children know you respect them, they let go of their hostility more easily and solve problems more effectively. The fact that you initiate problem-solving sessions with the children also teaches them the ethics of consideration.

Parent Handout

What Do You Teach 'Em, Anyway?

Through my constant availability, scarce interruption, and lack of curriculum planning with the kids, I work toward teaching the following concepts and attitudes:

1. Feelings
   A. learn to identify feelings
   B. learn to verbalize feelings
   C. learn to accept feelings
2. Expectations
   A. learn to adjust the expectations of others and self to reality in the areas of giving, expression, dexterity, responsibility, etc.
   B. learn what behavior is not appropriate and/or acceptable (hurting others physically or verbally, some behavior that does not hurt but is just not safe or is "too much" in a group in a small space)
3. Age differences (affects development and needs)
   A. verbal
   B. manual dexterity

    C. memory

    D. needs

4. Interpersonal relations

    A. appreciation and enjoyment of differences, age, temperament, interests, etc.

    B. nurturing, comforting, protection, advocacy, defense of others and self

    C. fairness; turns, sharing, the Golden Rule

5. Self-confidence

    A. I can do it, I can learn it, I can remember, I can use self-control, I can do without and wait, I can learn things that I couldn't learn last month

    B. I can help, teach, make others happy without compromising personal dignity or integrity, and it makes me feel good

    C. I can be honest, even about my mistakes, and I can take responsibility for my own attitudes, feelings, and actions; I can change my own attitude or "head space"

6. I am a valuable and special person — and so is everybody else. Self-respect and respect for others

7. trust and security (consistency in discipline, limits, and expectations foster feelings of trust and security)

8. value of friendship — environment forces children to become interdependent and fair with one another, and to form firm, important relationships with one another, sharing feelings, experiences, and learning to cooperate for the happiness of each member of the group

9. freedom with responsibility — an abundance of equipment, activities, and materials is available to the kids, each carrying its own small responsibility for care

10. problem-solving — kids are led to take responsibility for their own problem behavior, to talk out differences, make compromises, and set rules of acceptability for their own behavior in relation to others

10

Behavior Problems

The various techniques and subjects I have described in preceding chapters are premised on the assumption that the day care children trust you to oversee their lives for the entire day. This trust is based not only on their implicit acceptance of you as a final authority but also on their implicit faith that they are safe in your care. These two facets of their trust complement each other. Children learn happily and independently with each other in an environment that guarantees their safety but also has known and reasonable rules. To ensure this environment, certain kinds of behavior must be eliminated — fussing is the least disruptive, physical violence of one child against another the most disruptive — and each new addition to the day care home must know your rules and policies on these behaviors. The most common behavior problems among preschool-age children are fussing, spitting, name-calling, biting, hitting, and dirt-throwing. Each is discussed below. In addition, it seems appropriate to discuss here the possible abuse of children by adults, since an adult's response to specific behavioral problems can be an important clue in deciding how best to handle a difficult situation.

New children in day care will undoubtedly engage in one or more of these forms of behavior, either as a reaction to the new environment or as a test of your ability to maintain authority over that environment. Your response must be immediate, definite, and consistent in all instances.

Fussing

The behavior I find most difficult to tolerate, which is found most often in toddlers, is persistent fussing. If you can determine the cause of the fussing, you can sometimes eliminate this problem. Usually the cause is simply that something has not gone according to the toddler's plan: someone else is in the chair she wants, the preferred toy is in use, or Mother has gone to work. Sometimes if you offer the fussing child an alternative activity or an alternate chair, she will accept the suggestion and stop fussing. At other times the child will be persistent and single-minded in her thinking. These children have probably found fussing a very successful method in obtaining their goals. The parent has communicated to the child, "Anything, anything; just stop fussing." The child in her turn fusses when she wants anything. Understanding this, I employ the opposite response. If a child fusses for a toy, even if the other child is willing to give it up, I do not allow the fussing youngster to have the desired item; instead, I put it away for another time, explaining, "You will not get what you want when you fuss. When you tell me in another way, I will be glad to listen to you, but fussing will not work." If the child is unhappy for a reason not involving a thing, I first give her time to express her feelings. I might say, "You are angry to be left here," or "You want Brianna to be the mother and she doesn't want to play that game." Then I give the child permission to stop: "You can stop fussing now. You don't have to keep crying." Sometimes children need to be reminded that they do not *have* to act as they usually do; they seem to forget that they do have the power to change their own behavior. I then say, "Okay. You are all finished now. Stop fussing." Many children accept this direction gladly.

If the child seems to want to fuss but you and the other children have had enough, invite him to go to the time-out room to cry by saying, "The kids will be glad to play with you when you are finished." If the child does not budge, take him by the hand, or if necessary pick him up, and move him to the time-out room. (This is the same procedure described in Chapter 5 for dealing with tantrums. It is very central to my method of discipline.) Leave the door ajar. Wait beside the door, and as soon as there is a pause, even a short one, invite him out. "Would you like to come out now and play?" Usually this provides the opportunity the child needs to escape his unpleasant, self-inflicted situation. Sometimes I put a child in the time-out room when he is crying and very angry. When he emerges he may begin yelling again immediately, so I put him back in immediately and explain, "You have to do your yelling in here where it doesn't bother the others. When you are through you can come out, but you have to stay here until you are finished." Continue this pattern until the child understands that you mean what you say and that you intend to follow through. After you have been through this process once or twice with a child, it will not be necessary in the future. You need only say, "If you want to fuss, you can go into the other room." The fussing magically stops and the child is able to move on to a more productive and enjoyable activity.

Children do not enjoy crying and throwing tantrums, but they often indulge in this behavior because of the effect it can have on those around them. When the audience is removed, so is the motivation for the behavior, and it very quickly ends. Any child will be much happier if you help him or her eliminate this form of behavior and its attendant unhappiness.

Spitting

I have found that you can easily stop spitting by having the child spit directly into the toilet for at least two minutes, longer for repeated spitting incidents. Two minutes can be a long time to stare into a toilet and work up saliva. Explain to the child that spit carries germs, and some of these may be sick germs. It is important to try not to send our personal germs into the room to other people. For this reason people spit into the toilet or tissue only.

Name-Calling

Usually the offended child will come to you saying, "Danny said I was stupid." My standard reply is, "Do you think you are stupid? Can Danny make you stupid by calling you stupid? No? Then you don't have anything to worry about." If his feelings seem genuinely injured, I will say, "I bet your feelings are hurt because Danny is angry with you about something." If the child is six years old or older, I will suggest that he return to Danny and work out the problem. Many times the "victim" has initiated a conflict and uses the role of victim to escape responsibility. If you decide to get involved in this particular situation, you may approach Danny, take him from his activity, and help the children with their problem-solving only as much as they really need. When you simply let the children know that name-calling is not acceptable, by stating, "No name-calling," it is rarely a problem.

Biting

Because my approach to biting will be frowned upon by many, I seriously considered just leaving out the problem. But because almost all children seem to experiment with biting and because repeated biting is intolerable in a day care home, I will risk criticism.

Most children experiment with biting and may continue if they find it effective and if they are not stopped very early. With other forms of aggression, such as pushing, hitting, or yelling, the victim will often retaliate, and the aggression may be returned or repelled. But biting evokes a different response. After a child is bitten, he or she immediately withdraws and does not usually retaliate. The child gives in to the attack.

My son, Sean, got his teeth early. By eight months he had two uppers and two lowers in opposition. Because he was still nursing, it was very important to me that he stop biting immediately. With the very first little nip I took him off the breast, abruptly put him down with a stern "No biting," and walked away, refusing to comfort his angry cries. Only two more times did he test the consequences, and fortunately for me, he never did bite hard. If he had been older or in day care, I would have used the "cure" after the second instance.

Every child I have accepted in day care has tried biting when they have been between the ages of one and a half and three. Because biting is singularly frightening and painful to children and because it is so potentially effective, it is important for you to make it very clear that biting will not be tolerated. When a child bites in day care, I go to the child, kneel in front of him, hold his chin in my hand, and state in a very stern voice, "Biting is not good. I will not let other children bite and I cannot let you bite anyone else.

It is too scary and hurts too much. That means that you cannot bite anyone for any reason at all. If you bite anyone again, I promise I will bite you back." This threat is rarely permanently effective. The second time the child bites, I go immediately to the child and bite him or her in the same place that the other child was bitten, saying, "Biting hurts, doesn't it? It is scary. You don't like it and neither does anyone else." This is the cure. I bite softly enough to avoid any kind of skin damage or bruising, but hard enough to hurt and leave an impression on the child. Only once has it been necessary to bite a child twice. I have not found any other method that is immediately effective, and in a day care situation it is very important to be immediately effective. Biting is probably the most frightening form of aggression. Once one child bites another in day care, the other children will try it too, unless they are convinced that there are severe consequences.

I am certainly open to suggestions about a better way to handle this particular problem. I am not comfortable with adults biting children any more than you are. On the other hand, my discomfort seems a small price to pay for the safety and peace of mind of the children. When I consulted other day care and preschool personnel, I found that children older than four have usually grown out of this stage. We are therefore here concerned with children under three, those most often cared for in a day care home. It is important that you develop your own policy on biting, and that if biting occurs with a particular child, you discuss the problem with the child's family. If the family is unable to keep the child from biting and a verbal and time-out approach does not work, it is important that the family give you the authority to deal with the biting problem in your own way.

Hitting

Children go through a short hitting experiment at about eighteen to twenty months. If they learn that it is not acceptable behavior, that it does not solve their problem or get them what they want, and in addition that continued hitting leads to isolation, the hitting, pinching, or scratching will be short-lived. I have also noticed that discussion is not enough at this age. It is necessary to use time out on a chair or to send the child to the nap room for a short time as a consequence of antisocial behavior.

Dirt-Throwing

Throwing dirt is another mode of behavior I find intolerable in children, and children usually find it extremely upsetting. Here again, I first attempt to change the offending child's behavior by talking to her and explaining why this behavior cannot be tolerated. I will also use the time-out method to isolate the child and give her time to think about what I have said. Nevertheless, I will not tolerate a child's failure to respond to a clear definition of the rule. If she refuses to obey the rule and throws the dirt a second time, I will take drastic action. A second occurrence of dirt-throwing, for instance, has prompted me to give a child some experience in being on the receiving end of a handful of dirt in the face. The child inevitably no longer finds the situation humorous or powerful and also develops immediate self-control over the urge to throw dirt. Whatever method you ultimately rely on, children will expect you to be completely fair and consistent; you must be prepared to use the same tactics with all of the children, after taking differences in age into consideration.

Preventing Abuse

Child abuse is a problem that is finally beginning to receive the attention and concern it warrants, and the seriousness of the problem for the child should compel every day care operator to examine her methods in fairness and reasonableness. Child abuse is not known to be a problem in day care homes, but that does not mean that it does not or cannot happen in day care. It may happen, and every day care provider must be prepared to examine her feelings for the sake of the children's safety. Child abuse most often occurs when an adult reaches his or her limit of tolerance for a certain behavior of a child, although the child's behavior may be perfectly reasonable — asking questions, crying, refusing to eat dinner, or playing noisily. The adult's response may range from excessive but controlled anger to any form of unkind speech or to physical aggression against the child. The purpose of this discussion is to help you recognize the possible different responses in yourself or in others in contact with the children.

We all have different tolerance levels for various behaviors. Which of the behavior problems mentioned in the last section is the most threatening to your peace of mind? If you find that you have negative feelings about a child when he spits, that is one thing. But if you find you still have negative feelings about that child when he has stopped spitting and is happily playing, then you must give yourself time to change your attitude. If you find this is impossible, you must help the parents find a better place for the child. Your home is not a good place for him if he is getting negative messages from you.

I have to admit to personality conflicts with two children during my tenure as a day care mother. I simply could not muster friendly feelings for these two children. Recognizing the necessity of protecting children from this nonproductive experience, I began calling other good day care homes. To my surprise, I found that these children had been at other homes and had encountered the same problem. After discussing the situation with a trusted colleague, I concluded that a day care center would probably be a better environment for these children. In a center there are usually several adults who share the responsibility and relationship with a problematic child, and the structure of the center can dissipate the effect of the personality that I and other individual day care operators found so difficult to deal with.

If you find that your negative feelings appear only in response to certain behaviors, then the child can stay and the behavior must go. Whether the objectionable behavior is spitting, name-calling, physical aggression, ignoring communication, throwing toys, or writing on walls, it is important to remember that the child is not doing this to annoy you personally. This behavior is a manifestation of what is going on in the child. If you deal with children in a fair manner using the information in this book, you can be certain that this child is not after you, though he or she may be after the *authority* you represent. It is important that you do not become personally offended or angered by behavior, but rather handle it at a rational level. If you feel yourself getting angry, the safest thing to do is to remove the child to the nap room and take time to calm yourself before you deal with the problem. When you are ready, go to the child and proceed with your plan to eliminate the behavior.

If you find yourself responding to simple childhood behavior on an irrational level and the behavior itself does not seem to justify any reasonable level of annoyance, then you must consider whether the problem is within you rather than in the child's behavior. Are you having problems in other areas of your life? Are hormonal or physical changes affecting the level of your energy, patience, or self-control? Are you undergoing marital stress? Have you had an argument with a relative? Do you have problems with a neighbor? If you have problems in other areas of your life, get extra help during this time. Change the structure of day care for a week or more by arranging projects and materials to occupy the children and thereby keep the noise and activity to a minimum. If the weather is nice, insist that they play outside. Tell the kids the reason for the temporary change. Let them know that you know that you are crabby and that you do not blame them, but you need some time to get over your bad feelings. Let them know that sometimes when other things are bothering a person, that person may get angry with whoever is nearby instead of solving the real problem. Tell them you care about them so you want them to stay out of your way for a while, because you are upset about something else. Children can understand this and will be very cooperative and concerned. If you fail to take precautions and later treat a child in a manner you regret, there is no way to erase or undo the damage to that child or to your self-image and the trust of the parents. You must guard against this possibility above all, by monitoring and meeting your own needs.

I believe that the large family day care environment I describe minimizes the risk of mistreating children simply because it minimizes unnecessary contact with them. The contact that a provider has with children in this kind of environment leads to satisfaction and pleasure from teaching rather than to frustration from constant negotiation and judging. In addition, the rules are minimal and the discipline consistent. This means that children are satisfied more quickly in their testing behavior. There are also fewer confrontations in which an adult is likely to overreact.

If you should actually lose control, I cannot give you advice from my experience. I have been angry with children, but I have not abused a child. I do not know what you can do to heal the hurt that has been done. I would advise you to express your feelings to the child and call the parent and arrange for time to talk that same day. At this meeting, tell the parent what happened and how you feel; accept responsibility yourself. Do not blame the child for your loss of control. Next, find help through counseling and arrange for some time out for yourself.

Abuse is a very serious national problem, and we are a long way from dealing effectively with it through family and individual services. Most people who abuse children were abused themselves. This is the only obvious warning sign I know of. If you have a history as an abused child, you need help to heal the damage that was done to you. Most major cities now have organizations that offer services to abused women. Most of these services are oriented toward women abused in marriage, but the staff will be able to direct you to appropriate counseling or group therapy.

Most adults immediately recognize certain extreme forms of punishment as abuse, but there are other, more subtle, forms of abuse to children. Belittling, mocking, sarcasm, name-calling, and ignoring real needs are common problems children face in their relationships with adults. The result of these child-rearing practices is a feeling of worthlessness in the child. The damage that is done in this way is not physically visible, but can be just as serious as physical abuse. The subtle degradation of children can have life-long effects, and every adult should be concerned with protecting children from this experience.

I have gone to great lengths in this book to stress everything besides the superficial relationship between the child and the day care provider. In the end, of course, all these methods and the way you implement them will determine that relationship and the feelings between you and the child. Some people may view some of my methods as abusive when taken separately. But the test for distinguishing and defining abuse is the relationship between the adult and the child. The child must not come from the experience feeling stupid, unimportant, guilty, bad, or sinful. Punishment in the traditional sense is not part of my philosophy, because it is usually related to labeling children as bad. Children must have confidence in your sense of fairness and your underlying concern for their welfare and growth. They must know that you respect them as being equal in value to adults. If they trust you and *feel good about themselves* when they are in your care, your methods cannot be considered abusive.

The responsibility to be constantly aware and wise is a heavy one and difficult to fulfill. Day care providers are not super-humans; they do the best they can. I often feel guilty that I am not able to follow my own advice at all times. I sometimes slip into authoritarian attitudes, lose my temper when I feel I shouldn't, and blame the children instead of taking responsibility as I should. But I remind myself that no one can be the perfect parent or the perfect day care home operator. If the children are basically happy and trusting, if the parents are basically supportive and satisfied, and if you continue to choose providing day care as a good vocational option, you are a success. Children and their parents will forgive human frailty, and you will be doing more and doing it better than most day care centers and home operators.

11

Play and Playthings

So far, we have given very little attention to what children do during most of their hours in day care; as adults we tend to see everything from the perspective of what we must do when confronted with the needs of a child or a group of children. But day care is nevertheless a business that primarily concerns children and what they do. And in day care homes they play — freely, creatively, and continuously. The amount of equipment children use will vary from day to day. Some children will have a favorite toy or a favorite game, and others will appear never to play the same game twice. I believe in providing children with as many creative options as possible and letting them make the choices. On rainy days or days when everyone seems tired or cranky, I may organize a group activity, such as painting or board games, but in general I leave the children to their own devices. I expect to see children involved in different games scattered throughout the house or in the back yard. Various pieces of large equipment are arranged in different areas, and my home has been adapted to accommodate children's play safely in every area except our bedroom. The various materials and equipment described in this chapter can be included, omitted, or modified according to the style of your day care home, although I feel that children should have places to climb or dig or run and jump whenever possible. The descriptions of modifications made to the rooms themselves are more necessary, because they make the home safe and functional for children.

With the most sophisticated and expensive toys and equipment standing nearby, children will launch themselves into a complex, absorbing game that may require nothing more than a playmate or a single tattered bedsheet. Inside or out, this is the play that often most delights children and holds their interest the longest.

This is the play that most adults today will remember as typical of their childhood. In my youth most children played at home with other children during the preschool years, and had ample time to explore the world through imagination. Today fewer children than ever before have this opportunity. Large day care centers often prohibit the free and apparently unstructured games of inventive children and confine children to closely supervised, more sedate activities. This limits not only the imagination but also the peer interaction between children. If you doubt the importance of this interaction, children's vehement protest at adult interruption of their game should convince you. I begin with this form of play, then describe materials and equipment for play and equipment and modifications to make the day care home safe and functional for children.

I will offer only one word of warning, which many day care providers and parents will understand. Even if you supply only benign props, such as the kitchen items listed below, children will often use them in the most blood-curdling fantasies. I strictly ban toy guns, but find it unrealistic to ban bananas and fingers. I also hear children using the most unbecoming punishment with their "babies." I think it is true, as many psychologists say, that children play scary games to make frightening situations easier for them to manage. This form of play is a way of making adult authority and punishment seem less threatening — more understandable and acceptable to the child — when it emerges in real life. I do not try to prevent this kind of play, but I am glad that it is usually of limited duration.

Inside Games

Spooky House. The setting needed for this game should be obvious: shades down, curtains drawn, perhaps even a blanket hung to exclude that last bit of light seeping in around the edges of the windows. Props are flashlights, a night light, blankets or sheets, and any toys that make unusual sounds and noises. From outside the room (I have never been invited to participate) you will hear lots of squealing, roaring, yelling, and constant direction by several playing members. Usually at least one person is stomping around the room making scary noises (presumably under a blanket or sheet) while other children run about trying to avoid being caught.

Baby. This is also considered a private game. If the game is being used as a cover for body exploration, the door will be closed and I will be asked not to come in. The children will need a blanket, pillow, baby bottle, and perhaps diapers. There will be lots of play fussing, ordering the baby, and the baby refusing through a mouth full of thumb. Diaper-changing will give children the opportunity to observe the baby's genitalia. Often children will ask to use an ointment, but because of greasiness I usually tell them they will have to pretend. As with Doctor and other such games, I remind the children of the rules limiting their activity before they begin: (1) the ages of the children must be close; that is, the baby and the mommy must be approximately the same age; (2) all participants must want to be part of the activity; (3) the only toys or tools they can use are those in the doctor set, which I have examined for their safety; not even fingers should go in any holes (looking is okay and won't hurt); and (4) the game must be played in the private room (it probably will not be necessary to state this).

Doctor. Again, the children will demand privacy and will need blankets and pillows. Some children will probably pretend to be family members and hover around the patient with great concern, asking the doctor questions and trying to usurp the doctor's role in the game. The patient also has a prized role, and children will take turns in this role as well.

Pet monster. Usually this game needs no props and is an excuse for a younger child to have almost total authority over an older child, who is the monster. The monster crawls around the house making monster noises while the other child or children cajole him into cooperation.

Fort. One of the best sites for a fort is a large cardboard box such as a packing container for a refrigerator or other appliance. Sometimes the children will want a door and windows cut into the box; at other times they will want the box to be completely dark inside. In the end the fort will become a box for sitting on and good-natured bashing from children. If you have a fireplace, the destruction phase of the game will provide at least an hour of exercise and excitement while children tear the box into small pieces for you to burn.

Other sites for a fort or camp might be under a sheet draped over a clothesline, the corners of the sheet spread and fastened to the ground. If you allow children to move furniture, they will find all sorts of places for small camps, such as the space between the wall and a sofa.

House, restaurant, dentist, school, store, office. Any place of formal activity run by adults can be the subject of an imitative game. In my home the Community Playthings Climbing Gym is the preferred site for most of these games, although the setting is flexible, and stores and schools sprout wherever the children gather. These games all require extensive props in order for the children to be satisfied, since the main purpose of the game is to produce something, perhaps a page of printing, money, or food. A restaurant is more fun when there are things to serve and eat. I take advantage of this game to introduce raw vegetables. The school game requires paper and writing tools: a blackboard, chalk, rulers, and other materials will enrich the game. Sometimes the props will not be important, when children are more interested in the teacher–student relationship and in discipline.

Robot. No props are necessary. Children use this game to practice negotiation. The robot's actions are controlled by various "buttons," but only the robot knows where these are. The other child must learn to control the robot by finding out where the buttons are. The robot must maintain the enjoyment of the game for the other child by rewarding him or her often enough to keep the game going. The rest of the game involves the robot moving about making beeping noises and jerking limbs around, often blocking doorways and thereby making it necessary for the children to find the right buttons to move the robot out of the way.

Train, airplane, bus, ferry. The children arrange every movable chair in the house to form one row or two parallel rows. They negotiate for places, the first, second, and last chairs being the favorite seats. The specific journey is flexible and all pretend.

Car. A chair is turned over so that the top of the back of the chair and the front edge of the seat slide while a child drives the car by pushing the chair's back legs. We have an uncovered floor in most of my home, which gives ample scope for this game.

Outside Play

Water. Water is a wonderful experience that all children enjoy and of which they never seem to tire. Summertime back-yard water activity with a sprinkler, hose, spray bottles, and a shallow plastic pool are great for both the children and the day care parent. In the house, water is not much fun for the parent. I simply explain to the children, "Water is so much fun, isn't it! Water play doesn't hurt anyone and you love it, but there are too many children inside the house for water play. Water ends up on the floor and it ends up all over the house, where it makes the floor slippery and dangerous. You can use water outside and at your house, where there aren't so many kids." Children now save their flotation experimentation and pouring practice for the bathtub at home. If you have a room with a drain, a water table (a plastic sandbox on legs with a plug), or a large low sink, water play inside might be reasonable. But without this special equipment, water play should be reserved for yard and home.

Mud. Mud holds a special joy for children. I will not describe any games with mud; I will simply tell you my best mud story, which took place on the last day of school several years ago. That year I had six after-school children who arrived daily at 3:30 P.M. It was a wonderful hot day, rare in the early summer in Seattle, where I live. At the time the front of our house was not much more than a large dirt pit with a few stubborn blades of grass — the result of front-porch construction, not child activity. I was occupied with getting the toddlers up from their naps when I realized that the hose had been running for several minutes outside the house. When I looked through the window, I saw six school-age children and five younger ones stripped to the underpants or nude, delightedly covering each other with mud. I thought, "What can I do? Nothing, it's too late." I just watched and enjoyed it. Standing on the curb across the street were at least eight other children, watching enviously. In the window behind them were parents, watching with a variety of expressions: some were appalled, others looked tempted to play themselves. As each child tired of the play and came into the house, I carried him or her to the bathtub, where I used the shower hose to help the child wash. This was one of those events parents love to hear about but are glad they missed.

Drink stand. Beginning at the age of four, children enjoy playing hawker on the corner, usually selling some bright-colored, luke-warm liquid. A well-traveled corner is not essential but makes for an interesting afternoon. The kids enjoy making a sign illustrating the contents of the pitcher and naming it, more or less. They tape the poster to the front of a very small table, then haul it and a few chairs up to the corner. When they expect to spend the entire day at the corner, they also take a couple of toys and one or two books. A customer will request ice. The choice of drink depends on your personal values (mine are lax in this area).

My arrangement with the children is that I will give them money for the cups and drink mix and be reimbursed "right off the top" when the day is over. The kids learn about change, lending, invest-ment, product quality, customer satisfaction, and supply and demand. It is wise, I think, to come to an agreement about what to do with the profits *before* the profits are made. It is probably best to decide as a group where the money should go; for instance, the children may decide to have a party or buy a toy. In my home we have agreed that when the stand is set up during day care time, the proceeds should go into a fund used to buy special things for the group as a whole. You may choose instead to reinforce private enterprise, but in my experience the younger children lose out in a private enterprise arrangement. Fortunately, money does not seem to be the most important factor; the pleasure of the activity itself is enough to keep the stand open many days in the summer, even if there are few customers.

In addition to a fruit juice, children can sell popsicles. You will need a large box of sticks ($4 per thousand from a local crafts shop), several ice-cube trays, and a large cooler. The children will have to plan ahead at least one day to make hard popsicles; Kool-Aid or juice can be used (Kool-Aid makes harder popsicles). Juice popsicles are an excellent treat for day care children at any time, and I always keep about forty ice-cube-sized popsicles in the freezer. To prevent the children from littering your lawn with sticks, you can require each child to turn in a stick if he or she wants a popsicle at a later time. One summer I ignored the sticks until the end of each week, when we had a contest. The child who collected the most sticks got two popsicles, and any child who collected any sticks got one popsicle.

Clothing

Children love to dress up in old clothing and use cosmetics; I balk at cosmetics on principle, but both boys and girls enjoy it so much that I cannot object to it. In addition, old costumes, masks, and sheets are always used for different games.

Books and Magazines

Books and magazines suitable for children of different ages should be readily accessible in the day care home. I keep a box of disposable books — books that will be mutilated and chewed on by toddlers — in a large cardboard box on a bottom shelf, where toddlers can easily reach them. Children at this age love catalogues, telephone books, and magazines. For children aged two and a half to four, I keep a number of suitable books on a shelf they can reach. Books for older children are placed on a still higher shelf. On one of the highest shelves I keep books that can only be used with adult supervision. Two-year-olds will show interest in the books set aside for older children, so I explain to them that if they would like to use these books, they may select one, take it to the couch, turn the pages like a seven-year-old — carefully holding the top corner of the page with the thumb and finger and turning the pages slowly — and then return it carefully to its place. The children have come to respect books and treat them with care and concern, using them frequently and deriving great pleasure from them. Much of the pleasure is in finding out that they are able to follow my instructions: the physical control has its own reward. The toddlers watch the older children learning about these books and have the freedom to practice with their magazines and books without an anxious adult standing by to protect the book from damage. You will find an extensive book list organized by topic at the end of this book, included as Appendix B. All of the books listed are in print in 1983, but unfortunately, many other excellent books have been deleted from the list because they are no longer in print.

In addition to books I keep a photo album of day care children involved in their daily activities. Both children and parents enjoy seeing these pictures and reminiscing about their earlier years and children who have moved on. Pictures of activities and games may in turn instigate new versions of the old games. This visual documentary reinforces the children's sense of belonging and the continuity of their day care life.

Art Supplies

You do not need to spend a great deal of money on art supplies, and I would not recommend that you do so. Children can entertain themselves happily for hours with the simplest materials, as long as they are free to use their imaginations in their artwork. Children in my day care home regularly use play dough, paper and drawing pens or crayons, and finger paint.

Play dough. Below is a recipe for making play dough; children enjoy measuring, dumping, mixing, and selecting colors. If properly stored, the dough will stay soft for several weeks. I generally let children play unaided with the dough, but occasionally I give them cookie cutters, spatulas, buttons, or nuts and bolts to use with it.

Play Dough

4 c flour
4 T cream of tartar
1 c salt

2 c water with lots of food coloring
3 T oil

Mix together first three ingredients, then add water and oil. Mix and knead until smooth, adding flour if sticky. Keep in a covered plastic container; it is not necessary to refrigerate the dough. Sprinkle with a few drops of water and let stand in a covered container when dough becomes too stiff or dries out.

When the dough has lost its nice texture and *umph,* roll it out and cut
with cookie cutters to make tree hangings. Be sure to put small holes
in the top of each shape for the hanging string. Bake at 300° about
15 minutes, or till dough begins to darken slightly.

Sawdust Clay

6 c sawdust	2 T salt
5½ c flour	boiling water

Mix, gradually adding water. Blend thoroughly until it resembles a stiff
dough. Wrap in plastic or aluminum foil, store in cool place. Keeps
about one week.

Paper. Children derive great pleasure from paper, crumpled or
otherwise. I use discarded computer printouts (readily available
from businesses and colleges) and scrap colored paper and news-
print ends from printers. Usually at least one parent among the
families has access to this often-wasted resource and will be glad
to contribute to the children's store. If you do not have a screened
fireplace for paper deposit, you will need several paper disposal
baskets throughout the house for cuttings and rejected artwork.
Children can work safely with round-tipped scissors and paper
to create various kinds of artwork.

Pens and crayons. Nontoxic, washable, colorful felt-tipped pens
are a favorite material among day care children, but children must
be taught and constantly reminded to put the tops on tightly to
keep the pens from drying out. I have been most satisfied with
Crayola brand pens: the tips survive constant use and are well
shaped for the kind of varied line children like. They are reasonably priced (approximately $2 for a box of eight pens) and will
last a reasonable amount of time. Scented pens are delightful, but
are not recommended for toddlers, who think the pens should
taste as good as they smell. Crayons cost less than pens, but their
colors are not as bright, and children will generally prefer pens
to crayons if both are available.

Finger paint. Finger painting is always popular. I generally use
heavy paper designed for this activity, since lighter paper tears easily
and leads to disappointment for the children. The recipe following
is fairly simple, and children enjoy helping you make the paint.

Fast Finger Paint

Mix a very small bit of dry powder paint with lots of soap flakes and a little water, blending as you add drops of water. This is really fast and satisfying in texture (a little lumpy).

Cooked Paint

½ c laundry starch
1 c cold water
1 envelope unflavored gelatin or
  1 T glycerin
2 c hot water

½ c mild soap flakes or
  synthetic detergent
all-purpose RIT dye or powder
  paint

Combine dye and ¾ cup of the cold water in a saucepan. Soak gelatin in remaining ¼ cup cold water. Add hot water to starch mixture and cook over medium heat, stirring constantly, until mixture comes to a boil and is clear. Remove from heat; blend in softened gelatin. Add soap or detergent and stir until mixture thickens and soap is dissolved. Cool. Divide and mix in coloring dye or powder paint. Makes about 3 cups; recipe may be multiplied.
When paintings are dry, press with a warm iron.

Toys

I see no reason to invest in expensive, unusual, or exotic toys; a good supply of cars, trucks, dolls, stuffed animals, and other items can be collected from garage sales and community bazaars. If you are interested in obtaining specific items, make a list of these and the price you are willing to pay, and give the list to the parents. Most parents recognize that the quality of the day care environment is everyone's responsibility, and they will be willing to participate by helping you locate the toys you need. Some toys, such as those listed below, are especially popular because they allow free rein to a child's imagination.

Fisher-Price Parking Ramp–Service Center. This is a very durable toy and popular with boys and girls of all ages. It is used in conjunction with blocks, little people, cars, trucks, and so on, and helps children learn to share when playing. Most toys require the children to take turns rather than sharing; a toy that can truly be shared has a special value in the day care environment.

Fisher-Price Doctor Set. This is another popular item with all children, regardless of age. Children are interested in expressing their feelings about visits to the doctor and also in exploring their own bodies; this toy legitimizes their games to some degree, is designed to be safe, and is realistic enough to satisfy them. The pieces in the set are strong and well built, with the exception of the stethoscope, which will fall apart shortly after purchase.

Big Wheel. Although this toy will not last as long as a tricycle, it is so stable and inexpensive that it is well worth buying. Do not expect to find a used one for sale; children wear the toy out before they outgrow it. The Big Wheel needs a large flat area for riding, usually a sidewalk or driveway, and is too bulky for a back yard.

Table games and puzzles. There are many table games on the market for children of various ages. My favorite is one that several parents and I developed. I have found this unique game, called Trade, to be the most educational mathematical game available and suitable for a wide age range. The youngest children will enjoy fitting brightly colored wooden pegs into the holes; toddlers will enjoy matching and sorting and handling the pegs; and children about four years old will learn basic number concepts. As soon as the most elementary concepts are secure, after a few weeks of playing the game, a child can quickly move on to basic arithmetic. A full description of the game and information for ordering is given in Appendix C. Checkers, backgammon, Chinese checkers, Connect, Water Works, MAD, Sorry, Aggravation, and dominos are popular on rainy days or when I simply must have a little quiet. Younger children enjoy puzzles; the favorite ones are Simplex puzzles, which have pieces with red knobs that represent cars, people, animals, and so on and can be used separately when removed from the puzzle.

Puppets. Either homemade or commercial puppets offer an excellent opportunity for interage involvement. The youngest children like to arrange chairs, serve popcorn, and talk to the puppets and puppeteers, while older children like to rig up the stage by turning a table on its side or draping an old sheet between two chairs. Making puppets with small paper bags is a great rainy-day activity requiring only felt pens or crayons, dried beans, peas, popcorn, colored paper scraps, yarn scraps, and paste. More materials such as feathers, glitter, and beads can be added to make fancier puppets.

Musical instruments. A wide variety of percussion instruments are available for children. I recommend finger cymbals, tambourines, rhythm sticks, maracas, and homemade noisemakers such as sandpaper blocks and cans filled with beans.

Records. Listening to rhythm and music games on records by Ella Jenkins is a favorite pastime; her records are available from the public library in many parts of the country. Two very new exceptional music records for kids age 4 to 12 are (1) "In Search of the Wow Wow Wibble Woggle Wazzie Woodle Woo!" by Tim Noah, winner of the Parents' Choice Award given by the Parents' Choice Foundation of Massachusetts. This record is available from Noazart Productions, P.O. Box 30501, Seattle, WA 98103, and (2) "Circle Around" by the Tickle Tune Typhoon and available through them at P.O. Box 15153, Seattle, WA 98115. Both records will be available nationally in the future as the word spreads. Abundant material on music for children is available from libraries, bookstores, schools, colleges, and day care organizations. If music is your strength, you undoubtedly will be able to offer numerous musical games that will delight children. If music is not your strength, you can still include it through radio programs, records, or tapes during some part of the day. As I described earlier, my kids enjoy a daily dance session twice a day after clean-up.

Kitchen toys. Plastic fruit, kitchen utensils, and pots and pans are essential for many games of make-believe. Infants and toddlers will take immense delight in the amount of noise they can create with pots and pans as well as the novel experience of manipulating something large and bulky. Older children will use the equipment in more complex games of playing House or Restaurant.

Molded plastic car seat. This is not properly a toy, but children find many uses for it and it quickly becomes indispensable. By inverting the liner over the exterior shell, my children immediately turned the seat into a magic egg, from which emerged many fascinating animals and characters over the years. This egg will accommodate even a five-year-old. The chair is also used extensively in games of Baby and can be pushed around the house like a baby carriage.

Equipment

In addition to numerous toys and materials for play, I have found several larger pieces of equipment essential to the day care environment; children like to build, climb, and dig, and a day care home must enable them to do so. None of the pieces of equipment described below is very expensive, but all (or similar pieces) are worth the initial investment.

Blocks. A good set of wooden blocks is one of the most important items in any day care home. You can buy a set, order a set from a local carpenter or toymaker, or make your own set. Hardwood blocks are best, since they are not easily damaged. To make a basic set of blocks, cut a two-inch-by-four-inch piece of wood into lengths of twelve inches, six inches, and three inches. You can easily add to this set as time passes. Children from ten months to ten years will use the blocks, building creations together, since blocks are one of the few playthings that children can share and enjoy together. The blocks should be stored on a low shelf for easy accessibility and safety, and used on a carpeted area to keep the level of noise to a minimum.

Pounding bench. Children love to pound at a bench, with or without nails and pegs. You can construct a sturdy bench with a few wooden boards; the design is not important, as long as the bench is sturdy. The wood should be a softwood and of good quality to eliminate splinters. With twine, I attach a large hammer and with flathead nails a plastic container of large building nails to the inside of one of the legs. Children under three prefer using a rubber-headed mallet to hammer dowels into a board with holes drilled to fit them.

This toy will occasionally produce a bruised finger; soak the finger in cold water with ice cubes to prevent swelling. Children do not seem to mind an occasional injured finger from the play and continue to hammer at the bench off and on for several years.

Children's play furniture. Child-sized furniture gets constant use and should be sturdy and safely designed — no protruding nails or dangerous edges. Plans for a sink, stove, refrigerator, bed, and cupboard are available from do-it-yourself carpentry books. You can design your own, hire a carpenter, or purchase the finished items. Individual items are available from Community Playthings; pieces range from $40 to $100, depending on quality, design, and so on. On page 185 are designs of the child-sized furniture we use in my day care home.

Indoor jungle gym. A climbing apparatus that folds up when not in use will save your nerves and the furniture and cut down on running through the house on days when the children cannot play outside. Community Playthings makes an excellent climber/gym with a detachable slide that is well worth its cost (about $220). The climber has two adjustable platforms, which enable children to use it as a setting for innumerable games and fantasies. A sheet makes it a tent; adjusting a platform to table height and adding two small chairs inside convert it to a school, restaurant, or office. Two platforms can also be used as play bunk beds. My climber has had eight years of constant rough use and is still as solid as the day I bought it. It folds to a convenient storage size and can be moved by one person. If I intended to provide day care for many more years, I would invest in many items made by Community Playthings; their toys and equipment are well designed, exceptionally crafted, and almost indestructible. They also carry a reliable warranty. If you are planning any major equipment purchases, you should investigate this company's products. The company is located in Rifton, New York 12471.

Swings. Old tires can be made into safe swings. I was initially given a traditional swing set with two swings, but it is too dangerous for unsupervised play because feet fly through the air at head height. Traditional swings can be replaced with tires, designed as shown on page 186.

Digging place. The sandbox is a joy for children and a headache for the day care parent. I prefer to limit sandbox play to children three and older, and do so by locating the box in the front yard. If you have an assistant who can supervise the sandbox, younger children would certainly enjoy this play. In the beginning of sand play children will throw sand and test the rules. Since most children quickly experience sand in the face, they are usually convinced that they must not throw sand or play with it in such a way that it blows into someone's face or hair. On two occasions in my day care home children threw sand at others and thought it a great joke, though; the culprits had not experienced being on the receiving end of such a stunt.

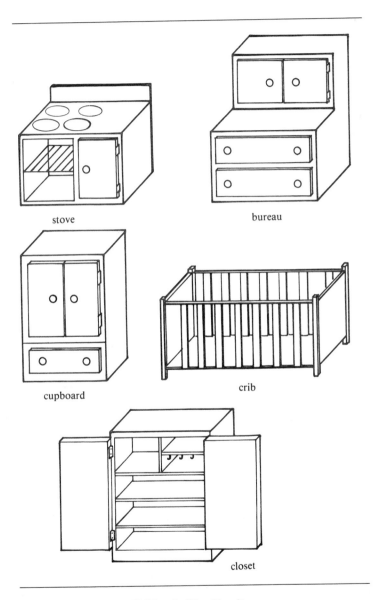

stove

bureau

cupboard

crib

closet

Children's Play Furniture

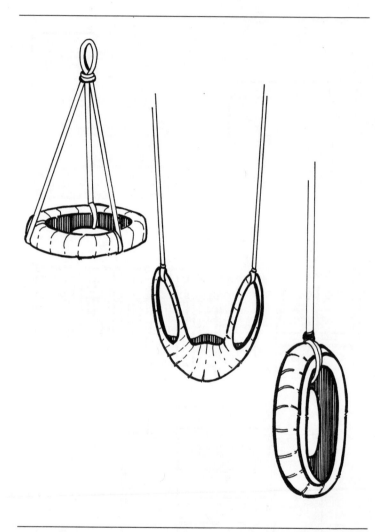

Tire Swings
All of these swings are made from tires. The middle swing is a tire
cut lengthwise, as shown, to form a bucket to sit in.
The swing suspended by one rope is used mostly for climbing,
whereas the top one is suitable for up to
three small children who want to spin.

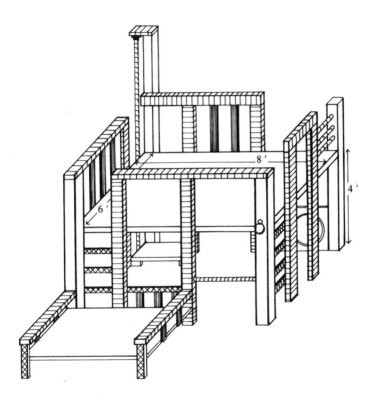

Outside Jungle Gym

Here's a picture of the jungle gym we used. Roughly, the structure stands 4' high, 6' deep, and 8' wide.

If you do not want to cope with a sandbox, you can still give children a place to dig by filling a small plastic pool with rice, lentils, or the like. The pool can be kept inside and the filling is easy to clean up.

Outside jungle gym. The first spring after I started my day care business, I designed a permanent outside climbing structure, which is illustrated on page 187. I bought secondhand lumber and some new lumber, stained the materials, and invited the parents to build the climber with me on a weekend. After several hours the fourteen adults and innumerable children were ready for a big spaghetti dinner. The children had had the wonderful experience of seeing their parents involved in their day care, watching the structure grow, and seeing the good relationship between their parents and me. This kind of experience can be very important in gaining children's respect, confidence, trust, and cooperation.

The jungle gym we built is designed to serve any purpose children can devise for it: it can be climbed, lived in, or used as a ship. A jungle gym need not be complicated as long as it allows children of varying ages to climb and explore in their imagination.

Television

To defend programming containing violence and aggression, television supporters often use the argument that children play violent games of their own volition. I see a significant difference between a child's fantasy, regardless of its content, and the realistic scenes presented to children on TV. Children have no control over television images, TV leaves little room for interpretation, and TV idols are macho beyond any real man's abilities and certainly beyond any woman's desires. I have seen countless children imitating superheroes of all kinds; the characters have no softness, no sense of compromise, no flexibility. There is no gray area between right and wrong, no hint of common human frailty or social cause of evil. Some children acquire inappropriate fears from TV and cannot handle them. Others may acquire a belief in their own invincibility or position above and apart from society at large, and may feel free to exhibit antisocial behavior for personal profit or satisfaction.

But to my mind the most detrimental effect, even from watching educational television, is the time lost. This time could be spent in developing stronger family and sibling ties, in interacting with peers, and in learning from real experiences rather than seeking vicarious pleasure from TV adventure. Children invest themselves in TV fantasy and superheroes instead of in their own family and community.

If you are tempted to use television to give you time to make dinner quickly, you might consider giving the children a carrot to hold them for an hour. Or you can invite them to assist in the dinner preparation. The result will be a late dinner, but also an hour of interaction with children and a learning experience for them in family participation and cooperation. You may have less difficulty with a picky eater if he invests himself in the preparation of the food. Children will also learn about the energy that goes into meal preparation and may feel they are more valuable family members as a result of this participation. If you do not have time to involve children in dinner preparation, invite them to bring a puzzle, book, or drawing into the kitchen. While your child works or plays, your presence will be felt. This is an opportunity for communication or for quiet parallel activity.

It is unquestionably a struggle to limit children's TV consumption, but the less time children spend watching, the less they want to watch. Although they feel it is important to know what happened on the "Six Million Dollar Man" when they talk to their friends at school, they can usually guess what happened. Furthermore, children who do other things have more to offer and are accepted and liked for their own wealth of creative ideas and their knowledge of the larger real world.

With this in mind, I must admit that I do use TV occasionally. I average about one hour a week, and I limit viewing to educational children's programming. Mr. Rogers has certainly addressed some important issues in ways that children can accept and understand, and I have learned from him ways to address the questions of my children.

When do I resort to TV? On those long summer days when the children have been hard at play outside and they are really too exhausted to do anything else. On a rainy day when every single child who could show up actually does. Once in a while, when I just can't take it — the whole thing — I let the kids watch TV and take time out myself.

Home Arrangements

The large number of small children and the variety of materials and equipment needed for their play require that the day care home be carefully organized and arranged. My home may look messy and my housekeeping standards lax, but every room has been arranged to accommodate children and their play. The kind of day care home I have been describing throughout this book — the large family environment — cannot be accommodated in one or two children's rooms. For the home to run smoothly and safely, each room and each aspect of the children's day must be considered. The detailed drawing of the plan of my home on page 192 will show you the general layout of a day care home as I describe the specific arrangements made in each area. I moved the larger pieces of equipment around in the hope of finding an arrangement that would give added empty floor space, but I eventually gave up on this goal. With many children and many pieces of equipment you will never have much empty floor space; the best you can do is to use folding and stacking pieces to provide floor space for certain activities.

Porch. Children will make very good use of all kinds of space adults neglect. The front porch can be a special place for toddlers, especially when all the older children are playing in the front yard. On page 195 is an illustration of a gate for the porch stairs; the gate confines toddlers to the porch but allows older children and adults to step over to the stairs.

Inside Play Areas

There are three main play areas inside my home; the large pieces of play equipment can be moved from one to the other, but I try to keep certain storage items in the same place so that children can easily find whatever they might be looking for. Three play areas are not necessary, but certain items should be readily available in these areas for children.

Cubbies. Cubbies are individual storage places for the children's property, such as clothing, toys, and artwork. They can be plastic buckets lined up against a wall, hung from pegs, or placed on a shelf. You can also use wide shelves with dividers for individual cubbies. In my home the cubbies are in an entryway, which is a secondary play area, and children need to be reminded to use them. To keep this kind of direction to a minimum I also use a large five-gallon plastic bucket, in which children put their shoes and socks as they discard them. The bucket is kept in the main play area, and after children learn to use it they have fewer lost socks and shoes. If you can persuade parents to buy only one style of socks for their child, you will have even less difficulty locating and identifying a child's clothing. Carl wore only red cable-knit knee-highs and lost fewer socks than anyone because they were easily identified and there was never any controversy over ownership.

Clothes trunk. I keep the dress-up clothes in a separate topless trunk that children can open and close easily, leaving them free to start this play whenever they feel like it. I found the trunk to be easier for the children than a small clothes closet with hangers. Occasionally a child's clothing will be mixed into the general collection of dress-up clothes, so this is a good place to begin looking for a lost article of clothing.

Shelving. Adequate shelving is a necessity, not only to maintain a semblance of order but also to teach children the importance of putting things away when they are finished. In the main play area we have separate shelves for blocks and, on the other side of the room, for books, arranged by age of the children. There is also a large cushion nearby, where children can sit and use the books or magazines. Toys should also be arranged on shelving according to the ages of the children: toys that can be used by the youngest children on the lowest shelves, toys for older children on upper shelves, out of the reach of infants and toddlers. Any adult materials should be on the highest shelves.

Storage drawers. A large bureau of six drawers is also a necessity. In the top drawer are swimsuits; in the second drawer, paper diapers, tape, bottom-wipes, ointment, and plastic disposal bags; in the third drawer, lost and found articles; in the fourth drawer, extra T-shirts, jerseys, sweaters, shirts; in the fifth drawer, extra pants; in the bottom drawer, mittens, hats, and scarves. Extra clothing is always needed; during play children get dirty and some-

Layout of My Day Care Home

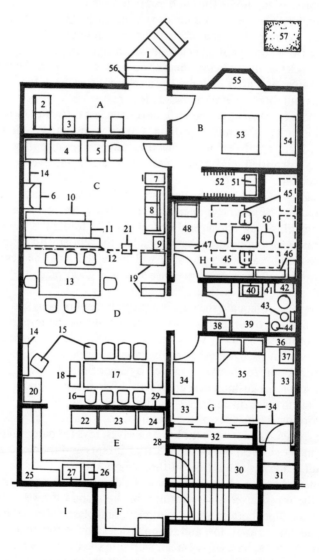

one thousand square feet total floor space

Key to Floor Plan

A   Front porch with 4½ ' high, closely
    spaced slats on front, side, and end
B   Entry area with coat and cubby
    area
C   Living-room space, carpeted to
    archway, indicated by dotted line
    across the space
D   Dining-room area
E   Kitchen
F   Back porch
G   Master bedroom, used as nap space
    and time-out room during day care
    time. All sleep-on things fold or
    stack
H   Kids' room
 I Back yard
1   Step-over gate at top of porch steps
2   Porch swing
3   Rocking horses (the kind suspended
    in a frame by large springs)
4   Typing desk
5   Large plastic bucket used for shoes
    and socks for everyone
6   Fireplace
7   Stacking steel file drawers used to
    store extra clothes, diapers,
    swimming gear, etc. Sides used to
    display photographs of children —
    taped on
8   Very old, beat-up sofa
9   Bookcase used to house building
    blocks
10 Bookcase, 4 ' high, books arranged
    with child's height in mind
11 Large pillows
12 Floor-to-ceiling shelving unit for
    equipment and toy storage
13 Child-sized table and stacking
    children's chairs
14 Radiator
15 Adult-sized chairs — some at the
    table with 4 " booster pads
16 High chairs with arms and backs
    removed to stack
17 Dining-room table, adult height
18 Benches, a little higher than regular
    chair height
19 Playhouse equipment — sometimes
    set up in the entry space and re-
    placed by the indoor climbing gym
    here
20 Sewing-machine cabinet
21 Johnny Jump-Up seat, suspended
    from archway by a large spring
22 Stove

23 Portable dishwasher with wooden
    chopping-block top
24 Refrigerators
25 Countertop with kitchen cabinets
    above and below
26 Kids' cup pegboard drainer/storage
27 Sink
28 Wall-sized blackboard/corkboard
29 Walls used to display children's
    artwork
30 Stairs to basement
31 Closet to master bedroom
32 Recent built-in closet space
33 Folding playpens for napping
34 Crib mattresses (stack well or flip
    up against the wall)
35 Queen-sized water bed
36 Shelving for stereo and records
37 Bedstand for clock radio
38 Cupboards for storing linens
39 Bathtub
40 Sink with drinking fountain
41 Hand towel fixed to wall
42 Toilet
43 Potty chair
44 Bucket for bath toys
45 Cots stacked and set up against the
    wall for storage during play time;
    dashed lines indicate placement for
    nap time
46 Floor-to-ceiling shelving unit for
    toy and equipment storage
47 Stacking steel storage drawers used
    for children's clothing and supplies
48 Bunk beds
49 Folding table (child-sized)
50 Stacking child-sized chairs
51 Cubbies — plastic buckets stacked
    on their sides pyramid style
    between the walls
52 Coathooks and little shelf above
53 Indoor climbing gym (Community
    Playthings), sometimes switched
    with playhouse area or set up in
    kid's bedroom (folds easily); set up
    in living-room area when used with
    the slide attachment. Slide is stored
    behind the couch in living-room
    area.
54 Dress-up clothes trunk
55 Window seat with storage
    underneath
56 Storage for Big Wheels and
    sandbox equipment under porch
57 Sandbox

times soaked, so change them into something dry and comfortable. I buy secondhand clothes at thrift shops and garage sales in case of emergencies and let the children keep whatever I put on them. Children often take a liking to these novel outfits and find the experience of discovering a strange item in the drawer of extra clothes a minor adventure. You may also need to keep several pairs of boots of different sizes so that all children can play outside during damp weather. Extra pairs of heavy socks will make the boots fit.

Furniture. When you enter the day care business, you must put in abeyance any plans for a formal living room. Children will follow any rules you lay down for the treatment of your furniture, but you cannot prevent normal wear and tear. Put any good pieces of furniture in storage and buy a comfortable secondhand sofa and whatever else you might need. Anything delicate or valuable will not survive the day care years, and the children should not be put in the impossible position of having to restrict their play for your furniture. The children are the most important consideration here, and your home should reflect that. In addition to a sofa I used large floor cushions; cushions from discarded sofas are a good size for children. A large mattress that can be occasionally dragged to the living room is good for tumbling and jumping.

Wall space. Throughout the play areas children will want to display their prized artwork, and several wall areas are needed for this. Which artwork is displayed is entirely up to the artist, regardless of how the parent or provider might feel. The two-year-old will want to display a piece of folded computer printout, and another child will want to view her splash of red paint. Some children will produce work daily, and you will need lots of wall space.

Suspended infant jump seat. A suspended infant jump seat is a necessity if you have infants and older children. The seat should be hung in the main play area, where the infant can watch the other children play and interact with them and yet be protected from being stepped on.

Dining Area

The dining area in my home is also a favorite spot for play; children can sit at the table and work with play dough or draw

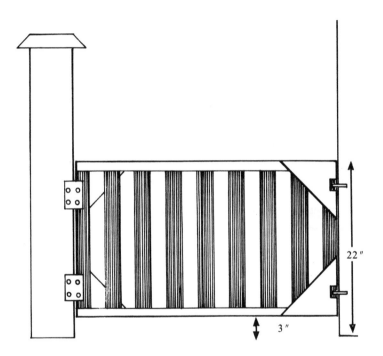

Porch Gate
Be sure to use the heaviest, strongest hinges available,
because kids like to stand on the gate. Hinges that swing
both ways may be most suitable. This gate was used for
five years without significant wear and is now in use at
another day care home. Be sure to keep both bolts shut to
distribute and support the weight of the gate and kids.

or read. Nearby is an area large enough to accommodate either the indoor jungle gym or the children's play furniture. Since children make their artwork in this area, I keep several wall areas free for display.

Children's table and chairs. The most functional table for children is one with adjustable legs; if you begin by caring for toddlers, you may have the same children for several years and will want furniture that can grow with them. A table that you can extend with leaves is another option. If you intend to have a second table, it should be collapsible, requiring as little permanent space as possible. Small children's chairs that can be conveniently stacked and set aside will also give more area for play. Other chairs of varying heights, suitable for children of different ages, should also be available in the home. Leave enough space around the dining table and chairs to allow for easy clean-up.

Hanging infant chair. A hanging infant chair needs little storage space and allows the infant to sit at the table with other children (see illustration on opposite page). The chair is suitable for children aged seven to twelve months.

High chairs. Children aged one to three seem to be most comfortable eating in a high chair if other children are eating at an adult-sized table. Remove the tray and scoot the high chair up to the table with the other children. At this age children do not need the back of the chair for safety or support if the chair is placed against a wall. I remove the arms and backs of old high chairs, leaving only the legs with a connecting bar (to climb up) and the seat, which allows me to stack the stools. Secondhand high chairs that can be disassembled can be had at thrift shops and garage sales for less than $5.

Kitchen

Children will not go to the kitchen specifically to play, but their games will spill over into this area, and the kitchen should therefore be equipped with safety devices. In addition, you will want to purchase a few items to make serving meals to children easier and safer.

Plates, bowls, and cups. I recommend plastic or enameled plates, bowls, and cups for serving children. The bowls and cups should

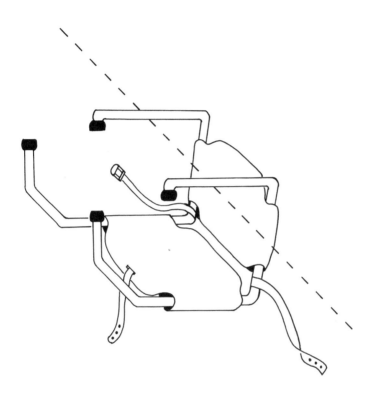

Hanging Infant Chair
Constructed of aluminum tubing with plastic caps on each
end to protect table. Seat and back made from heavy
semi-flexible plastic. Bottom easily snaps off at one side,
enabling chair to fold for flat or hanging storage.
Safety straps attached at sides and front of seat.
Dotted line represents edge of table top.
We are looking through the table top to see the seat and
front legs of chair which support the suspended chair
with the weight of the child pressing up through those legs.

have wide bottoms. In my home the cups hang on a pegboard mounted on a cupboard near the sink, making them accessible to the children by chair. If you use a dishwasher, make sure the plates and so on will fit before buying a set.

Garbage disposal. This can be a necessity if you are serving lunch and snacks to a large group of children every day. Consider it a business expense and buy the one with the best safety features and longest guarantee.

Cupboards. Child-proof locks are a necessity on all drawers or cupboards that contain knives, sharp cooking utensils, breakable bowls, cleaning fluids, or any other items that could injure a child. Toddlers enjoy playing with pots and pans, and if you can tolerate the racket, you can leave a lower cupboard of pots and pans accessible to them.

Refrigerator. You can house a second refrigerator on a back porch or in a closet and will need it for storing milk, fruit, and vegetables for the children. This is not a necessity, but it will allow you to limit grocery shopping to once a week.

Kitchen step. You will need a safe two-step stool in either the kitchen or the bathroom, wherever you want the kids to wash their hands. Following is a design for a step that will not tip over, no matter how a child steps on it. Children will use it in the kitchen to reach cups and in the bathroom to reach the sink or toilet.

Bathroom

The bathroom need not be the most dangerous room in the house if you take simple precautions. This is not ever considered a play area, and children will abide by simple, reasonable rules for its use.

Drinking fountain. A drinking fountain mounted on the sink will save time and reduce the number of dirty cups and mild colds you experience. Fountains for the home area are hard to find, but sinks with fountains on them are sold for service stations. For the years of convenience and service it provides, a drinking fountain/sink combination is worth the search and the cost.

Cupboards. All medicine, soap, shampoo, and household cleaning materials should be kept in a high, locked cupboard. Most children will ignore these materials, but there will be one who will make you glad you installed the locks. Keep ipecac syrup and other

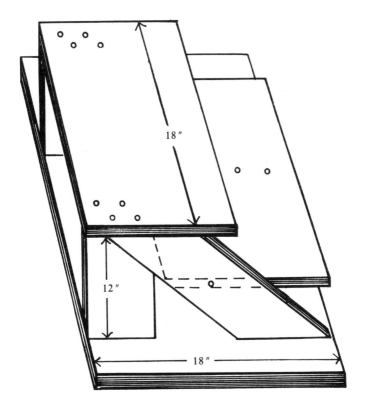

The Tipless Step
Pieces fit together in grooves and are then screwed together.
Another piece of 2' × 4' is cut and screwed in under the
bottom step to support the middle of the step.

medicines for children in a locked but readily accessible cupboard or toolbox.

Safety pins. Keep diaper pins stuck in a bar of soap; the pins will be much easier to use and always be where you can find them.

Towels. Buy secondhand towels to use in the bathroom, at the beach, for cleaning up children, and as rags. One towel should be fastened securely near the sink where children can use it but not remove it.

Bathtub. The bathtub should have a hose with a showerhead attachment, for cleaning children after a day in the dirt or at the beach, and a rubber mat. If you decide to allow water play, keep the necesary toys in a plastic bucket near the tub.

Potty chair. I recommend two potty chairs if you have children under three. The plastic chairs are unstable and tip easily; I buy secondhand wooden chairs that have square, solid bottoms at garage sales and thrift shops.

Water temperature. Adjust the hot-water heater to keep the temperature at 130 °F. Although this may not feel very hot to an adult, brief contact with water even a little hotter can scald a child. Fortunately, I had lowered the hot-water temperature before a two-year-old somehow unscrewed the handle on the hot-water tap in the bathroom sink, unleashing a warm geyser that rose almost to the ceiling. That incident prompted the "no play in the bathroom" rule.

Nap Room

The nap room is used for both taking naps and giving children time out. It is also the adult bedroom, housing the queen-sized bed and bounded on three sides with children's sleeping places. This room is never used as a play area, with the exception of the games of Doctor and Baby. The other bedroom is converted into a nap room daily by laying out the cots, which are otherwise kept stacked and hanging in the corner on the wall. Some children go to sleep more easily and sleep longer than others. Children who need the least sleep are placed near the door; children who need more are placed farthest from the door. I arrange the children head to toe or toe to toe whenever possible. Children will usually fall asleep in five minutes if you follow these arrangements and stand in the doorway, hushing any noise.

Stairs and Open Doorways

All stairs and any open doorways that lead to areas not open to children should be closed by gates or doors with latches or locks. Any closed door leading to stairs that might swing open if pushed by a child should be latched at the top.

Outside Play Areas

Outside play areas should be clearly defined for the children. A back-yard play area for young children should be fenced in; the limits for play on the sidewalk should be clearly marked, either by telephone poles or some other physical landmark. I keep a sandbox in the front yard and a jungle gym, hammock, picnic table, and tire swings in the back yard. Any outside play area should be carefully searched for sticks, broken glass, and poisonous plants. See the next page for a rendering of my back-yard play area.

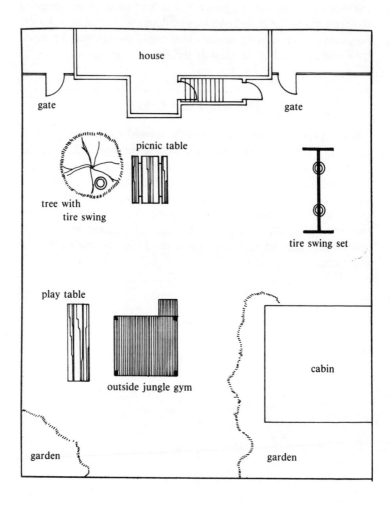

Back-yard Play Area
800 square feet, aerial view

12

Structure and Rules

People often say my day care home looks "unstructured," yet it has a complex structure, one that is not at first apparent to the casual observer. The structure designed by the adult sets the tone of the day care home and reflects the provider's personal values. Children will sometimes grasp this definition far more quickly than their parents do.

Rules and their consistent enforcement are the basis of a child's feeling of security, at home or away from home. Children are more comfortable, more secure, and more confident of their ability to fulfill expectations when they know the rules. Through consistent enforcement an adult will gain children's confidence and respect as they learn that the adult is above all fair and predictable. When rules are formed with the children's needs as well as the adult's needs in mind, they help to ensure that children are not put into impossible situations. Rules define outer limits and help children control behavior that they find frightening.

In a way, it is true that "rules are made to be broken." When children know a rule but are still free to decide whether or not to break it, they and the adult have an opportunity to examine the rule, the required behavior, the rationale for change, the responsibility of the individual, and future intent. When children participate in examining their own social order and take responsibility for the consequences or chaos of breaking rules, they more readily work to support their social system.

Specific rules define expectations for children based on their individual maturity and development, and realistic expectations are an important part of the structure of a day care home. There is no rule that a three-year-old must buckle his or her own shoe, but there is a flexible expectation that children will become independent and at the same time help another in need. The three-year-old is expected to try to buckle his own shoe before asking for help; and when he has learned to buckle his shoe, he is expected to help others.

For most people, the most obvious sign of structure in a day care home or center is a schedule of activities. Many adults seem to feel that a strict schedule of activities means constructive adult attention, whereas a lax or open schedule means that the children are not given anything to do and are not learning. To focus on scheduling activities for children is to deny them the freedom to follow their imaginations and create their own structure. A reasonable set of rules for safety and courtesy gives children the required framework within which to develop their own social system and subrules and to abide by them. Allowed to define their own structure within safe limits, children will negotiate rules for games and solve complex problems. They will learn self-discipline and self-control. A child denied the opportunity to explore his or her capacities in this way may grow into an adult who must have rules in order to know what to do.

School-age children can appreciate and enjoy a democratic approach to determining rules, and rules established in this way will be more effective than rules ordained by a parent or provider. Children are very serious about rules they define themselves and will be quick to ensure that those rules are working. Children four years old and younger are not yet ready for this type of rule-making; a democratic meeting is usually too remote in time from the relevant situation to be meaningful. Children at this age will learn the principles behind the rules if you discuss feelings as problems arise. Gradually they will learn that the rules protect each child and ensure the safety and happiness of the group. Children who are standing nearby will listen, and before long all the children will have heard the rules related several times to real situations. If a rule is not somehow related to a specific situation, a child may feel that it is arbitrary and try to reject it. Children are reasonable about rules as long as they can understand or sense a purpose behind them.

Keep rules simple in the beginning. Restrict only those activities that might be harmful to a child or might needlessly destroy property. Also restrict those activities that you cannot tolerate. Children will understand and accept your needs if you make them known. If you cannot tolerate the squeak of balloon-rubbing, keep balloon play in a separate room. If you cannot tolerate fussing, say so and use the time-out method.

Developing Rules

Through posing the following questions and experimenting with answers, you and the children can come to an understanding about the need for and implementation of specific rules.

How do you like to be treated?
— Fairly. You want your friends to make sure that you have a turn.
— With consideration. You want your friends to think about how you feel; you want them to talk to you in a nice voice; you want them to tell you how they feel when they are unhappy or angry with you so you know what is going on; you want them to tell you what they need; and you want them to ask you for things instead of grabbing or bossing.

Do you like to be included?
— You want the other children to include you in their activity and give you a turn to be the character you want to be in the game; you want the kids to change their game sometimes to make room for you, even after they have already started to play.

Do you want to have time playing with just one other person sometimes without interruption from others?
— You want the other kids to understand that you don't have very much time to play with this person and you need some private time with this friend.

Do you need privacy and quiet time once in a while?
— You want your friends to respect your need to play alone.

Do you expect your friends to accept your apologies when you make a mistake?

Do you expect your friends to be sorry when they hurt you or your feelings accidentally?

Do you want to be allowed to leave a game if you change your mind about playing?

Do you want to have the choice to play a game regardless of
whether it seems to be a game for younger or older children,
boys or girls?

Does being teased hurt your feelings or make you angry?

General Principles

However questions are posed to a child and whatever the specific
answers might be, certain general principles emerge that should
be reflected in every individual rule. No child wants to be made
to feel small or hurt or less than equal and worthwhile. Each child
has a responsibility to be treated as she or he would like to be
treated. These are simple principles to recognize and articulate,
but they require effort to follow every day. To ensure that no one
loses sight of these values, I describe them in three examples —
saving face, copycatting, and being fair.

Saving Face

Saving face is very important for children and should be a consideration when disciplining them. The most important element in
allowing the child to save face is the tone of the adult's voice. A
matter-of-fact tone, a tone of concern or even sometimes a tone
conveying alarm is appropriate. A tone suggesting shame, humiliation, belittling, ridicule, or excessive anger is not only nonproductive but very often will cause resentment or hostility. When disciplining the child, it is important to state the situation in terms of
"I" rather than "you," such as "I can't stand yelling in the house."
In addition, to help the child accept discipline without resentment,
do not allow any other child to comment on the disciplining. This
"no comment" rule helps keep the conversation focused on the
specific incident and prevents other children from assuming an
unequal, authoritarian role. Two books, *How To Parent* and
Between Parent and Child, offer excellent advice on communicating
with children, and I have found them to be the most useful for
help in solving interpersonal problems with children.

Copycatting

There are two kinds of copycatting. The first is an intentional mimicking in order to tease or anger another; it is frequently used for verbal revenge. This type of copycatting comes under the rule that forbids teasing or hurting of any kind.

The second kind is different; it is an expression of admiration or desire to learn a behavior or skill. When older children understand that a younger child sometimes mimics because "she likes you and wants to be like you, she wants to learn to do the things that you do and to talk like you do," they often accept this form of copycatting as a compliment, and understand that it is important for the younger child.

Being Fair

I have used the term *fair* in many places as the mainstay of your relationship with the children. What does *fair* mean to them, and how do you interpret *fair*? To a child, *fair* often means that each person gets the same-sized piece, that each person has to help clean up the same number of toys, or that the discipline is predictable regardless of the person involved. Adults recognize that being fair is not as simple as it may seem to a five-year-old. Each child has the right to be considered as an individual, different from other children. Children can be taught to understand that individual differences in age, development, and social sophistication necessitate treating children in different ways to some degree. How much responsibility can a one-year-old bear in the 11:30 A.M. clean-up effort? You can help older children accept these inequities by helping them to recall earlier times and situations when they felt overwhelmed by some expectation. You can point out that it is not fair to expect a three-year-old girl to act like an eight-year-old boy. Each person's life is different from every other person's life. The fair thing to do is to consider each person in light of his or her uniqueness. Design the expectation, or the size of the plate of food, or the discipline, in terms of that child's maturity. What must be consistent across all differences is the consideration and respect to which all children, as well as adults, are entitled.

Rules on Property and Safety

I try to keep the rules in my day care home to a minimum, limiting them to what children need to know in order to feel secure and safe. Many of the rules listed here have been discussed earlier, but I repeat them here to give a complete list of the rules of my home. Most of these are on proper use, proper care, and proper behavior. Because children have a great deal of freedom in my home, they enter many situations that require guidelines.

What Not to Bring to Day Care

- A child should not bring toys that cannot be shared. We take turns with all the things in my home; toys and equipment are for everyone. Anything a child brings will be treated like the other things, even though it still belongs to the child.
- Food should not be brought to day care unless I have pre-arranged it with the parent for some special occasion. There is plenty of food for each child at day care; the food is good, and we share food together.
- No gum or candy can be brought to day care. Young children cannot keep gum in their mouths; it ends up on the rug or in someone's hair. Candy is not nutritious; the body doesn't need it and it causes teeth problems. There are other good things to eat that taste sweet but will not hurt a child's teeth.
- Children should not bring jewelry except sturdy costume jewelry; if they bring jewelry, they should know that it may be broken or lost by accident. Jewelry is delicate and does not last long when many kids are anxious for a turn. Rings are very small and will probably get lost.
- Party clothes are fun to wear. If a child wears dressy clothes to day care, he or she should bring play clothes too.
- Children should ask Mom or Dad before bringing anything to day care. Sometimes a parent will have different ideas about what should leave the house with their child.

Rules on Safety

- Children are not allowed to go into the basement.
- Children may never go through the gates in the back yard. They must go through the house to get to the front yard from the back.
- Children are not allowed to open the medicine chest. Medicine is dangerous unless given by an adult.
- Throwing anything is not permitted in the house.
- Children are not allowed to hurt each other or me.

Rules for Adult Property

- Children are not to touch anything on my desk.
- Children are not to touch the stereo system in my bedroom.
- Children are not to open drawers in my bedroom or in the sewing-machine cabinet.
- Other. (Add rules protecting your valuables.)

Rules for Toys

Big Wheel

The tricycle known as Big Wheel is a favorite toy: It is easy to stop, comes in several sizes, and makes a child feel powerful. Our home is on a hill with a moderate slope. For this reason I have set a limit far from the bottom corner to allow plenty of room for stopping. This leaves children about 150 feet in which to build up speed and scrape to a stop. They will rise up from their powerful chariots with appropriate grins and swagger up to the next kid awaiting a turn. Rules are as follows:

- Children must wear shoes, and no loose clothing hanging down.
- No running in front of or behind Big Wheel.
- No jumping from ramps or boards set up to form jumping platforms.
- Children must stop at the designated boundaries.
- No crashes; reckless driving means loss of driving privileges.
- One child at a time on each Big Wheel.

- No skidding to a stop by sudden turn of the front wheel. (This wears it out too fast.)
- Big Wheel must be brought back to the yard after each ride.
- Big Wheel must be in the storage area under the porch before 5:30 P.M.

Water Play

- Squirt guns can be used outside — but only with others who have a squirter. I prefer spray bottles to squirt guns: They last longer, are cheaper, and are not shaped like a gun.
- An adult must control the water hose (on or off, and how much water). Children are allowed to handle the hose when the sprinkler head is on. Children over three years can play with the sprinkler and about four inches of water in the plastic pool under loose supervision. Younger children need close supervision, even in what seems to be a harmless amount of water.
- No water play in the bathroom. Playing in water does not hurt anyone, but there are too many children in day care for water play inside.

Seesaw (Tube frame, metal)

- Children should stop when someone wants to get on or off.
- The maximum number is three kids at a time.
- Do not turn the seesaw upside down to use as a bridge; it is not strong enough.

Play Dough

- Children should take as much as they can hold in two hands. (Sometimes older children have a project in mind that requires more; you can make exceptions.)
- Play dough should be kept at the table.
- It should not be mixed with toys. (Children may want to do this occasionally, but this severely limits their imaginations.)
- If all the play dough is in use and a new child comes to the table, each person must contribute a little to the new child.
- Children should put play dough back into the plastic container and put its top on tightly when finished.

Art Supplies

- Fine-tip pens can be used by children four and older. In the hands of younger children the tips are easily pushed inside the pen and cannot be retrieved.
- Cone-shaped or Crayola pens may be used by younger children.
- Tops should be replaced on all pens except those in immediate use.
- Paper is used one piece at a time. Children take care of it when they are finished — put it on the wall, on the shelf to go home, or in the fireplace or basket.
- Only scissors with rounded tips may be used. Children pick up their own cuttings.
- Watercolors can be used by children over four. (Younger children enjoy finger paint, but do not have the dexterity to handle watercolor brushes.)
- Poster paints with heavy brushes can be used by younger children.
- Children should keep crayons and pens on the table and replace all in container when finished.

Puzzles

- Only one puzzle should be taken down at a time by a child.
- A child should finish any puzzle he takes down. If he needs help, he should ask an older child. Replace the puzzle on the proper shelf before taking out another.

Books

- Books are for looking at and reading and discussing; they are not to be played with or incorporated into games such as Store or Office.
- Books must be kept inside the house except when taken outside by the adult for group use or with adult permission.
- All books are to be returned to their proper places after each use.

Dress-Up Clothes

- After children select an outfit, they should put all unwanted clothes back in the trunk.
- The timer can be set to allot specified amounts of time with favorite costumes.

Indoor Jungle Gym

- The jungle gym and its platforms are to be moved only by an adult.

Battery-Operated Toys

- Batteries should be inserted for use and removed when children are finished with the toy.
- These toys should be returned to their proper places when play with them is over.

Records

- Before playing a record, the children should decide who is currently in charge of operating the record player and who is in charge of choosing the records.

Toy Box

The toy box is a cardboard box or boxes for small toys that do not have a special place on a shelf. Two-year-olds can pick up their toys in a reasonable amount of time (fifteen minutes of supervised and directed activity) and deposit them in the toy box. It is fun and good experience for the children occasionally to sort the toys into smaller containers labeled with words and pictures. If there are many younger children (under one and a half), older children find it frustrating to do the sorting for the younger ones at clean-up time, so let the sorting be done at other times as an activity if younger children are enthusiastic about putting things away and need to learn to put things in the right containers.

Toys that can be sorted are little cars, little people, puppets, doll-house furniture, dress-up clothes, art materials, dolls, tools, marbles, Legos, blocks, Checkers, dominos, play dishes. Toy boxes are especially helpful in enabling the youngest children to share in the pick-up responsibility to the best of their ability. (Full boxes of toys can be easily stored in the top of a closet until needed. The children will later greet these as new toys.)

Other Equipment

In general, whatever a child can reach without using a chair is intended for his or her use. If a chair is required, the equipment probably needs adult supervision. Equipment in the closets or the private special boxes belonging to my own children may be used only with my children's permission. If my children bring anything out during day care time from these boxes, the toys will be shared and used by all children of the appropriate age.

13

Enriching the Day Care Experience

Children who go to day care five full days a week may spend more of their waking hours with the provider than with their parents. Day care can be the significant fact in a child's life. Here children make new and lasting friends, discover new ideas and values, and explore a larger world than many have previously known. But the day care world is often something that parents know little about.

It is the provider's special responsibility to integrate the child's day care world with the rest of his or her life and to integrate the parents into the day care world. Drawing together families and children in a network that gives a wholeness to each individual's life will enrich the day care experience for all. Usually day care children live too far apart to visit and play on weekends, but their friendships are important to them, and they want to show each other their homes and parents and favorite toys. Parents, on the other hand, are often preoccupied with the idea of giving children a special time — so-called high-quality time — that will make up for the lack of time they spend with them. Working closely with the provider to ensure that children are doing the many things that parents consider important — including special trips to zoos and other places — will help parents realize that the only thing their child might lack is quiet time with them. When they recognize the fullness of the day care experience, parents realize that they can enjoy their time at home with their child simply and quietly. The child will enjoy more simply being with the parent in their own home in the day-to-day routine of living, and the parent will be able to give the fundamental nurturing that children thrive on. Parent and child can make dinner together or play cards, knowing that they have both had a full and busy day and can now enjoy the quiet pleasure of each other's company.

There are many ways to enrich the day care experience for parents and children — and all should be fun and interesting. The more parents become involved in these events, the greater will be their satisfaction with day care, and in turn, the happier their children will be. The events and methods described below are only examples of what a provider can do; there are many more possibilities than those listed.

Progressive Dinner

I planned a progressive dinner to coincide with Christmas, which also coincides with Willow's third birthday, but no special occasion is necessary. It seems to be particularly important to children aged two and a half to four years to be part of this event. You can invite the other children, younger and older, if the group is not too large, or you can limit this event to the younger children and plan another event for the older children. The first year we limited the group to five families with children between two and a half and four years; we had eight children and their parents. You will want to limit the evening to about four hours, which may be too long for most adults but is essential to get all the homes in.

The day care provider will have to do the organizing, planning, and scheduling, and may have to help some families prepare for the part of the party taking place in their homes. Be sure you take a camera or arrange for two other people to take pictures. These tangible reminders bring untold delight to the children in the months to come.

We gathered at the day care home at 4:00 P.M. on Sunday afternoon. Each family was given a list of addresses and a schedule, and we drove to the first home, about three miles away. I planned the route so that most of the driving would be done early in the day, thus avoiding the possibility of losing people later because of fatigue and darkness.

The first stop was Willow's house. We gathered in the living room, sang "Happy Birthday" and Christmas carols as well as other favorites, and ate vegetables, dip, and pineapple upside-down birthday cake. Children are always glad to start with dessert.

There seems to be no problem with this order when children know that there is spaghetti and another dessert yet to come.

At 5:00 P.M., on schedule, we departed in our respective cars, but children could ride in any car they chose. Some cars had no children, and others had several, but not the child belonging to that family.

Second stop: David's house. We trooped down to the basement shortly after everyone arrived and after David had shown everyone his room and favorite things. Our hostess, David's mother, brought down the spaghetti dinner, and each parent served and ate with his or her own child. When the children finished, I passed out Christmas presents. Each child unwrapped a small box of fabric crayons and a plain white T-shirt, one size too large. The T-shirts were a cotton-synthetic blend to ensure the success of the fabric crayon designs. I set up an iron and ironing board while the children drew pictures. There was lots of scribbling, but each child had an individual scribble. Parents encouraged children to put lots of color on the paper to ensure an impressive shirt. As the children finished they brought me their shirts and papers, and I ironed a design on each shirt by turning the drawing face down on the shirt and using a hot iron on the back of the paper. (You can lift the corner of the paper to see how much of the crayon is transferring to the shirt. When the design is nice and bright, the shirt is finished. The design is permanent; it does not run in the wash or stain other clothing.) The children were delighted with their new outfits for the evening. As soon as the last child finished this project, we moved on to the next home, leaving the mess for later.

Next stop: Teo's house. Teo, aged three and a half, and her father, Ted, hosted a tree-decorating party. The children had made decorations from play dough in day care (see the recipe and decorations in Chapter 11), an important personal investment for them. They also enjoyed making and hanging paper chains. One parent stapled the loops together as the children finished them. Parents enjoyed this chance to meet each other and learn about their children's friends. At 7:00 P.M. we left for the last home, Kristi's house.

Kristi, three and a half, lives two blocks from my day care home. The children ate ice cream and opened another set of presents. We hung a piñata stuffed with small toys and packages of corn nuts. Each child took a turn in order of size, with the shortest child first. Blindfolded, the youngest needed an adult's guiding hand to make contact with the piñata. As usual, the last child broke the piñata, and kazoos and toys and corn nuts scattered along with the kids. Piñatas are a useful tool in teaching consideration and fairness, since the oldest children invariably scoop up the most loot, leaving the youngest with very little, if anything. Although the young children may not care, we always end by sitting in a circle and trading until everyone seems content. The older children are encouraged, and are usually more than willing, to make sure that all the children feel they have what they need. Often this does not mean having exactly the same amount of everything. For some older children, getting the goods is the important part, and it is easy for them to give to a smaller child and enjoy being generous and receiving the child's gratitude.

By the end of the evening the children were happily tired and the parents had established new links to their children's daily lives.

Trick-or-Treat

Trick-or-treating is an activity that will center around children three and a half and older. On one occasion children dressed in Halloween costumes gathered at my home, and parents took turns accompanying them around the neighborhood. Another time we took the young children in one car to each family's house for a short trick-or-treat visit, followed by cider and donuts at one home and Pin the Tail on the Donkey and Blind Man's Bluff at another. The evening always began with face-painting at the day care home.

This can be an especially important event for parents. Many adults remember a mild October evening spent trick-or-treating in their youth, but consider the practice today less safe for children. By arranging a Halloween party, the provider can assure the children of the opportunity to continue a tradition their parents knew and assure the parents of a safe and enjoyable evening.

Potluck Dinner

A potluck dinner or picnic is always successful. The Fourth of July offers an occasion for day care families to gather, and the potluck dinner or lunch can be held in a private home or in a nearby park, while children spend the afternoon playing games. Children enjoy the holiday and fireworks and the chance to play with their friends in a different environment.

Weekend Outings

A weekend trip for day care families requires extensive planning, but can be less work than expected. In order for the parents to have time with the children, the provider should plan to do most of the cooking, with occasional adult help. If each family cooks separately, no one will have time for the children. Rent cabins at a nearby resort for one night and plan a dinner for the evening. The parents and children will have time to play and explore and help with the food preparation as needed.

Field Trips

Field trips are fraught with hazard, but can benefit both parents and children. If there is a special event parents want their child to experience, the provider can organize a field trip for all day care children. As a general rule, I never took more than eight children on a field trip and never took any child who did not immediately follow directions or whose judgment I questioned. This means that no children were under four years old. If you decide to take three-year-olds, you will need to hire another adult or to limit the size of the group. In a group of three-year-olds, there must be enough adults to hold each child by the hand.

Field trips to museums, zoos, parks, libraries, and even parents' offices offer children variety and new experiences and reassure parents that their children are not missing valuable opportunities. These trips should be spaced so that children understand that they are special events that complement the regular day care schedule. You will not be able to take children on field trips every day or even every week throughout the year; the summer months are best, but worthwhile programs for children are available throughout the year.

Summer Schedule

During the summer you will probably have some full-time school-age children, increasing the number of children in your home throughout the day. Cities and towns schedule a number of activities for children of all ages during the summer months, and the day care provider can arrange for children to participate. Because of the increased number of activities and children during this time, you should hire an assistant.

During the spring, collect information from the various organizations that offer programs for children during the summer: parks, YMCA, YWCA, schools, churches, libraries, arts councils and so on. Using a large piece of cardboard, draw up a calendar of all possible events — swimming lessons, reading groups, painting classes, puppet shows — and post it in the entryway of your home; if there is a fee for any event, list that too. As the summer advances, you can choose from the available activities, depending on the weather and the composition of the group. On some days you will spend most of your time driving children to one or another activity; on other days you may want to stay at home with the younger or nonparticipating children while your assistant drives. Older children will enjoy the variety and excitement of new activities; younger children at home will enjoy the calm and smaller size of the day care group.

If few activities are offered in your area, plan to take the children on picnics to the beach or park. Children will find this change as exciting as the most exotic field trip. You will need to take enough equipment to occupy children after they are finished exploring; following is a list of things to take on a picnic with children.

Picnic Ideas

Take:
  blanket
  first-aid kit
  towels
  washrag or two
  large piece of plastic
  juice can opener
  spreading knife
  plastic bag
  game book

Beach toys:
  scooping-pouring things
  sieve, funnel
  large spoons
  squirt bottles
  plastic bucket

Lawn toys
  balls
  frisbee
  squirt bottles

Foods:
  frozen juice
  juice container with lid
  cut raw vegetables in a little
    water in tightly closed
    plastic container
  fruit in its skin
  pickles
  hard-boiled eggs
  cooled squares of spinach
    soufflé

  popcorn
  container of sandwich mix
    and loaf of bread
  rice-cake crackers and cheese
  yogurt fruit salad
  shredded raw vegetable salad
  cornbread
  muffins
  string cheese

Take kids to beach in swimming clothes; use plastic to cover car seat for the ride home. Avoid taking shoes and socks when possible, or take one container for all the shoes, socks, and other clothing.

Parent Meetings

The day care home environment does not usually lend itself to meetings, but parents involved in day care homes have most of the same needs as parents involved in day care centers, where there are meetings. After having been involved in a large day care center, I realized that parents will come to gatherings organized for them if they are interested in the agenda or a particular subject scheduled for discussion. In most large cities, speakers are available to address small groups of parents. PET (Parent Effectiveness Training) people are always interested in talking to groups of parents, and members of the public health department, children's hospitals, and universities are also available.

On one occasion my day care parents raised questions about the sexual activity of their children in day care. I arranged an evening gathering to enable parents to discuss the general topic of values and sexual behavior of young children with a member of the education department of Planned Parenthood. This proved to be a very interesting evening. Parents were so enthusiastic that we arranged a second meeting, to which several parents invited friends from outside the day care group.

Informational meetings on topics of interest to your parents will make your job easier. When you introduce speakers with formal credentials, you can avoid telling parents things they may not want to hear or accept but from which they can benefit. These meetings provide parents with new information on the problems we all face in raising children.

Baby-Sitting Co-op

The day care home is an ideal starting point for baby-sitting exchange; you can begin with known families and expand on the basis of personal contact and experience. On the following page is a list of by-laws for a baby-sitting exchange that has been successful in several communities across the country. Not all neighborhoods will want to adopt this system, but it is usually successful with families of young professionals interested in developing

Baby-Sitting Co-op By-Laws

1. Membership will be limited to forty families.
2. The position and the responsibilities of secretary will rotate every two months.
3. Members earn one credit per hour of sitting time, one additional credit for each meal provided, and one additional credit if sitting after midnight.
4. One credit is donated by each family to the secretary each month as compensation for his or her time.
5. When members need a sitter, they should call the current secretary with the request. The secretary will find a sitter, and the sitter will call the requesting party to make arrangements. Requests should be made as far in advance as possible.
6. The sitter will come to requester's home for evening sitting.
7. The requester will bring children to the sitter's home for daytime sitting.
8. Hours of debt will be limited to ten, but credits may be earned without limit.
9. Members with the highest debt will be called first for sitting in an effort to give members the opportunity to remain active.
10. The requester may ask the secretary not to call certain members without explanation.
11. The sitter will call the secretary and report credits earned within three days.
12. When leaving the co-op, members will pay $1.50 per hour of debt in order to hire a sitter to make up their time.

Each new member will receive a current list of members, which will continually be updated.

strong community ties. This structure will provide a group of forty families with reliable adult child care on an occasional or frequent basis without exchange of money. It is a good tool for forming friendships in a community and for finding playmates for children before they enter school. Sitting in each others' homes gives the participants greater experience with the members of their community and increases feelings of belonging and security.

Lending Library

Parents will be enthusiastic users of both your children's and your parenting books. Begin your library with those listed on the following page. Keep a notebook near the bookshelf for parents to record the name of the book they borrow. If you want to increase your library, discuss a lending fee with parents; the fee will enable you to expand the selection. The public library is a good resource, but is not always convenient. Children, especially, will want to take home books in which they have immediate interest. Day care families can contribute books to the library for a few months or suggest books to buy. Reserve a high shelf for this library.

Bulletin Board

Some cities and towns publish a list of children's activities. This and material from the public library, park department, community college, and other organizations should be posted where parents can see it. I use a large corkboard in the kitchen for this.

Clothing and Toy Exchange

You will accumulate leftover clothing, which should be visible for parents to claim. You can expand this to include an area for the exchange of outgrown items. In some cities charitable organizations will collect donations at your home and you can dispose of unwanted items and start over. Before giving anything away, I pin leftover clothes on a clothesline on the front porch for one week; if they are not claimed in that time, I donate them to charity.

Photographs

Photographs of day care children and activities reinforce the bonds that children develop in day care by allowing them to see themselves and their friends of the present and previous years and enjoy the continuity in their lives in day care. I keep an album of these photographs on the bookshelves and a bulletin board of individual photographs in the entryway. The pictures stay posted as long as there is a child who remembers the children in the photograph.

There will be times when you know your day care children will be changing; suddenly three children are too old for day care, and a younger child is moving. When this happened to me, I called upon two parents to help with a photograph. I arranged for *all* of the children to be present on the last day of school, which was the last day of day care for all four children. The parents took photographs, and I selected one that showed at least the face of every child. From this photograph I had a large black-and-white poster made for each child (not each family). The children will have these for years to come as a reminder of their day care family and friends — their first community of friendship.

Books for Parents and Day Care Providers

Boston Children's Hospital Medical Center, and Elizabeth M. Gregg. *What To Do When "There's Nothing To Do."* New York: Dell, 1968.

Dodson, Fitzhugh. *How to Parent.* Los Angeles: Nash, 1970.

Dreikurs, Rudolf and Vicki Soltz. *Children: The Challenge.* New York: Dutton, 1964.

Fraiberg, Selma. *The Magic Years.* New York: Scribner's, 1959.

Ginott, Haim. *Between Parent and Child.* New York: Avon, 1969

Gordon, Thomas. *P.E.T., Parent Effectiveness Training.* New York: New American Library, 1975.

Hainstock, Elizabeth G. *Teaching Montessori in the Home.* New York: Random House, 1968.

Marzollo, Jean and Janice Lloyd. *Learning Through Play.* New York: Harper & Row, 1974.

McPhee Gribble Publishers. *Cover-Ups: Things to Put on Yourself.* New York: Penguin Books, 1978.

Montessori, Maria. *The Home School.* Bethesda, Md.: Elad Enterprises, 1963.

Parents' Choice, Box 185. Waban, Mass. 02168. Magazine published every other month reviewing all media for children, including books, music, TV programming, movies, games and toys.

14

Closing Up for
New Beginnings

Day care is a unique business — it is both demanding and
rewarding in very personal ways. There are few occupations in
life in which individuals can have such a significant impact on
others' lives as they can in day care homes. The demands and
rewards can remain in balance for many years, and the business
and its participants continue to thrive. To be aware of the need
for this balance will keep the provider alert to any problems that
she must solve or changes that she must make. But for some, a
time will come when the rewards no longer balance the demands,
and the need to remain in this particular business no longer exists.
The provider should ask herself periodically, "Would I choose
to do this again today?" If someday the answer is no, it is time
to consider moving on to other things — perhaps work related
to day care or to children, perhaps something else. For whatever
reason you choose to leave the day care business — another job,
a move to another state — you should plan this aspect of your
business as carefully as you have planned every other. You must
consider the emotional investment children and their families have
made in your day care home; the transition in your life will be
an important transition for them also.

When I decided to leave the day care business, I realized that
it would mean a major change in the lives of each child and family,
and I began to plan the transition several months in advance. I
informed each family individually of my decision. The first consideration was keeping the children together. A day care home is like
a large family, and children are led into an association with each
other that cannot and should not be abruptly broken. The emotional fabric that makes the day care home a success needs special
care during a major transition.

Finding a New Provider

Some providers may find it easier simply to refer the parents to other day care homes, but this is only a last resort. With effort and time you will be able to find a new provider to take over your day care family, but you will probably have to interview several people several times before you find a satisfactory replacement. I talked with several women who simply would not believe that the day care business can be successful. Others would have been interested earlier in their children's lives or before undertaking other careers. Still others lacked qualifications I had come to believe were of primary importance: one lacked the support of her husband, and another had serious marital problems. A third woman had provided day care successfully for two years, but quit to seek employment away from home and been unable to find anything that paid as well, and was reconsidering day care — but she was tentative and therefore not a good choice. I met another prospective provider in my favorite thrift shop. She had worked as my assistant one summer, done very well with the children, had a three-year-old child, and was considering leaving her job to have a second child. She was enthusiastic as well as qualified. My day care children would be especially fortunate in entering a new home with a provider they already knew.

Finding a New Location

The new home should be as near the current one as possible. Location is usually a factor in the parents' original decision, and this must be taken into consideration. Schoolchildren need a day care home that is near their school or qualifies for transportation to it. In Seattle, for instance, children who live or attend day care less than two miles from the school must get there on their own; children who live farther away are eligible for school-bus transportation. It is important, therefore, to locate the day care home either *very* close to the school, so that children can walk (perhaps five or six blocks), or far enough away to qualify for busing. The provider should not be responsible for the children's transportation to and from school, because it is almost impossible for one person to combine the schedules of preschool and school-age children.

In my case, both the new day care mother, Heidi, and I searched for an appropriate house to rent. We found several, and narrowed our choices to two. Heidi chose the one she preferred, then spent several weeks preparing the home. She purchased my day care equipment. We agreed that I would continue day care until the last day of school — a natural point to make a change.

Ending and Beginning

For my group, the change from one day care home to another was a passage that deserved a formal marking. To meet this need I planned a special weekend outing. I reserved nine cabins at a nearby beach resort for the current day care families and a few families from the past. The grounds consist of fifteen cabins arranged in a horseshoe shape, with a large, well-kept grassy area in the middle and a beach at the open end. The gradual slope of the beach allows children to go far into the water safely, and the beach is rich with horse clams and fine sand for play. Since I began to plan this career change three months in advance, parents had ample time to make plans for the weekend. Heidi, the new day care provider, did more planning and the shopping, whereas I chose to do the cooking. There was a constant stream of parents in and out of the cabins, visiting and helping throughout the weekend. Children and parents swam, played on the beach, and dug for clams. At one meal we had potluck; at another we barbecued.

What did we gain from this weekend? In addition to bringing the families closer together and strengthening their ties in preparation for the adjustment to come, we gave the children a concrete event that would link one home to the next. For Heidi, this was a chance to meet the parents as a group; for the parents, it was a chance to transfer their loyalty to their new day care provider. For me, it was a celebration of accomplishment and my last gift to the group as a whole, given in appreciation of the constant support I received during the previous five years.

APPENDICES

Appendix A
Information Handouts for Parents about Sexuality.
These handouts were developed by Seattle-area residents
and the Harborview Medical Center's Sexual Assault Center.
I suggest that you look for materials from similar
organizations in your own city.

Appendix B
Children's Book List.

Appendix C
TRADE Instructions and Description, with drawing
and details for use of this unique numbers game with
children of different age groups.

A

Information Handouts for Parents About Sexuality

What To Do
If Your Child Has Been Sexually Molested...

Be Aware That:

1. Children are usually molested by people they know — often a relative or friend of the family.
2. Children are usually not violently attacked or hurt physically during a sexual assault.
3. Children very seldom lie about such a serious matter.
4. Not all children are able to tell parents directly that they have been molested. Changes in behavior, reluctance to be with a certain person or go to a certain place may be signals that something has happened.

What To Do Immediately:

1. Go with the child to a private place. Ask the child to tell you what happened in her/his own words, and listen carefully.
2. Tell her/him s/he did well to tell you, that you are very sorry this happened, and that you will protect her/him from further molestation.
3. If you suspect your child has an injury, contact your regular physician or Harborview Medical Center's Emergency Room immediately.
4. You may call the police immediately and a uniformed officer will come to your house to take an initial report.
5. You may call the Sexual Assault Center, 223-3047 (Monday–Friday, 8:00am–5:00pm) or 223-3010 (24 hour coverage, ask for the Emergency Room Social Worker) for advice and information about what to do. 632-RAPE and Children's Protective Services, 464-7333, are also available 24 hours/day.

Helping Your Child Following the Assault:

1. Continue to believe your child and do not blame your child for what happened.
2. Consult with your physician or the Sexual Assault Center regarding need for medical examination.
3. Instruct your child to tell you immediately if the offender attempts sexual molestation again or bothers her/him in any way.
4. Give your child reassurance and support that s/he is okay and safe.
5. Respond to questions or feelings your child expresses about the molestation with a calm, matter-of-fact attitude but do not pressure your child to talk about it.
6. Respect privacy of child by not telling a lot of people or letting other people question her/him.
7. Try to follow regular routine around the home (expect usual chores, bedtimes, rules).
8. Inform brothers/sisters that something has happened to the child, but that s/he is safe now and will be okay. Do not discuss details of assault with brothers/sisters. Make sure that all children in the family are given enough information to protect themselves from the assailant.
9. Take the time to talk over your feelings privately with someone you trust — your spouse, a friend, a relative, a counselor; express your feelings. Do not discuss situation repeatedly in front of your child/children.

Most Common Immediate Problems of Sexually Molested Children:

1. Sleep disturbances (nightmares, fear of going to bed, wanting light on, waking up during night, fear of sleeping alone).
2. Loss of appetite.
3. Irritability, crankiness, short-tempered behavior.
4. Bedwetting.
5. Needing more reassurance than usual, clinging to parent.
6. Fears.
7. Behaving as a younger child (regression).
8. Changes in behavior at school or in relating to friends.
9. The adolescent may also act out her/his feelings, i.e., running away, skipping school, being rebellious.

These are normal signs of upset. Your child may have some of these problems or none at all. They usually will last a couple of weeks. Try to notice all changes in usual behavior, and discuss with your counselor.

No one knows for sure about long-term emotional effects, but we believe that if the situation is handled in a direct and sensitive way at the time it is revealed, your child need not suffer permanently from the assault.

Contact the Sexual Assault Center, 223-3047, for help: medical care; counseling for parents and the child; reporting to police and going to court; getting help for the offender; and any other concerns. You are not alone.

A report must be made to Children's Protective Service if there is any potential for further abuse of the child.

Sexual Abuse within the Family

The Problem

About one-half of children who are sexually assaulted are victims of intra-family sexual abuse. Seventy-five percent of the situations involve girls as victims and twenty-five percent are boys. The most common pattern is the oldest daughter being abused by a father, and in forty percent of the cases where there are other children, subsequent daughters are also abused. Children are also molested by older brothers and extended family members, e.g., grandfathers, uncles. Almost all offenders are male adults or teenagers. The abuse generally begins when the child is between six and nine years old and often continues for many years. The sexual contact may include fondling, forced masturbation, oral-genital contact, or vaginal or anal intercourse. Sometimes the incest is disclosed inadvertently, but more frequently disclosure occurs after the child has acquired enough independence to seek outside help. When disclosure occurs, the child and family are in a state of acute crisis.

Treatment Philosophy

The Sexual Assault Center treatment approach is based on the philosophy that incest is the outlet for the offender's sexual behavior disorder and that he (offender) must assume full responsibility for his behavior. Children are vulnerable targets for sexual abuse because of the natural authority that adults command and the powerlessness of the child within the family unit. For this reason, force is rarely used to insure submission and the child often has ambivalent feelings toward the offender. Pathological family dynamics usually result from this unhealthy distortion of the parental roles, and all children in these families experience some degree of emotional disturbance. All cases are reported to Children's Protective Service (CPS) as state law mandates, in order to provide the legal authority to protect the child.

Goals

The immediate goal of intervention is to protect the child from further abuse. Accomplishing this protection usually requires separation of the offender from the child until he has received adequate treatment. The focus of ongoing intervention is to meet the long term needs of the victim by providing extensive supportive assistance to the child as well as to the non-offending parent (usually the mother) and as appropriate, other children in the family.

Services

Referrals are accepted from any source: individuals, law enforcement, Children's Protective Service, social agencies, mental health practitioners, and clergy.

1. *Crisis intervention:* Counseling by professional social workers is available 24 hours a day, either through the Emergency Room or the Sexual Assault Center: initial assessment of the child, information, reassurance, assistance in treatment planning to ensure a safe and supportive environment for the victim.

2. *Medical care* by specially trained pediatricians: emergency and follow-up medical care, treatment of injury or infection, documentation of legal evidence, reassurance for patient and family.

3. *Advocacy:* Initiation and coordination of involvement with the criminal justice system and/or Children's Protective Service, accompaniment and support for the victim throughout the process, liaison between the victim and family and the criminal justice system. The victim and family are helped to understand the system and the court proceedings and the role of criminal justice system involvement as part of the victim's process of dealing with the emotional effects of the assault.

4. *Ongoing counseling* by telephone and in person: counseling is available for the victim and her family to build a sense of emotional well-being, change maladaptive or self-destructive behavior, restore the child to appropriate developmental level of functioning and repair mother-child relationship where indicated.

Individual counseling helps both the victim and mother clearly understand the offender's responsibility for the assault. The victim is helped to understand her feelings about herself, the offender, the other parent. The mother or non-offending parent is helped to better understand and fulfill the parental role with the child. Family counseling and parent-child counseling may occur concurrently. Victims and other family members may, as well, participate in group counseling. The type of groups offered at any time vary and may include: groups for child and adolescent victims; groups for the non-offending partner; groups for siblings of child victims; groups for couples (offender and partner) who desire to reunite.

5. *Offender services:* SAC provides crisis intervention and referral for treatment and evaluation to the sexual offender. While not offering ongoing offender treatment, SAC is closely aligned with expert offender treatment programs locally. Following referral of the offender, SAC maintains close case coordination with the appropriate offender treatment

resource and acts as a liaison between offender treatment and the family. The process of family decision-making regarding visitation and, in certain cases, the reuniting of the family, is a joint process involving the family, SAC, CPS and offender treatment.

A Few Hints — Communicating with Your Child about Sex

Do not use fables, myths or vagueness

Do use correct names, terms when explaining

Do not talk animals when your child wants to talk people

Do be patient — the same question may be asked over and over

Do not preach or lecture when your child simply wants information

Do listen to your child's ideas about sexuality

Do answer with honesty always

Do share with your child freely and often your values about sexuality

Do tell your children what they want to know using words they can understand

Do not wait until your child asks you — *You* may start the process

Do not postpone answering your child's questions

Do talk about sexuality in the context of everyday life

Do learn more about sexuality — if you don't know an answer, find out

Normal Sexual Development in Children: Major Landmarks

A. Birth through Two Years of Age
1. Family decides to encourage either a male or female identity.
2. Family and other significant adults teach either a positive or negative attitude to body parts, especially genitals.
3. Child naturally begins exploring genitals along with other body parts, unless stopped by parents.
4. Child first experiences awareness of genital pleasure.
5. Family either builds or discourages the development of trust and self-esteem in the child.

B. Three and Four Year Olds
1. Family continues to reinforce a male or female identity. The child becomes aware of gender differences.

    2. Child naturally seeks to stimulate genitals for pleasure, unless trained not to touch.

    3. Body exploration with children of both sexes is common.

    4. Child begins developing attitudes towards the opposite sex as well as his/her own sex.

    5. Child often wishes for a special relationship with the opposite sex parent and may see same sex parent as a competitor for the attention of the favored parent.

C. Five through Seven Years of Age

    1. Gender identity is now fixed as either male or female.

    2. Child usually gives up wish for special relationship with opposite sex parent and seeks a stronger identification with parent of the same sex.

    3. Mutual body exploration, primarily with children of the same sex, is common.

    4. Daydreams of fantasies about sex begin for many children.

    5. Confused feelings, even hostility, towards opposite sex are not uncommon.

D. Eight through Twelve Years of Age

    1. Peer group has increasing influence on the child's self-image.

    2. Beginning of separation from parents.

    3. Early menstruation begins in some girls.

    4. Body changes (breast growth, penis growth, pubic hair, etc.) in many girls and some boys.

    5. Strong feelings of modesty are common.

    6. Some children will begin masturbation. Orgasm is possible.

    7. Any sex play that occurs is hidden from adults.

E. From Age Thirteen

    1. Puberty and following body changes continue in boys and girls. Menstruation occurs in almost all girls by age 16. Ability to ejaculate in boys by age 15 to 16.

    2. Ovulation begins in girls usually 18 to 24 months after first menstrual period.

    3. Separation from parents as authority figures accelerates for many teenagers.

    4. Masturbation and sexual fantasies are common, especially for boys.

    5. Sexual attraction to the opposite sex becomes stronger...or awareness of a lack of attraction.

    6. Mood swings are frequent, especially regarding feelings toward body, from extremely self-critical to overly vain. More attention is paid to personal appearance and dress.

    7. Behavior towards opposite sex often follows norms of culture (i.e., dating, petting, etc.)

Books on Sexuality for Children, Ages 3–9

Baker, Gayle Cunningham and Vivian M. Montey. *Special Delivery: A Book for Kids About Cesarean and Vaginal Birth.* Charles Franklin Press, 18409 90th Avenue West, Edmonds, Washington 98020, 1981, $5.95.

Dragonwagon, Crescent. *Wind Rose.* Harper & Row, 1976, $4.95. The simple story of love, conception, birth and joyous welcome to new life. Rhythmic and poetic in style, it is excellent for reading aloud. (SIECUS Report, Nov. 1978).

Farrell, Sherrie. *Gabriel's Very First Birthday: A Book About Birth for Children.* Sherrie Farrell and Pipeline Books, 1976, $3.95 paper. Very simple text illustrated by very explicit photographs shows a pregnancy, a home birth, nursing, and describes parents' feelings.

Gendron, Lionel. *Birth, The Story of How You Came to Be.* Grosset and Dunlap, 1972. Excellent and clear illustrations presented in school text fashion. The text covers human reproduction and sexual organs, impregnation, fetal growth, birth, twins, and genes. No animals or plants! Excellent description of intercourse. This book is particularly appropriate for the child interested in a more detailed explanation than provided by any of the other books listed for this age group.

Gordon, Sol and Judith. *Did The Sun Shine Before You Were Born?* Ed-U Press, Inc., 1979, $3.50 paper. Primarily intended to be read aloud by a parent but also suitable for the beginning reader. The illustrations are excellent pencil drawings. The warm and straightforward approach in this book is striking. Developed to help parents communicate facts about sex, reproduction and the family to their children. Especially appropriate for the three and four year olds.

Gordon, Sol. *Girls Are Girls and Boys Are Boys — So What's the Difference.* Ed-U Press, Inc., 1979, $3.95 paper. Debunks sex role stereotypes in a clear and simple way. Illustrates physical differences between boys and girls. Other topics described briefly include intercourse, conception, birth, pubertal changes, masturbation, feelings. Best for ages 5 and up.

Gruenberg, Sidone Matsner. *The Wonderful Story of How You Were Born.* Doubleday, 1973, 95¢ paper. Storybook style text. The drawings are outstandingly beautiful as well as informative. The text is conversational rather than technical. A guide for parents is printed on the inside jacket cover. More appropriate for the five and six year old.

Knudsen, Per Holm. *The True Story of How Babies Are Made.* Children's Press, 1973. Multi-color, bright and colorful illustrations. The text is clear, simple and sparse and focuses on intercourse, conception and birth. Presents these concepts in the simplest form of all books listed.

Mayle, Peter. *Where Did I Come From?* Lyle Stuart, Inc., 1973, $10. Multi-color cartoon illustrations in a large book format. The text covers

very well intercourse as well as orgasm. Human characters are chubby
and humorous. Love and being loved receives the focus. This book
may offend the parent who objects to a light-hearted humorous
approach to the subject. Also fetal development and childbirth are not
well described either in the text or by illustrations. On the other hand,
children usually respond with enthusiasm and delight to this book.

Nilsson, Lennart. *How Was I Born?* Delacorte Press, 1975, $5.95. To
be read by parents with their children, this book tells the story of
reproduction and birth using a combination of the famous Nilsson
photographs of fetal development with warm family scenes and other
illustrations. (SIECUS Report, Nov. 1978)

Sheffield, Margaret. *Where Do Babies Come From?* Alfred A. Knopf,
1973, $6.95. Beautiful color illustrations. Gentle, clear text. Excellent
illustration of childbirth for the younger child. This book is the favorite
for many parents for this age group.

Sinberg, Janet. *We Got This New Baby at Our House: How a Child Feels
When a Brother or Sister is Born.* Avon, 1980, $3.95.

Sweet, Phyllis E. *Something Happened to Me.* Mother Courage, 1981,
$4.00. Read-along book for parents and children about abuse.

Waxman, Stephanie. *What Is a Girl? What Is a Boy?* Peace Press, 1976,
$3.95 paper. A simple written, nonsexist message for young children:
names, hair lengths, interests, clothing, and emotions do not identify
a person as a boy or a girl — only a person's genitals can do that.
Excellent photos, including those of nude babies, children and adults.
For all curious children — especially those with only same-sex siblings.
(SIECUS Report, Nov. 1978)

A Bibliography for Parents
on the Sex Education of Their Children

Berenstein, Jan and Stan. *How to Teach Your Children about
Sex. . . Without Making a Complete Fool of Yourself.* Ballantine Books,
1980 (1970 originally), $2.95. This paperback humorously approaches
the topic of parental discomfort with sex education. Although limited
in scope, it may potentially serve as an ice-breaker.

Bernstein, Anne. *The Flight of the Stork.* Delacorte Press, 1977, $7.95.
What children really want to know about sex and when they want to
hear about it. Bernstein's book is based on her own studies and the
theories of Piaget, both of which suggest there are definite stages of
thought that each child progresses through. The author suggests that
unless the parent can gear the sex information to the level of the
thinking child, the information will not be "heard" or will be
misconstrued. Good reference for the analytical parent.

Block, William A. *What Your Child Really Wants to Know about Sex
— and Why.* Fawcett, 1972, $1.50. Analyzes the reasons behind the

questions children ask, and advises how parents can respond while fulfilling the psychological need conveyed in such questions.

Brenton, Myron. *Sex Talks.* Fawcett World, 1973, $1.25. Recognizing
the need for clear communication about sex between man and woman,
parent and child, this book suggests how such communication can be
achieved.

Brown, Rev. Thomas E. *Concerns of Parents and Sex Education.* SIECUS
Study Guide No. 13, Behavioral Publ., $1.00. Written in a question-
discussion format, this SIECUS Study Guide identifies common
situations parents experience in teaching their children about sexuality.

Calderone, Mary S. and Eric W. Johnson. *The Family Book about
Sexuality.* Harper & Row, 1981, $14.95. Sol Gordon calls this "By far
the best parents' sex education book to date." The book is designed
to be read by anyone from preteens to grandparents. The book attempts
to be all-inclusive covering a range of topics from reproduction to sex
problems and the family's role in the development of children's
sexuality. Each chapter includes several excellent illustrations. As an
overview, this book is very complete and human.

Child Study Assn. of America. *What to Tell Your Children about Sex.*
Pocket Books, 1974, $1.50. Frequently revised since first published
almost forty years ago. Still full of good ideas.

DeLora, Joann S. and Carol A.B. Warren. *Understanding Human Sexual
Interaction.* Houghton Mifflin Co., 1977. A good general textbook
on human sexuality.

The Diagram Group. *Child's Body: A Parent's Manual.* Simon &
Schuster, 1977, $7.95. This copiously illustrated manual gives parents
an objective description of children's growth and development from
conception through adolescence. Medical jargon has been eliminated,
practical advice is offered, and flexibility encouraged. This national
bestseller is also available in pocket-sized format.

Gordon, Sol. *Let's Make Sex a Household Word.* John Day, 1975, $8.95.
An excellent resource book for parents. The author and other con-
tributors thoughtfully discuss a wide range of issues, such as concerns
of the single parent and of the parent of the handicapped child. Includes
Gordon's popular "Bill of Sexual Rights and Responsibilities."

Gordon, Sol and Judith. *Raising a Child Conservatively in a Sexually
Permissive World.* Simon & Schuster.

Gordon, Sol and Irving R. Dickman. *Sex Education: The Parent's Role.*
Public Affairs Pamphlet No. 549, 1977, 50¢. A short, practical guide
for parents. The text is clear and readable and the advice is straightforward. Typical questions young people ask are included. Alternative
approaches to the same situation/problem are not presented.

Gordon, Thomas, M.D. *P.E.T., Parent Effectiveness Training* and *P.E.T.
in Action.* New American Library. An excellent resource for the parent
who wishes to approach communication with their children about
sexuality in the context of re-examination of their entire parent-child
relationship.

Katchadourian, Herant and Donald Lunde. *Fundamentals of Human Sexuality.* Holt, Rinehart and Winston, 1972. One of the best general textbooks on human sexuality.

King County Rape Relief. *He Told Me Not to Tell: A Parents' Guide for Talking to Your Child about Sexual Assault.* King County Rape Relief, 1979, 50¢. An outstanding booklet which provides excellent ideas for discussing the difficult subject of sexual assault in a positive and constructive manner. Myths are debunked, specific discussion techniques and games are suggested. What to do if your child has been molested and community resources related to sexual assault are also included.

Kirkendall, Lester A. *Helping Children Understand Sex.* Science Research Associates, 1969. This 55-page booklet provides a quick summation of normal sexual behavior in children and suggests appropriate parental responses to a number of situations.

Lanson, Lucienne, M.D. *From Woman to Woman.*Alfred A. Knopf, 1975. An excellent, nontechnical discussion, in question-and-answer format, of female sexuality and medical concerns. Useful for providing information on menstruation, etc., to daughters (and sons).

Lewis, Howard R. and Martha E. Lewis. *The Parent's Guide to Teenage Sex and Pregnancy.* St. Martin's Press, 1980, $12.95. Many facts about adolescent pregnancy and sexuality are included in a readable, somewhat documentary type style. Parents are given tips for discussions with their teens as well as a range of approaches they may wish to take regarding premarital sex. Also included is a detailed list of options and resources for pregnant or sexually active adolescents. This book fills a void in the area of sex education for parents of teenagers.

McCary, James L. *A Complete Sex Education for Parents, Teenagers and Young Adults.* Van Nostrand & Reinhold Press, 1973. A better than average guide that approaches sexuality with warmth as well as frankness. Several sections, namely "How children become adults" and "How people express their sex drives" are particularly helpful.

McCary, James L., Ph.D. *Sexual Myths and Fallacies.* Schocken, 1973, $1.95. This book offers "remedial sex education" by debunking common misconceptions about sex and sexuality. Seventy sexual myths about pornography, female sexuality, homosexuality and contraception are explored in the light of the best information available.

Minto, Lee. *Parents are the Facts of Life?* Planned Parenthood of Seattle/King Co., 1978, 40¢. An eloquent explanation of the rationale for parents consciously discussing sexuality with their own children. Gives suggestions about vocabulary, answering questions appropriately, and modeling positive attitudes toward sexuality. The pamphlet is tastefully presented and would be inoffensive to the majority of readers.

Money, John and Patricia Tucker. *Sexual Signatures: On Being a Man or a Woman.* Little, Brown & Co., 1975. This book offers a concise explanation of the physiological and psychological aspects of masculinity and femininity, developmental stages from conception to maturity, sexual identity problems and sexual orientation.

Morrison, Eleanor S. et al. *Growing Up Sexual.* D. Van Nostrand Company, 1980, $9.95. "This book is based on anonymous autobiographical papers by students in a human sexuality course at Michigan State University." The authors' order categorize the students' common experiences in order to describe psychosexual development. Themes of ignorance, misinformation, and guilt as well as pleasure in sexuality build a case for providing adequate sex education.

Pomeroy, Wardell B. *Your Child and Sex: A Guide for Parents.* Dell, 1976, $1.50. Addresses problems of communication about sex. Uses knowledge of human behavior to provide information to parents which would help them be more free and open with their children in discussing sex.

Preston, Harry with Jeanette Margolin, M.D. *How to Teach Your Children about Sex.* Books for Better Living, 1974, $1.25. While providing information on what to teach your children about sex, this book puts emphasis on the importance of both parents' own patterns of relating as models for children and the way in which children's questions are answered.

Rush, Florence. *The Best Kept Secret: Sexual Abuse of Children,* McGraw-Hill Book Co., 1980, $5.95.

Sanford, Linda Tschirhart. *Come Tell Me Right Away: A Positive Approach to Warning Children about Sexual Abuse.* Ed-U Press, P.O. 583, Fayetteville, New York 13066, $1.95.

Sanford, Linda Tschirhart. *The Silent Children: A Parent's Guide to the Prevention of Child Sexual Abuse.* McGraw-Hill Book Co., 1982, $7.95.

Silverstein, Charles. *A Family Matter: A Parent's Guide to Homosexuality.* McGraw-Hill Book Co., 1977, $8.95. The author, a practicing psychologist and founder of the Institute for Human Identity in New York City, provides parents of homosexuals information and reassurance and suggestions on how to maintain or re-establish open communication and warmth with their gay children. The information included about homosexuality would make this an excellent choice for any parent.

Simon, Sidney B. and Sally Wenkos Olds. *Helping Your Child Learn Right from Wrong: A Guide to Values Clarification.* Simon & Schuster, 1976, $7.95. Simon argues that parents cannot teach values themselves. He suggests rather how parents can teach children a process for arriving at their own values. The system is based on an assortment of game-like strategies devised to help families examine their feelings about love, friendship, money, work and honesty, and responsibility to oneself, to others and to society.

Tepfer, Sheri S. *Starting Early Experience: A Parent's Guide to Early Childhood Sex Education.* Rocky Mountain Planned Parenthood

Publications, 1979, 50¢. Very readable, practical and well-illustrated; topics include: the effects of poor sex education, when to begin sex education, vocabulary, nudity, sex play, puberty, promoting a positive self-image.

Uslander, Arlene S., Caroline Weiss, and Judith Telman. *Sex Education for Today's Child: A Guide for Modern Parents.* Association Press, 1977, $6.95. "Helpfully, they (the authors) discuss such problems as the new atmosphere of freedom, using the correct words comfortably, helping children ask the right questions and such other difficult issues as homosexuality and parental nudity." A very practical down-to-earth approach is taken.

B

Children's Book List

Babies

Alexander, Martha. *When the New Baby Comes I'm Moving Out.* New York: Dial Press, 1979.
_____. *Nobody Asked Me If I Wanted a Baby Sister.* New York: Dial Press, 1971.
Ancona, George. *It's a Baby.* New York: Dutton, 1979.
Greenfield, Eloise. *She Come Bringing Me That Little Baby Girl.* New York: J.B. Lippincott, 1974.
Hoban, Russell. *Baby Sister for Frances.* New York: Harper & Row, 1964.
Holland, Viki. *We Are Having a Baby.* New York: Scribner's, 1972.
Sheffield, Margaret. *Where Do Babies Come From?* New York: Knopf, 1974.
Stein, Sarah. *Making Babies.* New York: Walker & Co., 1974.
Watts, Bernadette. *David's Waiting Day.* Englewood Cliffs, New Jersey: Prentice-Hall, 1977.
Winthrop, Elizabeth. *I Think He Likes Me.* New York: Harper & Row, 1980.
Wolde, Gunilla. *Betsy's Baby Brother.* New York: Random House, 1982.
Wolman, Judith. *David's New Baby.* New York: Dandelion Press, 1979.

Multicultural Stories

Baylor, Byrd. *The Desert Is Theirs.* New York: Scribner's, 1975.
Blood, Charles. *The Goat in the Rug.* New York: Scholastic Book Service, 1980.
Ets, Marie Hall. *Nine Days to Christmas.* New York: Viking, 1959.
French, Fiona. *Aio the Rainmaker.* London: Oxford Univ. Press, 1975.
Goble, Paul. *The Girl Who Loved Wild Horses.* Scarsdale, New York: Bradbury Press, 1978.
Greenfield, Eloise. *Africa Dream.* New York: Harper & Row, 1977.
Jaynes, Ruth. *Do You Know What?* Los Angeles: Bowmar/Noble, 1967.
Leech, Jay. *Bright Fawn and Me.* New York: Harper & Row, 1979

Spier, Peter. *People.* Garden City, New York: Doubleday, 1980.
Vitenzon, J. *The Tale of Brave Yatto and His Sister Teune.* USSR: Progress, 1975.

Moving

Hickman, Martha Whitmore. *I'm Moving.* Nashville: Abingdon, 1975.
Hughes, Shirley. *Moving Molly.* Englewood Cliffs, New Jersey: Prentice-Hall, 1979.
Tobias, Tobi. *Moving Day.* New York: Knopf, 1976.

Handicaps

Adams, Barbara. *Like It Is: Facts and Feelings about Handicaps from Kids Who Know.* New York: Walker & Co., 1979.
Brightman, Alan. *Like Me.* Boston: Little, Brown, 1976.
Fanshawe, Elizabeth. *Rachel.* Scarsdale, New York: Bradbury Press, 1977.
Keats, Ezra Jack. *Apt. 3.* New York: Macmillan, 1971.
Larsen, Hanne. *Don't Forget Tom.* New York: Crowell, 1978.
Litchfield, Ada Barrett. *A Button in Her Ear.* Niles, Ill.: A. Whitman, 1976.
_____. *Cane in Her Hand.* Niles, Ill.: A. Whitman, 1977.
Peter, Diana. *Claire and Emma.* New York: Harper & Row, 1977.
Petersen, Palle. *Sally Can't See.* New York: John Day, 1977.
Peterson, Jeanne W. *I Have a Sister; My Sister Is Deaf.* New York: Harper & Row, 1977.
Sobol, Harriet. *My Brother Steve is Retarded.* New York: Macmillan, 1977.
Stein, Sarah B. *About Handicaps.* New York: Walker & Co., 1974.
Wahl, Jan. *Jamie's Tiger.* New York: Harcourt Brace Jovanovich, 1978.

Self-Reliance

Bruna, Dick. *Miffy at the Seaside* and *Miffy at the Zoo.* Chicago: Follett, 1970.
Corey, Dorothy. *You Go Away.* Niles, Ill.: A. Whitman, 1975.
Jensen, Virginia A. *Sara and the Door.* Reading, Mass.: Addison-Wesley, 1977.
Watanabe, Shigeo. *How Do I Put It On?* New York: Philomel, 1980.
_____. *What a Good Lunch.* New York: Philomel, 1980.
Wells, Rosemary. *Max's New Suit.* New York: Dial, 1979.

Nontraditional Roles

Asch, Frank. *Running with Rachel*. New York: Dial, 1979.
de Paola, Tomie. *Charlie Needs a Cloak*. New York: Scholastic Book Services, 1976.
_____. *Watch Out for the Chicken Feet in Your Soup*. Englewood Cliffs, New Jersey: Prentice-Hall, 1974.
_____. *Oliver Button Is a Sissy*. New York: Harcourt Brace Jovanovich, 1979.
Goodyear, Carmen. *The Sheep Book*. Chapel Hill, N.C.: Lollipop Power, 1972.
Herman, Harriet. *The Forest Princes*. Berkeley, Calif.: Over the Rainbow Press, 1974.
Isadora, Rachel. *Max*. New York: Macmillan, 1976.
Levy, Elizabeth. *Nice Little Girls*. New York: Delacorte, 1978.
Mayer, Mercer. *East of the Sun, West of the Moon*. New York: Scholastic Book Services, 1980.
Takeichi, Yasoo. *The Mighty Prince*. New York: Crown, 1971.
Woldin, Beth Wiener. *Ellie to the Rescue*. New York: P. Warne, 1979.

Friends

Delton, Judy. *Two Good Friends*. New York: Crown, 1974.
Fujikawa, Gyo. *Let's Eat*. New York: Putnam, 1975.
_____. *Sleepy Time*. New York: Putnam, 1975.
_____. *Puppies, Pussycats and Other Friends*. New York: Putnam, 1975.
Jaynes, Ruth. *Friends*. Alhambra, Calif.: Borden.
Wittman, Sally. *A Special Trade*. New York: Harper & Row, 1978.
Zolotow, Charlotte. *Hold My Hand*. New York: Harper & Row, 1972.

Grandparents

Alexander, Martha. *The Story My Grandmother Told*. New York: Dial, 1969.
Baker, Jeannie. *Grandmother*. New York: Andre Deutsch, 1979.
Brooks, Ron. *Timothy and Gramps*. Scarsdale, New York: Bradbury Press, 1979.
Farber, N. *How Does It Feel To Be Old?* New York: Dutton, 1979.
Kirk, Barbara. *Grandpa, Me and Our House in the Tree*. New York: Macmillan, 1978.
Miles, Miska. *Annie and the Old One*. Boston: Little, Brown, 1971.
Newman, Shirlee. *Tell Me Grandma Tell Me Grandpa*. Boston: Houghton Mifflin, 1979.
Williams, Barbara. *Kevin's Grandma*. New York: Dutton, 1975.

Feelings

Alexander, Martha. *We Never Get To Do Anything.* New York: Dial, 1970.

Barkin, Carol and Elizabeth James. *Sometimes I Hate School.* Milwaukee, Wis.: Raintree Pubs., 1975.

Cohen, Miriam. *Lost in the Museum.* New York: Greenwillow, 1979.

———. *No Good at Art.* New York: Greenwillow, 1980.

———. *When Will I Read?* New York: Greenwillow, 1977.

———. *Will I Have a Friend?* New York: Macmillan, 1967.

Corrick, Carol. *The Foundling.* Boston: Houghton Mifflin, 1977.

Delton, Judy. *The New Girl at School.* New York: Dutton, 1979.

Feder, Jane. *The Night Light.* New York: Dial, 1980.

Hazen, Nancy. *Grownups Cry Too, Los Adultos Tambien Lloran.* Chapel Hill, N.C.: Lollipop Power, 1978.

Hoban, William. *Arthur's Christmas Cookies.* New York: Harper & Row, 1972.

———. *A Baby Sister for Francis.* New York: Harper & Row, 1976.

Keats, Ezra J. *Peter's Chair.* New York: Harper & Row, 1967.

Lystad, Mary. *That New Boy.* New York: Crown, 1973.

Scott, Ann H. *Sam.* New York: McGraw-Hill, 1967.

Steig, William. *Sylvester and the Magic Pebble.* New York: Windmill Books, 1969.

Surowiecki, Sandra. *Joshua's Day.* Chapel Hill, N.C.: Lollipop Power, 1977.

Waber, Bernard. *Ira Sleeps Over.* Boston: Houghton Mifflin, 1975.

Yashima, Taro. *Crow Boy.* New York: Viking, 1955.

———. *Umbrella.* New York: Viking, 1958.

Zolotow, Charlotte. *The Hating Book.* New York: Harper & Row, 1969.

———. *The Unfriendly Book.* New York: Harper & Row, 1975.

———. *William's Doll.* New York: Harper & Row, 1972.

Environmental Responsibility

Bartlett, Margaret F. *Down the Mountain, a Book About the Ever-Changing Soil.* New York: Young Scott Books, 1963.

Byrd, Baylor. *Guess Who My Favorite Person Is?* New York: Scribner's, 1977.

———. *Hawk, I'm Your Brother.* New York: Scribner's, 1976.

Klein, Leonore. *Tom and the Small Ant.* New York: Knopf, 1965.

Showers, Paul. *Where Does the Garbage Go?* New York: Harper & Row, 1974.

Lollipop Power

Multiethnic, nonsexist books
P.O. Box 1171, Chapel Hill, N.C. 27514
(donations tax-deductible)

Atkinson, Mary. *Maria Teresa*. 1979.
Chapman, Kim W. *The Magic Hat*. 1976.
de Poix, Carol. *Jo, Flo and Yolanda*. 1973.
Eber, Christine. *Just Momma and Me*. 1975.
Eichler, Margrit. *Martin's Father*. 1977.
Goldsmid, Paula. *Did You Ever*. 1971.
Goodyear, Carmen. *The Sheep Book*. 1972.
Gullette, Margaret. *The Lost Bellybutton*. 1976.
Lenthall, Patricia. *Carlotta and the Scientist*. 1976.
Pratt, Ellen. *Amy and the Cloud Basket*. 1975.
Surowiecki, Sandra. *Joshua's Day*. 1977.
Tompert, Ann. *The Clever Princess*. 1977.

Divorce

Caines, Jeannette. *Daddy*. New York: Harper & Row, 1977.
Perry, Patricia and Marietta Lynch. *Mommy and Daddy Are Divorced*. New York: Dial, 1978.
Schuchman, Joan. *Two Places To Sleep*. Minneapolis: Carolrhoda Books, 1979.
Sinberg, Janet. *Divorce Is a Grown-Up Problem*. New York: Avon, 1978.
Steptoe, John. *Daddy Is a Monster...Sometimes*. New York: Harper & Row, 1980.
Thomas, Ianthe. *Eliza's Daddy*. New York: Harcourt Brace Jovanovich, 1976.
Zolotow, Charlotte. *A Father Like That*. New York: Harper & Row, 1971.

Death

Aliki. *The Two of Them*. New York: Greenwillow, 1979.
Brown, Margaret W. *The Dead Bird*. Reading, Mass.: Addison-Wesley, 1958.
Carrick, Carol. *The Accident*. Boston: Houghton Mifflin, 1976.
de Paola, Tomie. *Nana Upstairs and Nana Downstairs*. New York: Penguin, 1978.
Fassler, Joan. *My Grandpa Died Today*. New York: Human Sciences Press, 1971.

Miles, Miska. *Annie and the Old One.* Boston: Little, Brown, 1971.
Stein, Sarah B. *About Dying.* New York: Walker & Co., 1974.
Tobias, Tobi. *Petey.* New York: Garden City, N.Y.: Putnam, 1978.
Viorst, Judith. *The Tenth Good Thing About Barney.* New York: Atheneum, 1971.
Wagner, Jane. *J.T.* New York: Dell, 1971.
Zolotow, Charlotte. *My Grandson Lew.* New York: Harper & Row, 1974.

Childbirth

Farrell, Sherrie. *Gabriel's Very First Birthday.* Seattle: Pipeline Books, 1976.
Sheffield, Margaret. *Where Do Babies Come From?* New York: Knopf, 1974.

Illness and Hospitalization

Rocwell, Harlow. *My Doctor.* New York: Macmillan, 1973.
Stein, Sarah B. *Hospital Story.* New York: Walker & Co., 1974.
Weber, Alfons. *Elizabeth Gets Well.* New York: Crowell, 1969.
Wolde, Gunilla. *Betsy and the Doctor.* New York: Random House, 1982.

All Kinds of Families

Adolff, Arnold. *Black is Brown is Tan.* New York: Harper & Row, 1973.
Brown, Margaret W. *Runaway Bunny.* New York: Harper & Row, 1972.
Cavin, Ruth. *Timothy the Terror.* New York: Quist, Harlin Books, 1973.
Dragonwagon, Crescent and Paul Zinadel. *Wild Rose.* New York: Harper & Row, 1972.
Eber, Christine. *Just Momma and Me.* Chapel Hill, N.C.: Lollipop Power, 1975.
Ehrlich, Amy. *Zeek Silver Moon.* New York: Dial, 1972.
Eichler, Margrit. *Martin's Father.* Chapel Hill, N.C.: Lollipop Power, 1977.
Graham, John. *I Love You, Mouse.* New York: Harcourt Brace Jovanovich, 1978.
Greenfield, Eloise. *Grandmama's Joy.* New York: Philomel, 1980.
Hegwood, Mamie. *My Friend Fish.* New York: Holt, Rinehart & Winston, 1975.
Keats, Ezra Jack. *Snowy Day.* New York: Penguin, 1976.
Lasker, Joe. *Mothers Can Do Anything.* Niles, Ill.: A. Whitman, 1972.
Mahy, Margaret. *Ultra-Violet Catastrophe or The Unexpected Walk with Great-Uncle Pringle.* New York: Parents' Magazine Press, 1975.
Maury, Inez. *My Mother the Mail Carrier — Mi Mama La Cartera.* Old Westbury, N.Y.: Feminist Press, 1976.

Merriam, Eve. *Mommies At Work*. New York: Scholastic Book Service, 1973.

Nolan, Madeena S. *My Daddy's Don't Go To Work*. Minneapolis: Carolrhoda Books, 1978.

Schick, Eleanor. *One Summer Night*. New York: Greenwillow Books, 1977.

Scott, Ann H. *On Mother's Lap*. New York: McGraw-Hill, 1972.

Simon, Norma. *All Kinds of Families*. Niles, Ill.: A. Whitman, 1975.

Thompson, Susan L. *One More Thing, Dad*. Niles, Ill.: A. Whitman, 1980.

Waterton, Betty. *A Salmon for Simon*. New York: Atheneum, 1980.

Williams, Barbara. *Kevin's Grandma*. New York: Dutton, 1975.

Cognitive Development

Baylor, Byrd. *If You Are a Hunter of Fossils*. New York: Scribner's, 1980.

Feeney, Stephanie. *A Is for Aloha*. Honolulu: University of Hawaii Press, 1980.

Fife, Dale. *Adam's ABC*. New York: Coward, McCann and Geoghegan, 1971.

Fujikawa, Gyo. *Gyo Fujikawa's A to Z Book*. New York: Grosset & Dunlap, 1981.

Hoban, Tana. *Circles, Triangles and Squares*. New York: Macmillan, 1974.

_____. *Is It Red? Is It Yellow? Is It Blue?* New York: Greenwillow Books, 1978.

_____. *Over, Under and Through and Other Special Concepts*. New York: Dutton, 1978.

_____. *Push Pull Empty Full*. New York: Macmillan, 1972.

Holzenthaler, Jean. *My Hands Can*. New York: Dutton, 1978.

Showers, Paul. *Your Skin and Mine*. New York: Harper & Row, 1965.

Simon, Norma. *Why Am I So Different?* Niles, Ill.: A. Whitman, 1976.

Wosmek, Frances. *ABC of Ecology*. Los Altos Hills, Calif.: Davenport May, 1982.

Adoption

Caines, Jeannette. *Abby*. New York: Harper & Row, 1973.

Wasson, Valentina. *The Chosen Baby*. New York: Harper & Row, 1977.

Sexuality

Waxman, Stephanie. *What is a Boy? What Is a Girl?* Culver City, Calif.: Peace Press, 1976.

_____. *Growing Up Feeling Good*. Los Angeles: Panjandrum, 1979.

Kids' Favorites

Alexander, Martha. *No Ducks in Our Bathtub.* New York: Dial, 1971.
_____. *Nobody Asked Me If I Wanted a Baby Sister.* New York: Dial, 1971.
_____. *I'll Be the Horse If You'll Play With Me.* New York: Dial, 1979.
_____. *When the New Baby Comes, I'm Moving Out.* New York: Dial, 1979.
_____. *We Never Get To Do Anything.* New York: Dial, 1970.
Aliki. *At Mary Bloom's.* New York: Penguin, 1978.
Berger, B. *Animalia.* San Francisco: Celestial Arts, 1982.
Berenstein, Stanley and Janice. *Inside Outside Upside Down.* New York: Random House, 1968.
_____. *Old Hat New Hat.* New York: Random House, 1970.
Carle, Eric. *The Grouchy Ladybug.* New York: Harper & Row, 1977.
_____. *The Very Hungry Caterpillar.* New York: Philomel, 1969.
Carlson, Natalie S. *Marie Louise's Heyday.* New York: Scribner's, 1975.
Cummings, E.E. *Fairy Tales.* New York: Harcourt Brace Jovanovich, 1975.
de Paola, Tomie. *Bill and Pete.* New York: Putnam's, 1978.
Eastman, Philip D. *The Best Nest.* New York: Beginner Books, 1968.
Freeman, Don. *Corduroy.* New York: Viking, 1968.
Heilbroner, Joan. *The Happy Birthday Present.* New York: Harper & Row, 1962.
Hergé. *The Adventures of Tintin series.* Boston: Little, Brown.
Horsfall, Carrah and Bruce. *Bluebirds Seven.* Portland, Ore.: Audubon Society, 1978.
Jeschke, Susan. *Victoria's Adventure.* New York: Holt, Rinehart & Winston, 1976.
Kaufman, Joe. *How We Are Born, How We Grow, How Our Bodies Work and How We Learn.* New York: Golden Press, 1975.
Kellogg, Steven. *The Island of the Scogg.* New York: Dial, 1973.
_____. *Can I Keep Him?* New York: Dial, 1971.
_____. *Won't Somebody Play With Me?* New York: Dial, 1976.
Keolling, Caryl. *Silly Stories, Mix and Match.* New York: Delacorte, 1980.
Kraus, Robert. *Whose Mouse Are You?* New York: Macmillan, 1970.
Lionni, Leo. *Swimmy.* New York: Pantheon, 1963.
_____. *Frederick.* New York: Pantheon, 1967.
Lobel, Arnold. *Frog and Toad Together.* New York: Harper & Row, 1972.
_____. *Frog and Toad Are Friends.* New York: Harper & Row, 1972.
Marshall, James. *George and Martha.* Boston: Houghton Mifflin, 1972.

_____. *George and Martha Encore*. Boston: Houghton Mifflin, 1977.

Mathieu, Joseph. *Big Joe's Trailer Truck*. New York: Random House, 1974.

Merriam, Eve. *Bam Zam Boom! A Building Book*. New York: Scholastic Book Services, 1972.

Minarik, Else Holmeland. *Little Bear's Friend*. New York: Harper & Row, 1960.

Mosel, Arlene. *The Funny Little Woman*. New York: Dutton, 1977.

Palmer, Helen. *Why I Built the Boogle House*. New York: Beginner Books, 1964.

Sarnoff, Jane. *What? A Riddle Book*. New York: Scribner's, 1974.

Slepian, Jan. *The Hungry Thing*. New York: Scholastic Book Services, 1972.

Spier, Peter. *Crash, Bang, Boom*. Garden City, New York: Doubleday, 1972.

Williams, Margery. *The Velveteen Rabbit*. New York: Avon Books, 1982.

Yolin, Jane. *Brothers of the Wind*. New York: Philomel, 1981.

C

TRADE
Instructions and Description

TRADE is an exceptionally involving educational game for children which unfortunately is not available in stores at this time. It is an aesthetically pleasing game made completely of wood with bright, nontoxic colors added. TRADE consists of a playing block, a 6" × 10" hand-crafted piece of alder with thirty-two holes in eight rows of four holes each. Each hole has a wooden pin with a brightly painted head indicating its value. Below are the directions.

Purpose of the game. Players set their own "winning goal"; perhaps three of the pins of 128 value (a long game) or one pin of 64 value (a short game).

Pieces. There are four pins of each number. Each player chooses to use either the upper or lower set of numbers on the sides of the playing block. The top row of numbers is for use with young players (4–7 years) and the bottom row for older players. Use a jar of dried beans as a bank. Each bean equals 1 (is a substitute for the 1 pins when they are all in use). Player may use beans in combination with pins for trade to get more valuable pins (higher number).

Rules of the game (2 to 4 players).
1. First player rolls the dice. Take the fewest pins with values adding to the number rolled (i.e., a roll of 5 will take one 4 pin and one 1 pin when you are using the top number set, or one 5 pin if you are using the bottom number set).
2. The second player rolls and takes pins as above, perhaps adding the number rolled to pins already held and exchanging pins in hand for those of higher value on the board.
3. Take turns rolling and taking pins. When a player has pins that when added together, are equal to any higher-value pin, then he or she will call "trade" during his turn and will trade in his pins for those of higher value in addition to rolling the dice. The game progresses until a player wins by reaching the agreed-upon winning-goal pin.
4. When all pins of any number value are already in play, use beans from the bank and trade as though they are pins valuing 1.

Variations by age

Age ten months to one and a half years. Infants and toddlers will increase small muscle coordination and dexterity as well as hand–eye coordination by removing and replacing pins in holes.

Age two to three. Young children enjoy matching, sorting, and classifying pins by color as they remove them, changing the color order, making piles of different combinations, etc.

Age four to five. Add a set of dried beans to use as counters. If a 3, 5 or 6 is thrown with the dice, the child may count out this number of counting beans; grouping them in various ways will teach the child how small numbers are combined to make larger ones. This will help the child to decide which pins can be removed from the board with each dice throw. When trading pins in, children may use beans again to count out each pin and figure out their trade transaction. A parent will need to work with the child for some time before the child will be able to complete this procedure independently.

When children have practiced the game several times, they will outgrow their need for counting beans, and the beans can be removed from play as counters and used as the bank.

When children have mastered the game and begin to lose interest in the top row of numbers, at about age eight, they can begin using the lower set. This set has no color shortcut and will require the use of pencil and paper for figuring and keeping track of bank transactions. This is a version of TRADE that will maintain the interest of adults in a game situation with their children.

This game and detailed instructions are available by mail order from

Sunnyside Up
3920 Sunnyside Avenue No.
Seattle, WA 98103

and costs $20 plus $2 for postage and handling.

Colored dots identify proper pin row during play. Rainbow color arrangement of pins and labeling dots on board face.

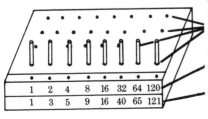

Solid hardwood playing board with 32 holes.

32 pins, 4 of each color; each row of 4 pins assumes the value designated in the front of the board.

Children under six use top row of numbers for pin values.

Older children use bottom row of numbers for pin values.

Index

Karen Murphy, formerly a social worker for the first school-age day care program in Seattle, ran a successful day care business in her own home for five years. She lives in Seattle, Washington, with her husband and two children, and continues to counsel parents with young children and those interested in starting home day care businesses.